HARMONY IN CHAKRAS

VOLUME 1

Written by
The Chakra Collective

Edited by
Olivia Whiteman

Published by: Positive Energies OM

DISCLAIMER: The material in this book is intended for general information purposes only. This book is not intended to replace or conflict with advice given to the reader by his or her health practitioner. Individuals who have concerns about their health or mental well-being should always see their health care provider before administering any suggestions made in this book. Any application of the materials, techniques, ideas and suggestions set forth in this book is at the reader's discretion and is his or her sole responsibility. The publisher does not have control over or assume responsibility for any author or their content.

Credits:
Cover Photography: Margaret L. Jackson
Project Editor: Olivia Whiteman
Developmental Editor: Tiziana Rinaldi Castro
Copy Editor: Heather Archibald
Copy Editor: Joan Carra

ISBN Number: 978-0-692-09117-3
Printed in the United States
First U.S. Edition
Library of Congress Control Number: 2018908553

THE CHAKRA COLLECTIVE
Contributing Writers

Alicia Armitstead
Ashni
Monica Bennett
Ivy Black
Carlos Cuellar Brown
Anthony James Canelo
Joan Carra
Tiziana Rinaldi Castro
Leah DeSanto
Nanci Deutsch
Heidi Elias
Denise Galon
Maria Gutierrez
Jo Jayson
Noelle Lauren
Rita London
Erolina
Munira Merchant
Desiree Mwalimu-Banks
Kaz Mirza
David Presler
Stella Preston
Yaffa Regev
Laurelle Rethke
Trent Rhodes
Deirdre (Dee) Savoie
Shanna Marie
Ashley Sperber
Elizabeth Tripp
Martha Vallejo
Carmela Villaroman Velarde
Lakshmi Voelker
Olivia Whiteman
Brenda Yarnold

ACKNOWLEDGMENTS

To all the authors of this book much gratitude.

Special thanks to Joan Carra, Leah DeSantos, Erolina, Trent Rhodes and Dee Savoy. Their feedback helped make this book move forward.

Heather Archibald, a poet and author of *Home-Home*. After meeting her I was inspired to take a poetry course at CUNY with her and three other poet instructors. At the time, I did not know that this class would impact how I would put this book together. I am forever grateful.

Tiziana Rinaldi Castro for sharing the love of this project and making sure the stories in this book are presented in the best light.

Joseph Adams, his humor and keen eye for details is much appreciated.

My friend, Michael DeUrso for always supporting me in any endeavor I take on.

Dominic Kay for her words of wisdom. She always shines a light within me.

Judy Goldston for her ability to listen and offer kind ways of thinking about people, and the circumstances life puts them in.

Sally Christenberry Roth, the host of *Coming of Age with Sally,* for sharing information on chakras with her YouTube viewers.

Margaret Jackson, a photographer with a beautiful eye and heart. Her perfect photo of Sedona makes the cover of this book.

My sisters, brother-in-law and nephews for always offering support, and although they are with me only in spirit, my loving parents.

BOOK CREDITS

Olivia Whiteman   Tiziana Rinaldi Castro   Heather Archibald   Joan Carra

Project Editor and Publisher: Olivia Whiteman is also a Completion & Fulfillment Coach who offers artists, musicians, authors, wellness professionals, teachers and entrepreneurs practical, holistic and customized options that allow them to complete what they start. Olivia conceived and developed this first book to inspire and encourage people to explore ways to balance their chakras and create greater harmony in their life.

Developmental Editor: Tiziana Rinaldi Castro is a transformational life coach at The Resonant Self, specializing in transpersonal and archetypal psychology. She is a published writer in Italy and in the US. Among some of her works: *Come della rosa* (2017), *Due cose amare e una dolce* (2007), *Il lungo ritorno* (2001), *Dai morti, (1992)*, *Embroidered Stories* (2014). She teaches Ancient Greek Literature at Montclair State University.

Copy Editor: Heather Archibald is formerly from St. Kitts and is an adjunct instructor of English at several CUNY colleges and, more recently, at Westchester Community College. She tutors and serves as a proofreader. She is the author of a book of poetry, entitled *Home-Home* (2016).

Copy Editor: Joan Carra is a psychic and a writer. Joan studied Creative Writing at Goddard College. She has written articles for Mystic Pop Magazine and the Greenwich Times newspaper. Her poems were in an award winning literary magazine called Pagan Place and she ran a poetry reading series in NYC. Her songs, performances and psychic work are discussed in the books: *Interdimensional Universe* and *Alien Rock*.

FORWARD

I knew nothing about chakras until I met Olivia Whiteman and she shared that she was putting together a book about chakras with over thirty people. Our conversation led to my interviewing members of The Chakra Collective for *Coming of Age with Sally,* my YouTube channel.

Coming of Age with Sally is about what happens when you get old, when your friends get old, or when your parents get old. Whether you are a caretaker or a person getting old, it doesn't matter. Everybody needs to know what's going on because a lot of people don't know what is going on when they are getting old. Some of them don't even know they are getting old, until one day they fall down or they go to the doctor and they get a bad report, or whatever. On *Coming of Age with Sally*, I talk about all the things that happen and what to do about it.

When I interviewed members of The Chakra Collective, the focus was on how aligning the chakras can be of benefit to the elderly. I know the information you discover looking through this book will cause a variety of reactions. It did for me. You may even apply some of the recommendations and suggestions to your life. I know I did.

Enjoy the book and I welcome you to visit *Coming of Age with Sally* on YouTube.

Sally Christenberry Roth
Host, Coming of Age with Sally

GREETINGS FROM OLIVIA WHITEMAN

There is so much more to chakras than anyone initially realizes. Chakras can benefit every part of your life and learning about them can shift your life into extraordinary and beyond. When I think chakras, I think WOW!!!

Having knowledge of the chakras and ways to balance them when they are out of alignment can enhance any and every aspect of your life throughout your lifetime.

What I love best about this collection of writings is the variety of understandings, insights and solutions presented. Just keep in mind that *all products or services mentioned in each chapter is the sole opinion of each author.* Therefore, other than a personal endorsement by a specific author, no product or service is endorsed by the publisher or any of the other authors. Responsibility for all aspects of your well-being is a personal decision. Do your research. Choose wisely.

Now, if you think that when your chakras are off it can only be a result of something negative, shift that viewpoint. Some of the happiest days of our lives: weddings, the birth of a baby, graduating from school or accepting awards also impact our chakras.

To offer you a deeper understanding of the chakras, you will notice that the word chakra is defined several times and that the definitions may vary depending on the focus of the chapter and the specialty of the writer. Therefore, if you read something that seems contradictory to another chapter chances are they're not incompatible. Should you have any questions, visit us on Facebook: https://m.facebook.com/harmonyinchakras.

In closing, may all that you want lead you to achieving great things in the world, including, contributing to peace in the world.

Olivia Whiteman
Publisher, Editor and Author

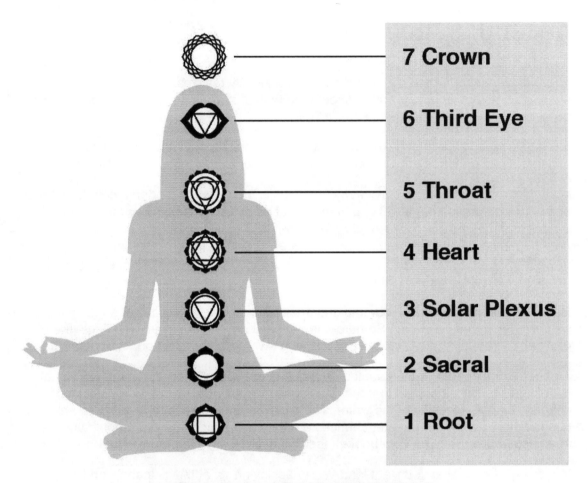

7 Crown

6 Third Eye

5 Throat

4 Heart

3 Solar Plexus

2 Sacral

1 Root

THE SEVEN MAIN CHAKRAS

TABLE OF CONTENTS

Photographer: Margaret L. Jackson

Each member of The Chakra Collective was asked the question, "How do you work with chakras in your personal or professional life?" Their answer precedes their chapter.

To learn more about the members, a brief biography is included after each of their chapters and even more information about the authors is available at the website harmonyinchakras.com/the_chakra_collective.html

The Feng Shui Master, Psychic Reader & Dream Interpreter

IVY BLACK
Feng Shui Master, Psychic Reader and Dream Interpreter

Raised in Asia and the United States, studying with highly-respected teachers around the world, I've combined a background in both eastern and western spirituality.

Feng Shui, Chi Reading, and Dream Interpretation are three ways I work with clients to assist them in getting their chakras back into balance.

Feng Shui – Literally translated as "wind-water," Feng Shui is an ancient Chinese art/science developed thousands of years ago to help improve life by creating an optimal and harmonious flow of energy within a space. To help clients change their lives by changing their physical space, I use a Chinese luopan compass to determine positive and negative chi within a home or work space, and offer what I call Alternative Feng Shui, providing easy-to-implement and affordable solutions to enhance the positive chi and minimize the negative chi.

Chi Reading – In Chinese, chi means the energy or life force within and around us. When performing intuitive or psychic readings, I tune into people's energies (tap into their chi) by holding objects belonging to them while in a meditative state. Through a process known as psychometry, I receive messages and impressions through the mind's eye as well as through my physical senses. The experience is similar to dreaming, when we see meaningful images, symbols and visions, or we experience deep feelings or emotions. Chi reading, a method of psychic reading, utilizes these same channels of intuition and insight.

Dream Decoding and Analysis – Understanding our dreams offers one of the most beneficial ways to clear chakra blocks. In my essay on "Dreams" that follows, I share the history of dreams, the benefits of remembering our dreams, and ways to remember them.

My life's goal is to help people improve their lives by offering my extensive spiritual training to help enhance their physical and psychic being. I am available for consultations and look forward to connecting with anyone who wants a chi reading, assistance with Feng Shui or a dream decoded.

DREAMS
Ivy Black, Ph.D.

HISTORY

Nestled in a valley in the Peloponnese Region of southern Greece are the remains of the Temple of Asclepius, god of medicine, health, and well-being. Formerly a sprawling complex beside the still-standing grand amphitheater at Epidaurus, it has been reduced by time to a field of twisted trees and rubble, yet once it was one of the most distinguished medical facilities in ancient Greece, at the forefront of scientific healing.

The Asclepeion at Epidaurus was among the earliest organized sanatoriums, active as early as the second millennium BCE (Before Common Era), attracting people seeking medical treatments and cures for their ailments. It is a key site of the history of medicine, bridging the gap between the belief in divine healing and the burgeoning understanding of science. It was from this site, dubbed "the cradle of medicine" by UNESCO, that medical practices spread throughout the rest of the Greco-Roman empire.

Dreams were understood back then to be an important piece of the puzzle of life and well-being. The Greeks believed that the sick would be visited in dreams by divine physicians with cures and remedies. Dream interpreters sought clues to combat illness by analyzing the dreams of the afflicted.

Throughout history – in the vanguard cultures of the ancient Greeks, Egyptians, Romans, Chinese, Native Americans and more – people paid high regard to dreams, believing they held a key to knowledge, health and power. Many temples were built in dedication to the gods of medicine and healing, allowing pilgrims to enter dream incubation chambers for one or more nights to receive a healing dream.

Over the ages, scholars, scientists and dream authorities have made countless breakthroughs regarding the importance of dreams, the functions of the brain, and the benefits of dreaming, yet how many dreams are forgotten or dismissed? How many people simply shrug and say, "It was just a dream?"

And what can we do to enhance, remember, and benefit from our dreams?

WHAT ARE THE BENEFITS OF REMEMBERING OUR DREAMS?

Nocturnal dreaming is the language of our soul and our subconscious mind. Dreams communicate to us through symbols, feelings and colors. Tapping into our subconscious mind is like discovering invaluable treasures, which help us to face our shadows, learn about our limitations, and conquer our fears.

Many significant ideas, breakthroughs and inventions were inspired by dreams – from Elias Howe's invention of the sewing machine to Nobel Prize-winning physicist Niels

Bohr's theory of the structure of atoms; from Mary Shelley's Frankenstein, based on her dream/nightmare, to Beethoven's musical compositions.

Nocturnal dreams are a bridge between our soul – our inner self – and our conscious mind. By understanding our dreams, not only can we acquire the wisdom and insights we need, but we can also change our lives. I believe – like the ancients, like our ancestors, like many generations before us – that we should treasure our dreams, as they allow us to unveil our true potential, reconnect with our authentic selves, and work toward understanding our life purpose.

In fact, one of my dreams not only impacted my life (getting me published in the book, "*Dreams that Change Our Lives*," from the International Association for the Study of Dreams), but also helped in a small way to combat illiteracy in South Africa. I shared a powerful dream with my husband, who is a fiction writer. He turned it into a story called "Project Hydra," which was picked up by a publisher in South Africa and the story became part of the book called "Ravensmoot: An Anthology of Speculative Fiction." In an effort to help underprivileged children, the publisher dedicated a portion of the proceeds from book sales to support schools and public libraries in communities across South Africa.

HOW TO REMEMBER OUR DREAMS?

Each night when we fall asleep a sleeping cycle is initiated, consisting of five distinct stages: Stages 1 through 4, and rapid eye movement (REM) sleep. Stage 1 is light sleep; it is when the sleeper is easily awakened. As the subsequent sleep stages progress from stages 2 through 4, our brainwaves gradually become slower, longer, and steadier. During the REM sleep cycle, the quality of our dreams become visually vivid, meaningful, and more powerful. During REM sleep, the long-term memory cells are turned off. As a result, it is challenging for us to remember our dreams. However, a few simple methods can help improve our dream recall dramatically.

- Before going to sleep, massage the soles of your feet with either lotion or essential oil while setting an intention to remember your dreams.

- If you have a crystal, such as clear quartz or amethyst (I personally use Moldavite, which is excellent for dream-work), hold the crystal in your hands or in front of your mind's eye, the third-eye chakra, while setting the intention to remember your dreams. Then place the crystal under your pillow. When you get up the next morning, place the crystal on your mind's eye and repeat to yourself, "I now remember my dreams." While doing it, stay still and uninterrupted.

- Before bed, prepare a glass of water. Hold the glass of water close to your heart and/or solar plexus chakras while saying to yourself that you will remember your dreams. Drink a third or a half glass immediately after the affirmation and before going to sleep. While drinking the water, continue to say to yourself that you will remember your dreams. When you get up the next day, finish the rest of the water. While drinking the water, repeat to yourself, "I now remember my dreams," or say to yourself, "During the course of the day, I will remember what I dreamed last night."

- Place a dream journal next to your bed and write down anything you remember immediately upon waking up, even if what you remember is merely a fragment, a single dream symbol, a faint smell or feeling
.
- Like the ancient Greeks or other ancestors, create your own healing center/sleeping temple by removing all clutter from your bedroom, placing a pot of fresh flowers or bamboo next to your bed to help generate fresh air in the bedroom, and burn sage or incense to remove any stagnant or negative energy.

- If nothing works, keep trying. You will remember your dreams soon enough.

HOW TO USE A CENTER PRAYER OR GUIDED MEDITATION TO BALANCE OUR CHAKRAS

Have you ever had disturbing dreams or nightmares after watching a scary movie or negative news right before falling asleep? In my own experience, when I am tense and stressed, I am prone to insomnia or have difficulty staying asleep, waking up so often that it prevents me from progressing through the sleeping cycle to enter REM sleep. As a result, I have difficulty recalling my dreams and feel fatigued the next day.

Therefore, using a center prayer, guided meditation or an affirmation to help relax, de-stress or remove negative thoughts before entering our dream zone can induce a positive dream experience and increase dream recall.

An example of a center prayer/guided meditation that I created and use to quiet my mind, relax my body, balance my chakras, and remove blockages in my sacred sleeping temple before falling asleep follows:

> *Closing my eyes and breathing in fresh air, I let go of all my concerns, worries, fears and tension; I simply let them recede and fade away. I call on the cosmos to bring me love and to support and guide me to achieve my highest life purpose and allow me to clear away any residual fear of myself and others and any low vibrational energy that no longer serves my higher purpose, from my crown chakra all the way down to my root chakra, and to the tips of my toes, and fill my body with beautiful diamond white light.*

> *I am surrounded by infinite wisdom and unconditional love. I am protected by brightest sunlight.*

> *At this moment and from this moment onward, my life overflows with joy, peace and success. Divine abundance and prosperity are forever appearing every step of the way in my life journey. I prosper, thrive and flourish in everything I do. I experience the deepest awareness of synchronicity with the universe. My chosen*

destiny is fulfilled, as I know I am embraced by the most earnest, kindest and most loving presence.

As I give thanks for the blessing now flowing into my life, I gratefully share the blessing with others. I give thanks to Mother Earth, which makes me feel grounded and supported (root chakra). I give thanks to the ocean, which purifies and cleanses my body, mind and soul (all chakras). I give thanks to the moon and stars, which heighten my intuition (third-eye and crown chakras) and give thanks for their mysteries, which intensify my imagination and creativity (sacral chakra). I give thanks to the sun, which softens my heart (heart chakra) and brings light to my darkest days.

Ask and it is given. Infinite love, gratitude and possibilities are in my past, present and future – unlimited, forever and ever!

Amen.

CONCLUSION

I used to believe that time is linear: past, present and then future. However, in my nighttime dream world, I've learned that time is not linear but in fact all past, present and future are indeed integrated. Our consciousness is not merely linked to our bodies, but it is beyond and above our bodies.

Being a vivid dreamer ever since I was a young child, I was always fascinated by dreams, which led to my life-long study of their meaning and significance. In my nighttime dreams, I've found myself traveling through space and different dimensions with no limitations. Oftentimes I am able to connect with loved ones and family members who have passed; I experience events that have not happened in the physical world; I communicate with spiritual guides and ascended masters, who provide comfort and remind me that I am not alone.

In addition, dreams have allowed me to get in touch with my subconscious mind, which is a powerful and insightful tool to reveal and communicate to me any old wounds that need healing, any damage I need to mend, fears I need to overcome, or past experiences I need to forgive and put behind me.

I believe that we are all given a key – our nighttime dreams – to unlock, unveil and explore the infinite immeasurable treasures of our subconscious mind. Within us dwells our spirit, our higher-self, that subtle inner voice which has all the wisdom, insight and answers we will ever need in this life journey. With the right tools and guidance, we can decode this language of our souls, and integrate our past experiences, our nighttime dreams and daytime realities to equip us to be strong and resilient and achieve our life goals and ambitions.

© Ivy Black

Photo by Marco De Waal

ABOUT IVY BLACK, Ph.D

Website: www.whomovedmychi.me

IVY BLACK holds a Ph.D in Metaphysical Humanistic Science and has gained national recognition in numerous media, including *Minority Business Entrepreneur,* dedicated to the success of minority and women business owners, as well as *Natural Awakenings,* the *Jersey Journal,* the *Hudson Reporter* and *Chopsticks NY.*

Ivy came to the U.S. as a teen and put herself through college and graduate school, receiving her MBA in Finance. Making a successful career in the financial industry, she became a director, project manager, and team leader for a Fortune 100 investment bank, spearheading multi-million dollar programs and managing a team of direct reports across different countries. She has served as official Chinese translator for major events including the Hong Kong International Film Festival, the Far East Film Festival in Udine, Italy and the Otakon Asian Media convention in the United States.

As an intuitive consultant and dream-life coach, Ivy excels in psychometry and the exploration of nocturnal dreams. In addition, Ivy runs a successful Feng Shui business, which is centered on what she calls Alternative Feng Shui, updating traditional and orthodox beliefs to bring the ancient Chinese discipline into today's modern, fast-paced world, allowing people living a contemporary lifestyle to benefit from thousands of years of accumulated insights.

Ivy believes her life purpose is to help people improve their lives by utilizing her extensive spiritual training to enhance their physical and psychic space.

To learn more about Ivy and her services, visit her website.

The
Creatrix

DEIRDRE (DEE) SAVOIE
Founder of Embody the Goddess, Bestselling Author, Educator and Healer

One of the truisms of energy work is that people tend to wear the color of what they need. So the first thing I notice about my clients is what they have chosen to wear and how it relates to the color scheme of the chakras. This helps clue me in to what issues my clients will want to deal with.

When clients first come to me, I do an assessment of their energy field, including the chakras and the layers of the aura. This is done using a pendulum and other tools to douse the chakras and gauge the aura. Invariably, my assessment of the strengths and weaknesses of their energy field will gibe with the issues they are facing in their lives.

Once I know which chakras may need bolstering, I set about clearing them with energy work, crystals, aromatherapy sprays (which I make myself and sell) feather wands, sound healing and whatever other tools I need.

I also do a lot of womb work with clients, helping them to clear stagnant energies, traumas, grief, karma, ancestral and lived wounds and more. This is a deep dive into sacral energies, one in which the goal is to cleanse, recover and recalibrate womb energies for greater purpose, passion, juiciness and joy!

CONNECTING TO YOUR INNER CREATIVE POWERS
Dee Savoie

It is said that everything that exists, exists twice—first in the mind of its creator and a second time in the real world. For example, every skyscraper that towers over Manhattan was first dreamt of and realized as a set of designs to be implemented.

I, and many others, believe that everything exists three times—once in the real world, once in our minds where we plot, plan, set goals and fantasize about our lives and once, even before then, in our imaginal realm, existing as one of many possibilities that could come to pass in our lives. Jung called it the collective unconscious. Others call it the oneness or the akashic records or other names. But the truth is, we tap into this imaginal realm whether we dream at night, take a shamanic journey, daydream or simply imagine what could be.

So, the trick becomes to build our skills at both connecting to the imaginal realm and believing in our own capacity to anchor our desires into our life in a real way. Many people call this manifesting, but i prefer to call it womanifesting, as tethering our imaginal life to earth energies is central to calling it in, in a real way. In other words, we must not only envision our desires, but we must be open to receiving that which we desire. Receptivity, too, bears a feminine vibration.

Of course, if we want to make the greatest use of our imaginal energy, we need to tap into the creative energies in our own bodies. This isn't difficult to do, but it does require a consistent commitment to raising our vibrational level to keep our energy clear and flowing. Try the exercises and meditation on the next few pages to heighten and activate your energy.

Dance your chakras. Put on some music and move your body, focusing on each of your chakras in turn. Record any feelings, knowings, symbols, thoughts or ideas that come to you while you are dancing on the chakra chart. Dancing is an excellent way of both clearing and connecting with your energy field.

Develop the three greater intuition sites in the energy field. These chakras are the third eye, the heart and the sacral chakra. These three centers represent respectively the mind, the heart and the soul. Each center has its own type of intuitive energy. The third eye often deals with symbols, language, pictorial and aural forms of intuition. The heart deals with our feelings of happiness, joy, interconnection, relationships and sorrow. The sacral chakra is our center of knowing. It is also our center of connection with ancestors.

Hone in on the sacral chakra which represents our most creative energies. It is our connection with both our ancestors (as mentioned before) and our progeny. By concentrating on this energy, we focus on past and future energies and anchor ourselves within our family lineage. Thus, by exploring and healing our own stories we can impact both past and future generations, ameliorating past wounds and providing a more elevated foundation for our children and their children.

Within this chakra is also housed the four elements of creation—earth, air, fire and water. Each element represents a different type of energetic force in our life. In terms of creativity, air represents our mental effort, our conceptualization and ideas. Water represents the emotional component of our creative nature, the depths of our psyche and our shadows. Fire represents creative energy, that spark of impulse and activity. Earth represents our ability to ground and anchor our creations into reality. In the middle of this center resides Spirit, the heart of our sacral chakra.

The strength of each element and how these elements resonate with us and combine within us can help us understand our creative capacity and bring insight into our personal stories. In order to understand and activate this center, you can perform the Sacral Center Meditation available on the next page and complete the Sacral Center Map on the page that follows. If you desire, you can set a recording device before you begin the meditation so that you can speak any information that comes forward for you and then you don't have to worry about remembering everything afterward when you work on your map.

Sacral Center Meditation*:* Lie on your back and place your hands low on your stomach, covering your womb if you are a woman or your hara if you are a man. Connect with your sacral energy. First imagine yourself at the top of a beautiful mountain. Breathe in the cool, crisp air. Feel your lungs expand and contract as oxygen suffuses your body. Overhead you can hear the sound of eagles' cries. Focus on your thoughts. What ideas come into your mind? Do any animal totems or guides seek to connect with you? Does this part of your chakra have any message for you? How deeply do you resonate with this element?

Next imagine yourself looking down and finding a beautiful river running below the mountaintop where you are standing. You dive from your peak, falling and falling until you slide into the water. You dive deeper and deeper under the water until you find yourself swimming with cetaceans and sea creatures and even mermaids. You are now in the depths of your emotions. What feelings push to your surface? What animal totems or guides seek to connect with you? Does the water have any message to you? How deeply do you resonate with this element?

Emerge from the watery depths and find yourself around a beautiful bonfire. This energy represents our creative fire, our passion and vitality. Imagine looking into the flames and feeling their warmth on your skin. Do the flames have any message for you? Do any fire totems, guides or guardians seek connection with you? How deeply do you resonate with this element?

Finally, lie down on the Earth. Imagine yourself sinking into the cool, green soil. In the distance, you can hear the sounds of animals. How comfortable do you feel allowing the Earth to hold you? Do any animal totems, guides or guardians seek to connect with you? Does the Earth have any message for you? How deeply do you resonate with this element?

At the center of this energy vortex is a gorgeous jewel. It represents your pure connection with Spirit. What color is your crystal? Is it a strong connection or one that needs bolstering? What message does it have for you?

Once you have connected with all parts of this chakra, you can fill out the Sacral Chakra map with whatever words, pictures, colors or whatever else comes to mind as you play.

© Dee Savoie

16

SACRAL MAP

Courtesy of Dee Savoie of Embody the Goddess
EmbodytheGoddess.life

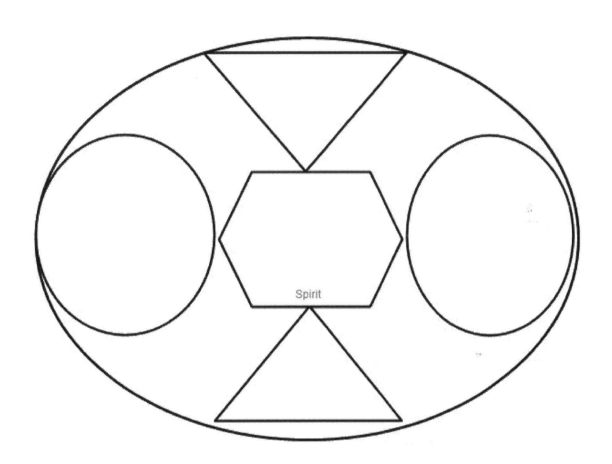

Spirit

CHAKRAS AND THE STORIES OF OUR LIVES
Deirdre Savoie

It has been said that story is the most basic unit of psychological understanding. When we want someone to comprehend us, we express ourselves in the form of story. Even the most primitive version of man used story to express meaning—first in the form of drawings, then oral storytelling and finally in written words. This explains the popularity of fables, myths, legends, and fairy tales, particularly as a vehicle for communicating meaning to children.

Mother Goose rhymes, The Brothers Grimm's tales (and their bowdlerized Disney counterparts), Biblical parables, ancient myths and rituals, Aesop's and other fables all serve as potent tales that help define what it means to be part of society, to fall in love or to fall out of favor with the prevailing culture. By tapping into the metaphor of myths and fables (rather than the actual details), we connect with the language of Spirit that has the capacity to guide and heal us.

Storytelling, along with singing, dancing, healing, dreaming and other activities, are some of the most sacred tasks that humans have taken part in since ancient times. They represent the many ways that we, even today, can be of service to ourselves and others in our community. When we explore our own stories, we become conscious creators of our lives and destinies. We bring light to the darkest parts of our own shadows and reclaim the creative power inherent in our own energy fields.

BASIC STORY ELEMENTS

Whether we are writing the book of our hearts, the memoir of our adventures or simply writing the story of our lives as we live them each day, we can add meaning to the tales we tell by being mindful of basic story elements. These include:

- **Theme:** What is the major issue that runs through your work? This is generally the same theme that will run through your life as we tend to work through the issues of our lives through our fictional products. Examples of theme can be trust, betrayal, love healing, avenging a wrong, taking a risk and many others. How you define the theme of your work will give your story grounding, a bottom layer on which to build.

- **Point of view:** From whose perspective are we telling the story? How "close" of a perspective is it? Are we telling our own story or someone else's? Are we a reliable narrator, or is our point of view clouded by our own biases, experiences or ideology?

- **Genre:** What type of story are you telling? Is it prose? Poetry? Fiction? Non-fiction? A love story? A tragedy? Your choice will dictate what can or should happen in your story. The deeper you get into certain genre, the more tightly the conventions of that genre can place constraints on your story or your life.

- **Plot:** What are the details of your story? In fiction, the action of the story, particularly in longer forms, can be described as a noose tightening around the neck of your protagonist until the climax. Desires, tensions and what thwarts or slakes them is the essence of a plotline.

- **Character:** Who is your protagonist? Perhaps the most important question you can ask about your protagonist is what does he or she want? The protagonist's goals, both internal and external and the motivations for wanting them are what move your story along and impart impact and meaning. A character's inner goals are things like true love, acceptance, revenge, redemption; external goals are financial gain, the death of a villain, home.

The worksheet on the next page can help you plan out your novel. Simply fill in each box with information about your story elements.

EXPLORE YOUR STORY

Fill in the boxes below to help you develop your work

NAME OF WORK: _____

THEME:
POINT OF VIEW:
GENRE:
PLOT:
MAIN CHARACTER:

© Dee Savoie

THE HERO'S STORY

Joseph Campbell, the author of *The Hero with Many Faces*, posits that every protagonist in any sort of story basically follows the same story arc, meets the same story characters and experiences the same types of incidents. In this way, every protagonist—from the most vaunted hero to the most common everyman—is believed to be on the same journey of discovery.

One of the most potent concepts that Campbell explores is an extension of the use of archetypes formulated by his mentor Carl Jung. Archetypes are vibrational patterns taken from the collective unconscious of humanity that can express themselves in familiar ideas, storylines and characterizations. For example, we recognize the significance of the mentor, the romantic rival, the ingénue, the wounded healer, the sidekick and other types of characters that might be present in any given story.

This hero's journey breaks down into twelve steps that start with the ordinary world, the call to action, the meeting of friends, allies and enemies, approaching the innermost cave, and end with the hero returning, transformed, changed and, perhaps, ready for the next challenge. Although not every voyage contains every step, the hero's journey provides a framework for story development that emphasizes the needs, wants, desires, successes and failures of the people who populate the tale.

More than anything else, it is the human struggle that makes each tale unique and meaningful. The more authentic and real the characters appear to be, the more we tend to root for them, to empathize with them and the more profound is our catharsis when the protagonist succeeds in the end.

THE CHARACTER'S THE THING

In order to form three-dimensional characters, we need to have some system of formulating or developing our characters. The chakra system is one way that has been underutilized but can be most helpful in exploring every aspect of a character's life, from their fears and foibles to their worldview and spiritual connection.

Crown: This is the center of our spiritual connection. Does your character adhere to a particular faith or spiritual path? Does this differ from that of their family and/or friends? If not, why not? Does your character believe the Universe is malevolent or benevolent or neutral?

Third Eye: The home of the imaginal realm, of psychic and mediumistic awareness. Is your character a plodder or a visionary? What is their perspective on life? Are they more driven by logic or by intuition? What are their dreams—both nighttime and their dreams for their life? Who is their hero(ine)?

Throat: The throat is the home of communication and intention. What are your character's intentions? Are they honest or dishonest? Do they stand by their word? In what ways do they communicate with those around them? Are they comfortable expressing themselves? In which situations?

Heart: This is the seat of both sorrow and joy, love and relationships. What close relationships does your protagonist have? Who is your character alienated from? Who or what does your character love? Hate? What sorrows or disappointments does your character harbor? What is their ultimate hope?

Solar Plexus: This is our power center, our connection to the ego, personality, and will. How strong is your character's sense of self? Are they confident or insecure? If so, what is the source of the lack? How does your character react when their ego is challenged?

Sacral: The sacral is our connection with family, creativity and creation? It is an intuitive center of *knowing*. What is your character's family background? Are they comfortable with or do they chafe against this background? Do they have siblings? If so, what are their relationships with their siblings? Are they creative in any way?

Root: The root chakra represents our most basic needs. Did your character grow up rich or poor? In a safe or dangerous neighborhood? Is your character having difficulty with money? What does your character fear? How does your character deal with fear (fight, flight or freeze)?

WHAT A CHARACTER!

The chakra system can help you formulate the characters of your story. Use this chart to delve into your character's issues or use it to log your own. Fill in each box with information relating to each chakra for your character using the questions on the previous page.

Crown:
Third Eye:
Throat:
Heart:
Solar Plexus:
Sacral:
Root:

© Dee Savoie

THE HEROINE'S JOURNEY

One other way we can relate the chakras to story is the tale of Innana. Innana, beloved of the Heavens decides to attend the funeral of her sister's husband—a death she may be responsible for. In order to attend she must venture to the land of the dead, presided over by her sister Ereshkigal. This journey is not without danger, as people who venture to the land of the dead tend to stay dead.

To visit her sister, Inanna dresses in all her finery, the gilded trappings of her role as Queen of Heaven. However to get into the innermost sanctum of the underworld, Innana must pass seven gates. At each gate, Innana must surrender an article of her raiment— first her crown, her necklace of lapis, her girdle and more. When she finally stands before Ereshkigal, Innana has been stripped naked and is no more than the shell of a body, which Ereshkigal commands to be hung on the wall on a meathook.

But Ereshkigal is not only suffering from the death of her husband, but heavily pregnant. She moans in both grief and pain. Two creatures, sent by Enki, god of the Waters, attend Ereshkigal's birthing. As a reward, they are given Inanna's corpse, which they revive.
As Inanna ascends from the underworld, her possessions are returned to her. However Inanna, has been transformed by her experience and no longer bears the haughty manner of Queen of Heaven, but becomes a wiser, more humbled Goddess, a true servant of her people, having come out the other side of the dark Goddess's lair.

Inanna's journey can be likened to that dark night of the soul, when we must face our deepest fears, the darkest aspect of ourselves, often unprotected by status, wealth, possessions, or the armor of our ego self. In this journey, we are broken down, stripped of all we think we are, in order to return to ourselves more whole, wiser, more in possession of our selves than we have been before.

If we want to view this as a journey of the chakras, we can imagine being stripped of our ego selves going down the front (or masculine side) of the chakras. This represents the way we present ourselves to the everyday world. Only then can we get to that dark place of the womb, the waters, the root, where our true power and creativity hide. It is only through examining our shadows that we can return wiser, more profound, more grounded, more sensual, more truly our whole selves as powerful creators and creatrixes, ready to birth new worlds, new lives, new ideas, and new stories.

© Dee Savoie

ABOUT DEIRDRE (DEE) SAVOIE

Website: EmbodytheGoddess.life
Contact: embodythegoddess444@gmail.com or 646-355-7934
Schedule a Call: bit.ly/2fHEqkV

DEE SAVOIE is an author, educator, healer, and coach. She started writing her first book when she was sixteen. It was during a family vacation to Martha's Vineyard where the beauty of the island had her dreaming of romance. Every so often she would pick up her masterpiece and do some work on it, then stick it in a drawer to be forgotten about for a couple of years. It wasn't until 20 years after she'd written her first word that she summoned the courage to actually send it out to an agent and a publisher for review. It was immediately accepted by the first agent who read it and eventually by the only publisher she sent it to. Since her first novel, *Spellbound* was published in 1999, she has published numerous more romance books.

She is–a nurturer, a mom at heart, a Goddess of the Earth. Her role is to teach, by word and example, to shine a light in the darkness for others to follow.

The
Psychics &
Mediums

EROLINA
Intuitive, Psychic & Pendulum Reader

The most important way to keep our chakras in alignment, I believe, is through healthy living. By eating organic and fresh foods rich in vitamins and minerals, exercising daily, getting a good night's sleep, and staying hydrated, it allows our brain and body to function at its best.

I select a rainbow of colors when I prepare my meals to provide tasty and nutritious options for my taste palette and my body. I go to the gym daily. I enjoy the hot sauna (it brings blood flow to my entire body and prepares me to move with less chance of injury or pain.)

I love to swim, dance, lift weights and stretch. I frequently use the Swiss ball (It is something you can use at the gym or in the comfort of your own home.) This is a great form of exercising. As we are multi-dimensional beings this allows me to work in many planes to optimize my functional abilities in the real world. I notice my day is better when I work out.

It releases endorphins, which help minimize or eliminate pain both emotionally and physically. On the occasions I miss a day, my body and mind feel the difference.

Eating well, exercising, drinking plenty of water and sleeping well is only part of the formula for feeling and living well. In the past when my mind was troubled, I would review a situation over and over again, or worry about it but it didn't change anything. Having a pendulum allows me to gain more clarity and open the door to solutions. It helps me focus and lights a path in which direction to move forward. I have been working with the pendulum for years for myself, private clients and as a party psychic. It doesn't matter if the client is eight or eighty, asking the pendulum a series of yes or no questions always leads to answers.

CHARM OF A PENDULUM
Erolina

As a psychic, I frequently use a pendulum. My pendulum is a chain necklace with a charm suspended from it; this way I always have it available. Some people have pendulums with crystals that end in a point, but it doesn't matter, there are many varieties.

You can use a pendulum yourself or you can go to a psychic. Reiki practitioners use a pendulum as well, often to scan the body to see if anything is out of alignment. The only caution with using a pendulum on yourself is that sometimes you seek certain answers so you must be careful that you are not unconsciously manipulating the response you want.

USING YOUR PENDULUM

The way a pendulum works is pretty straight forward. There are only a few rules.

- Be relaxed in both body and mind. It may be hard if you are worried about something to relax your mind, so take a few deep inhalations and exhalations before you begin, or visualize something that will get you to relax. You can imagine you're at the beach, soaking in the warmth of the sun, or see yourself on top of a mountain watching the sunset, or home on a comfy couch petting your cat, laughing with your child, or whatever brings a smile and calmness to your inner soul. You know yourself best, so use or do what works for you.

- Now that you are relaxed or in a more peaceful state, while sitting down, hold your arm in a horizontal position and allow the pendulum to swing free. If you want to rest your elbow on a table, you can, but it is not necessary. The goal is to get a feel of the pendulum. A pendulum moves mostly in these directions:

  - Side to side or front to back
  - In clockwise or counter-clockwise circles
  - In an elliptical or diagonal motion

  Once you're confident that you have a feel for your pendulum, hold the pendulum in one hand and with the other hand steady it. Usually, this is done by touching it to prevent it from swinging in any direction.

- Pendulums do mainly one thing. They answer "yes" or "no" questions. Therefore, you need to know when you have a clear sign for "yes" and when the pendulum is giving you a clear sign for "no." The directions are different for each person. Sometimes it will give you a sign for "maybe" as well. This shows that a final outcome is not ready. Sometimes we have to coast before we can land. The Universe will not give us the go ahead if we are not ready to receive it. It's OK, just be patient, the plane eventually has to land. Once we let go of all resistance this will happen. Keeping your eye on the pendulum, I ask out loud to the pendulum, "Show me a clear sign for *yes*," and then watch to see which way the pendulum moves. The faster the movement or the larger the motion the more powerful the answer. Then I say, "Show me a clear sign for, *no*." The pendulum will swing in a different direction or pattern. Same for asking it *maybe* watch the direction.

- Be sure that the pendulum is not being guided by you. Keep your hands and fingers still, with upper body and shoulders relaxed.

- Since the pendulum only responds with Yes, No or Maybe answers keep this in mind when asking questions.

- Once, you are ready to start asking questions, it is best to start with simple questions that you know the answers too. This will give you confidence that you are using the pendulum correctly and that the answers are accurate. I often start with these questions. "Is my name Erolina?" "Do I have a sister?"

- Once confident that you're in sync with your pendulum, you can begin to ask it more personal questions. Keep it to one question at a time. Don't ask multipart or vague questions like is it warm out or will I move? Try to be specific as possible with a date, time, place or name of a person.

That's it. It's pretty accurate and working with a pendulum will develop your inner eye (third eye chakra) of looking within which is great as often most answers we want are found if we look within.

© Erolina

ABOUT EROLINA

Website: www.psychicerolina.com
Contact: psychicerolina@yahoo.com

EROLINA is a gifted psychic. She mainly works with clients by phone to answer love and work related questions, but she also does parties and finds them fun to do and the participants find having a pendulum psychic awesome and different.

Erolina has expressed her intuitive abilities since age nine. Her gift enables her to read people's past, assess their current situation and offer guidance about the future whether it is regarding love, career, school, or family. She uses the pendulum to enhance her intuitive readings and to guide her client in answering any (yes and no) questions. It is best if you don't initially share information with her and just let her do the talking. All her services are available only on the weekends and by appointment. Her services include:

- One-on-One Readings
- Parties: Bachelorette, Bar/Bat Mitzvahs, and Birthdays
- Girls Night Out Gatherings
- Corporate Events

JOAN CARRA
Psychic & Medium

My hands are human x-rays; I can scan the human body and feel energy differences, such as heat and coolness. I often scan clients and pick up which chakra is closed. When my hands feel an energy dip, for example in the throat chakra, then I will tell the person that they do not express their feelings. They agree, and I suggest that they may want to explore chanting or singing so they can get their voice and their truth out. For one client, who had a difficult time standing up to her father, who she also worked for, I had her rehearse the word "no." When she first said the word no, it was barely a whisper. After many tries, she was able to say it as an empowered woman. The next time I saw her, which was months later, she was very happy and seemed like a new woman. She was able to assert herself to her father at the job. Now she was running her own department and had respect and encouragement from her dad.

For clients, who have their heart chakra shut down, I counsel them for their loss whether it is grief from the death of a loved one or a broken relationship. As a medium, I can connect to the spirit of the person they miss. I often see people leave smiling after I give messages from a departed soul. Love and communication continues after death and often situations are resolved. If it is heartbreak from a relationship, then I offer a meditation so they can renew their heart with love again. Over the years, I realized that we often fall in love with the illusion we have of the other person. We are infatuated with who we want them to be rather than accepting someone for who they really are. How many clients say, he would be perfect for me, if only he wasn't a player. Going deep with affirmations and meditations are very helpful for heartbreak. Sometimes a client cheers up knowing that the psychic sees another love coming with a happy outcome. We always learn about love and ourselves with each person we encounter. Forgiveness of yourself and the other person is also very healing, to help us move on to accept a new life when a relationship is over.

The palms of my hands not only can take a picture of someone's energy but can also emanate healing energies to the localized spot, so I often send a laser beam blast to the chakra that needs a boost. I also tell clients they can spin their energy centers counter clockwise to boost it even more. Thoughts are energy, so why not think that we can expand and harness the energy in our chakras. You are in control and you can learn to vibrate an inner current to yourself and to the world for greater healing and harmony.

CONNECTION TO SPIRIT WITH THE CHAKRAS
Joan Carra

How does a medium connect to a client and a loved one in spirit? For me, it is deep listening, which I call inner squinting. I also watch the pictures that flash in my mind's eye. When I go deep inside myself I am concentrating on my upper chakras: crown, third eye, throat and heart. My heart and voice are one with compassion and empathy. Often there is tremendous pain and trauma with someone's passing. Clients often feel guilty that they did not do enough or were not present when the person passed, even if they were miles away. Spirits often tell me to tell their family that they loved them all their lives and they are not going to hate them for this. Their passing was inevitable and usually they are not only in a peaceful new place but they are reuniting with family and friends who have already passed, even decades before. A client asked me, "Does my father know I adopted children?" Her father told me to simply say to her, "Skating" She gasped and then said, "I brought the children skating just this afternoon!" Loved ones in spirit are always watching over us. You can even talk to them yourselves.

People ask me if they can develop their intuition. The answer is yes. I often teach psychic development with techniques that stimulate the chakras to enhance intuition. First, you can start by imagining a funnel of white light entering your crown chakra. This is the primordial light of first creation associated with the sacred sound Aum. Ask for divine intelligence; an all knowing of the past, present and future. It's important to breathe deeply and slowly; breath means spirit and you are allowing invisible forces to find a home in your physical presence. Bring this ball of energy to your third eye and feel the effects of the indigo hue relaxing your temples, eyes and skull. Let go and feel light. Gently massage your third eye and believe you are opening awareness in your intuitive realm. With your next breath, direct the energy to your throat chakra. This blue light is breath from the sky and relaxes all the muscles in your neck area. Breathe and exhale with a soft sound and think how important it is to listen and speak with compassion and empathy. This energy is now surrounding your heart with a pink light that vibrates love in its highest form – unconditional and without judgment. Feel the tingling. As you breathe in and out, magnify this electricity throughout your body, the room you're in and beyond.

What if you can send this electrical current with an intention or thought? You will be amazed when what you are thinking about actually manifests itself in reality.

I hope this journey helps you feel the magic threads that connect us all.

© Joan Carra

ABOUT JOAN CARRA

Website: www.psychicjoancarra.net
Contact: psychicjoan@yahoo.com or (203) 531-6387

JOAN CARRA is a gifted psychic and medium, practicing for the past 25 years. Joan's spiritual counseling is recognized in six books including the first edition of *The 100 Top Psychics in America, Interdimensional Universe* and *The Rational Psychic*. She has been interviewed in Westchester's *WAG Magazine, The Wall St. Journal, Metro NY, AM NY* and *The Daily News*, in which she predicted the flooding of NYC right before Hurricane Sandy. In 2000, she predicted on WPIX television news that Hillary Clinton would not be America's first woman president; later on she predicted a Trump win. She teaches at the Edgar Cayce Center in NYC and taught at Lily Dale Assembly as well as many other venues. She does private readings on the phone or in person and is also available for parties and events.

Joan is also a lifelong writer and performer. Her cosmic songs were seen on the acclaimed television show *NOVA* and the TV show *Strange Universe.* Joan performed at the Village Gate in NYC and is in Mike Luckman's book *Alien Rock.* Her CD, *Mystic Bop*, is a compilation of poems and meditations. Her other CD is *Greetings from Outer Space.* She is mentioned in Phil Imbrogno's book *Interdimensional Universe* as an intuitive and songwriter and was written up in *UFO Magazine*.

YAFFA REGEV
Spa Owner, Nutritionist, Herbalist & Organic Chef

I have helped countless people to reach their health goals and maintain optimum health through my knowledge as a nutritionist, testing people for what vitamins and minerals they may need with special equipment that I have at my spa, and by creating delicious and nutritious vegetarian and vegan foods.

Sometimes though, I am so busy taking care of others, I don't schedule time to take care of myself. And sometimes, as much as I want to help someone, I am left unable to. Many years ago, my husband had MS. Although, he passed on, in wanting to find an answer to help him, I read everything about nutrition. It led me to discover ways to treat people with healthy eating and supplements and ultimately to co-own a health-food store.

In 2013, when a dear friend's daughter past away at age 33 from breast cancer leaving two beautiful small children without a mom, I wanted to do something. In memory of this beautiful woman, I decided to share my belief in the John of God Crystal Light Bed treatments and make it available to anyone who is a currently going through cancer treatments at no cost. Anyone else is welcome to come, yet there is a charge.

The John of God Crystal Light Bed balances your chakras with the use of seven crystals, the same colors as the colors of the rainbow and as the colors of the chakras; my chapter explains this further. There is a waiting list to schedule an appointment, yet anyone and everyone who contacts my Spa, Yaffa's Living Well, located in Brooklyn on Avenue M and 14th Street in New York gets an appointment.

Many people, not just cancer patients, have shared their personal experience with me after using the John of God Crystal Light Bed. Each person who has had a treatment has had a different experience. One woman, known for her talkative and friendly nature, after her session, couldn't open her mouth for fifteen minutes. Another person had a vision and clarity on how to proceed with a problem she was having. Yet another, who suffered from insomnia, was able to finally get a good night's sleep. The experiences vary and I'm always interested in what people share afterwards with me.

If you know of a person with cancer, please share my offer with them, or just come and try it yourself. Treatments last from twenty minutes to an hour. One of the things I like about the John of God Crystal Light Bed is that it requires nothing from you except to take the opportunity to relax, because the only thing you need to do is just lie down on a massage table and listen to soothing music.

CHAKRAS AND JOHN OF GOD CRYSTAL LIGHT BED
Yaffa Regev

When I first became aware of the John of God Crystal Light Bed, I was in Las Vegas on business. Several of the people I was with decided to try it. I was skeptical. During the trip, I witness a person with shoulder pain express he was pain free, and I observed an emotional eater stop over eating. That did it. I didn't even have to try the John of God Light Bed myself. I knew I wanted one for my wellness center as I thought emotional treatment, compliments the other treatments my wellness center offers. It was one of the best decisions, I made. When the bed arrived, I tried it. In my case, after suffering years of choking and never knowing what caused it, my choking episodes have completely stopped. At my first session, I felt someone touching my throat. Every session is different for everyone, but whenever I finish a session I get up feeling like I had a very deep sleep.

If you are like I was and don't already know who John of God is, let me share what I know.

John of God (João de Deus), was born Joao Teixeira de Faria. He is a medium who believes god gave him the gift to be a medium to channels the spirits (entities) of about 30 healers and doctors who have passed on, including King Solomon, Francisco Xavier and Drs. Augusto de Almeida, Jose Valdivino, Oswaldo Cruz and St. Ignatius de Loyola.

In 1979, he established The Casa de Dom Inacio (The House of Saint Ignatius) in Abadiania, Brazil. The Casa operates on the Principles of Spiritist Doctrine but, anyone, regardless of their faith or religious belief is welcome.

A John of God Crystal Light Bed session gives a person the opportunity to reset their body, mind and spirit. It consists of seven colored Vogel Crystals. Each light has a different vibrational frequency, matching the seven chakra colors (red, orange, yellow, green, blue, indigo and violet). The lights are made from pure quartz *crystals*. Each light is a crystal shaped diamond. It is the diamond shape, along with the colors, and the healing of the entities that give it its power to work on balancing the chakras.

THE CHAKRAS

Chakras are whirling energy centers. They are not physically present in the body. They exist on the metaphysical plane. There are seven major chakras. Each chakra spins in a circular motion and vibrates at a different frequency. The different frequencies are connected to different colors. Although, they have no real physical location, these subtle energies are represented as being aligned along the spine, from the base of the spine to the top of the head and correspond roughly to the sympathetic, parasympathetic, and central nervous system.

Chakras are associated with specific organs, glands and body systems. When our chakras are out of alignment we may think, feel and see issues relating to our emotions, body, or spirit.

Here is quick overview of each chakra: where it is located, its associated color and corresponding body system.

The first chakra or base chakra is located at the base of the spine. Its color is *red.* Red has the longest wavelength and the fastest vibrational frequency. It stimulates the immune system and governs our skeletal systems.

The second chakra or sacral chakra is located about two inches below the navel. Its color is *orange* and it relates to the reproductive system.

The third chakra or solar plexus is located in the diaphragm area. Its color is *yellow* and it optimizes the function of the digestive system.

The fourth chakra or heart chakra is located at the center of the chest. Its color is *green* and it manages our emotions, as well as balances the heart and circulatory system.

The fifth chakra or throat chakra is related to areas of the neck, throat, face and ears. Its color is *blue* (turquoise) and it is often associated with the endocrine system's thyroid gland.

The sixth chakra or so-called third eye is located in the middle of forehead and slightly above eyebrows. Its color is *indigo* (a dark blue) and its associated with the pineal gland and it balances the parasympathetic nervous system.

The seventh chakra or crown chakra is located at the top of the head. Its color is *purple.* Purple has the shortest wavelength, and the slowest vibrational frequency. It influences the brain, central nervous system, muscular system, and integumentary system, consisting of the skin, hair, nails, glands and nerves.

No matter what your reasons, if you want to experience the John of God Crystal Light Bed, it is important to enter a session with a clear intention of what you want. People, who do so, have found it to be worthwhile. The best way to understand what the John of God Bed is all about is to try it and evaluate your own response and result.

© Yaffa Regev

ABOUT YAFFA REGEV

Website: yaffaslivingwell.com
Contact: yaffaregevlivingwell@gmail.com or (718) 627-3438

YAFFA REGEV is a nutrition consultant, herbalist and organic chef. She owns Yaffa's Living Well and Organic Produce Club that helps countless people reach their health goals. She is fluent in Hebrew, Turkish and Spanish.

To experience the John of God Crystal Light Bed, call for an appointment. There is no cost to current cancer patients.

Address: Yaffa's Living Well - 1322 East 14th street, Brooklyn, NY 11230
Transportation: Q Train to Ave M or B9 Bus

John of God Crystal Light Bed

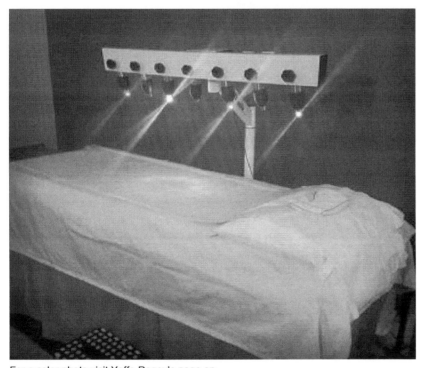

For a color photo visit Yaffa Regev's page on HarmonyinChakras.com

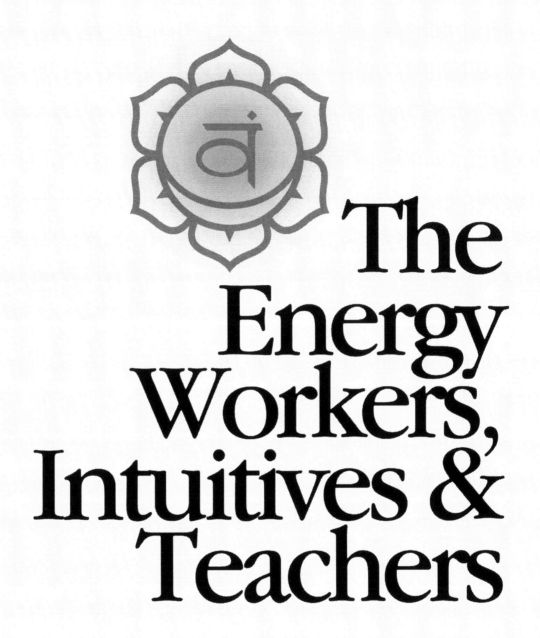

The Energy Workers, Intuitives & Teachers

LEAH DESANTO
Usui and Tibetan Reiki Master, Shamanic Reiki Practitioner and Empath

I love what I do and it brings me joy to help so many people live a more joyful life. The starting point in my work is to make a real connection with the people who come to me, both as clients and as students. Using the gifts of intuition and empathy, I explore with every person I meet through gentle questioning the root cause of blocked energy.

Reiki sessions are painless and the client leaves relaxed and with improved energy flow. The session requires the client to lie down on the Reiki table or sit in a chair. Then using my hands or a pendulum--and my intuition--I scan the body from the top of the head, the crown chakra, to the base of the spine also known as the root chakra. This scanning allows me to connect to an individual's energy system and assess if the chakras are performing optimally.

When I sense stagnant energy, I continue asking questions. Underlying emotional and physical traumas are often revealed as the cause of pain in just one session. As you read my chapter, you will learn about examples of how past traumas are revealed and healed.

Personal experience with neck and shoulder pain led me on this path of energy work. The pain was so intense that I made an appointment to see someone. I immediately noticed that he wasn't the average doctor. He was a chiropractor who applied energy transference.

I eventually told him that I was interested in learning how to work with energy to promote healing. He told me to research online and choose a modality that resonated with me. When I found Reiki, I knew that was the modality for me and committed myself to completing all courses necessary to become a Certified Reiki Master/Teacher.

Since attaining the Master/Teacher level, I have practiced in Queens, Long Island, Brooklyn and Manhattan. The rest, as the saying goes, is history.

REIKI & CHAKRAS: WHAT PART DO CHAKRAS PLAY IN OPTIMUM HEALTH?
Leah DeSanto, RMTP

CHAKRAS (ENERGY CENTERS)

First, let's briefly discuss what chakras are. Chakras are little swirls of energy, also called "Energy Centers." There are seven main Energy Centers that are located along the spine of the human body. Energy flows through them and creates harmony in the body when spinning optimally. There are minor Energy Centers throughout the human body as well that aid circulation of energy, but I will only concentrate on the seven main ones.

Each Energy Center has a color associated with it, as well as different emotions, physical organs and a spiritual connection. An Energy Center resembles a cone, where the center of the cone is narrower in the middle and gets wider as it protrudes out of both the front and back of the human body.

Each Energy Center vibrates at its own frequency; therefore, it is more attuned to a specific color in the spectrum. When working optimally, it is clear and bright with beautiful colors that rotate smoothly in a circular motion. When an Energy Center is not at its optimum, or shuts down, it may be cloudy, slow or blocked. If a person attracts negative energy in their aura, one or more Energy Centers may be affected and need to be balanced.

1st Energy Center (Base Chakra) - is located at the base of the spine, between the legs, and going down to the ground. The color is Red. It is associated with early childhood, how we see ourselves and Family.

2nd Energy Center (Sacral Chakra) - is located in the front of the body, two inches below the navel and lower back. The color is Orange. It is associated with money and relationships.

3rd Energy Center (Solar Plexus) - is located in the front of the body at the diaphragm and mid back. The color is Yellow. It is associated with how people see us and the God Center.

4th Energy Center (Heart Chakra) - is located in the front center of the chest, and between the shoulder blades in the back. The color is Green. It is associated with emotions.

5th Energy Center (Throat Chakra) - is located in the front by the neck/throat, and the back of the neck. The color is Blue. It is associated with the physical, the spiritual and communication.

6th Energy Center (Third Eye) - is located in the front by the center of the forehead, and in the back of the head. The color is Indigo Blue. It is associated with psychic abilities and clairvoyance.

7th Energy Center (Crown Chakra) - is located at the top of the head, vertically reaching the sky and through the body. The color is Purple. It is associated with the connection to the Divine Source.

REIKI - USUI & TIBETAN

What is Reiki? Reiki is a healing technique that uses energy transference directed by the Reiki Practitioner, using their hands onto their client. Reiki helps the body to heal itself. It is a beautiful and powerful natural healing system that involves placing hands above a person's body and directing the healing energy. Reiki is also used to direct energy at a distance when a person is in another country or state. It can also be directed to events in the past, the future and much more.

We are all a part of an energy grid or field where Ki (Chi) energy flows through our physical bodies, between us, and the space surrounding us. Invisible Ki (Chi) energy, or Reiki energy, flows through this energy field. This energy runs through each of us and is directed and transferred during a Reiki Session. It is an intelligent energy that goes to where it is needed in the human body. Both the practitioner and their client receive the benefit of a Reiki Session. The practitioner does not use her own energy. The universal life force energy, Ki (Chi), is channeled through their hands to the client. This is called energy transference.

THIS IS WHERE CHAKRAS (ENERGY CENTERS) MEET REIKI

When Energy Centers are not spinning optimally, Reiki energy is used to balance the body's energy and remove blocks to achieve optimal health. The cause of the imbalance could stem from an emotional trauma, a physical trauma, or both if not corrected over time.

EXAMPLES OF THE EFFECTS OF BURIED EMOTIONS

Jill had a huge argument with Jack and she said some very hurtful things that she didn't mean. She is really bothered by it, but will not apologize to Jack even though she knows she should. She buries the emotion. A little time goes by since the argument, and Jill is not feeling well. That emotion that was buried, and not expressed, is beginning to manifest itself into something physical. It can also manifest into an emotional block that could affect her current relationship or her next relationship. The emotional block affected her heart chakra.

Jill decides to go to a Reiki Practitioner. This is what I would do, as that Practitioner. I would scan her body with my eyes and hands. I would sense that she had an argument with someone and that she is suppressing an emotion that needs to be addressed. We would discuss what happened. I would have her close her eyes and recreate the argument. Then I would ask her in her mind's eye to apologize to Jack. Usually the client would have an emotional release after expressing the buried emotion. At that point, I would check the chakras to make sure that they are in balance and spinning optimally. The client feels better, and if necessary, will have the courage to confront any unresolved issues.

I would like to share this true story where I used my empathic and intuitive skills. While I was visiting my friend at his chiropractic office, two men walked in. One was hunched over in pain and the other one was helping him walk. The injured man did not speak English. I scanned the man's body with my eyes, and the message I received was very clear. I asked the interpreter to ask the man if he had an argument earlier that day. He said yes, and I knew I had to relay the message I just received. I gave it to him and told him he needed to pass it onto his friend. I said, "You need to tell this man that he caused great distress to the person that he had the argument with, and that for him to heal, he needs to apologize to him right away." The argument had created an imbalance in his chakras that needed to be corrected to achieve balance again.

Another true example is, when I was volunteering at Mt. Sinai Beth Israel Hospital, one of the psychiatrists thought it would be a good idea to send one of her patients for a Reiki session. The woman was in her 30's. A while back she had fallen down a flight of stairs and was injured badly. Thank G-d she overcame the physical issues, but the emotional issues that were brought on by the fall were not resolved. Her heart chakra and base chakra were blocked. I asked her if it was OK to go back to the accident and work through it with me. She was open to it. So together we went back to the accident through meditation. She relayed everything about the accident and what happened after it; her recovery process, etc. I saw that she was getting emotional so I reassured her that she is not alone, that I am with her and that she is safe. I asked her if she could let go of the fear. Her response was that she was used to it and she didn't want to let it go, it was familiar to her. I explained to her that she no longer had to hold on to it. As the emotion was trying to exit her body, she felt that it was located by her leg. I told her OK, let's help it travel down your leg and out through your foot. I needed to reassure her again that she wasn't alone, that I was with her and that she was safe. She finally let go of the emotion and the fear, and was crying. Her chakras were balanced once more. We both could see that a weight had been lifted from her being. We hugged and she left.

Ryan was a regular to my Shamanic Reiki Circle. He had problems sleeping. I gave him some advice on what he could do to help him sleep. A few weeks later, he mentioned that he was sleeping a little better but still had issues with getting a good night's rest. My intuition told me that something happened to him when he was a little boy and that it had a major effect on him. I mentioned it to him and he said he couldn't think of anything. I told him that together we could work on finding out what it is, when he was ready.

Ryan called to tell me he was ready for a private session to get to the root of the sleeping issue. While he was lying on the Reiki table, I took him on a Shamanic Reiki Journey into his past. I asked him what happened when he was seven years old that had had a major effect on him. He said that his parents were getting a divorce and he saw his mother crying. That was the very first time he ever saw his mother crying, and he had always looked up to his mother as a strong woman. This made him very sad and he started to cry. The thing that went through his mind at that time was that from now on he had to be the strong one and be there for his mother. He was no longer a child but the man of the house. He started to assume that role and it changed his life from that point on. As he was relating the story to me, tears were streaming down his face. I asked him to take the person he is today (the Adult Ryan), and go to the little child Ryan and give him a hug and tell him everything is OK. I am here, you are not alone. You are safe. Mom is OK. You no longer need to worry about her. He continued crying. I asked him to take a few deep breaths and release the emotions that were stored for so many years deep within him. At the end of the session, he smiled and said he was OK and thanked me. I called him a few days later to see how he was and he told me that for the first time in a long time he was able to have a good night's sleep. By going back releasing stored emotions and balancing his chakras, he could now move forward to a more joyful life.

One can use Reiki Energy to find the cause or root of an issue, and to get the Human Body Energy system flowing optimally by balancing the chakras. It really make a difference in the healing process.

© Leah DeSanto

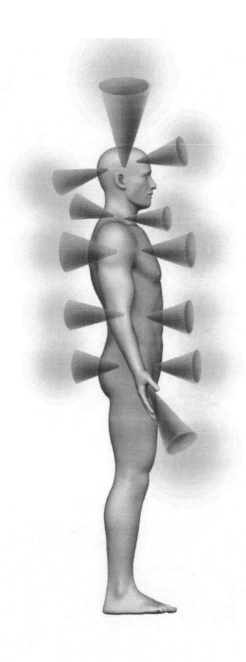

*Chakra means wheel in Sanskrit. Each wheel is a vortex,
spinning as it draws energy into its funnel.*

ABOUT LEAH DESANTO, RMTP

Website: www.reiki-relaxed.com
Contact: brachas18@gmail.com or 917-575-6182

LEAH DESANTO is a Certified Usui and Tibetan Reiki Practitioner (Master Teacher level), and Shamanic Reiki Healer. She utilizes her formal training, together with her intuition and empathic skills to get to the root of an issue or block. Leah was certified as a Reiki Practitioner, Master Teacher Level, in 2001. She studied Shamanism with Itzhak Beery through several workshops, Shamanic journeys and Soul Retrieval/Mending classes.

In addition to teaching Reiki, holding private sessions and the Shamanic Reiki Circle at the Edgar Cayce Center in New York, Leah was a volunteer and Reiki Practitioner at Mt. Sinai Beth Israel Hospital for three years, alternating from the main hospital to the Center for Health and Healing. The physicians at the Center for Health and Healing highly recommended Leah to their patients and were grateful for her presence.

Leah is not your typical practitioner. When necessary, she guides clients on a Shamanic Journey using drumbeats to go back in time and to find and clear deep-rooted trauma that may prevent them from having a joyful life. Whether you are new to Shamanic Reiki or have previous Reiki experience, you will feel very comfortable speaking with Leah. If you are new to Shamanic Reiki and Reiki, Leah will explain what the difference is and how she uses it to remove emotional and physical blocks. Reiki offers the opportunity to be more relaxed, peaceful and happy.

She teaches Reiki 1 and Reiki 2 Courses and is developing an online Reiki 1 course.

Leah facilitates a Shamanic Reiki Circle at the Edgar Cayce Center and at other facilities in New York where her students can practice and receive Reiki and how to use their intuition to get answers. All are welcome.

To be put on her membership list to receive newsletters and upcoming information about classes, workshops and discounts, send her an email and in the subject type "Reiki Sessions or Reiki Courses".

Leah looks forward to releasing blocks, teaching and sharing Reiki with you!!!!!

NANCI DEUTSCH, LCSW
Therapist, Coach, Speaker, Trainer and Radio Show Host

A large part of the work I do is helping clients tune into their truth and allowing the energy of the Divine to flow through them. I do this by using intuition, hypnosis, visualization and other modalities. It brings me great joy to help people clear energetic blocks that keep them from manifesting a peaceful and joyful life filled with loving relationships.

When I found out you can go to the realm of the soul, I became a hypnotherapist. Hypnosis is one of the ways I help people connect to their thoughts, those that are known and those that are hidden from them. This allows them to understand themselves and awaken to the truth of who they are in ways they may never have been aware of consciously. When clients are in a hypnotic state, they are able to communicate what they may need and want. At the end of a session, I always say to the person, "You will remember everything that has happened and will 'wake up' feeling relaxed." I will restate what we worked on and use positive suggestions that will support and inspire them. Many clients have had issues healed and gained understandings using this modality.

I love working with hypnosis and working with the chakras, (our chakras are portals to the different dimensions), as they can reveal the secrets of your deepest truths and wounds. When you connect with your soul, you have clarity. There is more peace and acceptance. There is harmony in your relationships, and your relationship with yourself grows so you feel more self-confidence, compassion, joy and gratitude. Interested in knowing how you score in relationships? I have a gift for you - a Relationship Chakra Assessment. Visit NanciDeutsch.com/chakraassessment to receive it.

Using my intuition is an important part of my work. I can receive information by hearing, seeing, sensing, knowing or feeling. When I am working with people, it amazes me what occurs as I trust my intuition to help them. I also help my clients to work with their own intuition and to trust the answers they receive.

On Tuesdays at 6:00 pm EST is my radio show *Inspired & Empowered Living* on healthcafelive.com. Every week it's a different topic, but it's always about having a better relationship with yourself and others. I invite people to write in the chat room. I really love to work with people to clear their blocks, accomplish their goals, develop their intuition, connect more deeply with their Higher Self and soul, and become more empowered.

I look forward to connecting with you!

THE SECRETS OF YOUR SOUL REVEALED IN YOUR CHAKRAS
Nanci Deutsch

Imagine living the life of your dreams! You feel happy, joyful and fulfilled. You are living your life's purpose. You have loving and joyful relationships. You feel healthy and vibrant. Money is flowing and you are prosperous. You are spreading joy and love from yourself to others and to the world. You are truly living an inspired and empowered life!

Within each of the cells of our being and within each of our chakras (chakras are portals to the different dimensions), our destiny and Divine Blueprint are encoded. Truly the secrets of our soul and our ability to live the best life possible are within our being. We are given ideas and we are meant to overcome any obstacles to make our vision a reality!

At the core of our being, we are pure awareness – source energy. But to experience a third dimensional existence, our spirit needed to create a stepped-down version of it so it created our soul. And our soul needed a means of expressing itself in physical form to live life on this planet, so our chakras were created to help us experience physical reality.

We are constantly receiving messages from other dimensions through our intuition to create the life of our dreams. However, if there are blocks, this will keep us from receiving the messages our soul and spirit have for us. Our job is to be able to heal the blockages and clear our channel so we become better expressions of the Divine within us.

Our spirit is already healed and whole, but our soul is not. For us to experience the truth of our spirit--the already healed being, we need to heal our soul from any pain and trauma from this or other lifetimes.

Like our soul, the chakras store pain. Our chakras also store the healing! For us to be whole and empowered, the first step is to clear our chakras.

When I am working with clients, we assess where in their body they feel the blockage or sensation so we can clear it allowing them to have a sense of freedom and relief. For example, when someone feels a lump in their throat, their throat chakra (5th chakra) is being affected. When they are feeling nervousness in their stomach, it usually relates to the third chakra (Solar Plexus). First it's important to understand the chakras.

UNDERSTANDING THE CHAKRAS

The actual meaning of the word chakra means "spinning wheels of light". These "wheels of light" are energy centers that are lined up along your spinal column. There is an actual energetic column coming down from your Divine Consciousness that extends down into the earth helping you have a physical body. Martial artists call this spinal column of light the Hara line. Along this column are seven major chakra energy centers. Although there are many chakras in your energy field, these seven are the most well-known and the ones we will work with.

Each of the seven major chakras hold your patterns and beliefs that affect how you see, feel, and experience yourself, your relationships, and the world. As we work with each chakra, beliefs and feelings that are negatively affecting us begin to clear.

THE SEVEN MAJOR CHAKRAS

The first chakra is also called the root chakra. It is at the base of the spine and the color associated with it is red. When you have blockages in your first chakra, you could have thoughts surrounding survival, not feeling safe, and questioning your reasons for being on this planet. So any issues concerning finances, your body and health, food, or anything dealing with your physical being will be affected by this chakra. Also, how you relate to your family, culture and heritage is associated with this chakra. When the first chakra is open, you are in present time and you feel grounded, centered, connected to yourself, the earth and your life.

The second chakra is also called the sacral or spleen chakra. It is located in the pelvis area about two inches below your navel (depending on body) and the color associated with it is orange. It is associated with your emotions, relationships, creativity, sensuality, and sexuality. When blocked you can't feel your emotions, desires, and needs. When this chakra is open there is a sense of abundance, well-being, and pleasure. You feel your emotions, needs and desires, and express your sensuality, sexuality, and creativity.

The third chakra is also called the solar plexus. It is about two inches above the navel (depending on body) and the color associated with it is yellow. It is connected with issues of self-worth, self-confidence, self-esteem, and issues around power in relationship to others and your uniqueness in the world. When you are wounded you can't express your uniqueness. When this chakra is open and healthy, you feel confident and more in control of your life; you are able to connect more deeply to who you really are to feel your power.

The fourth chakra is also called the heart chakra and it is in the center of the chest just above the heart and the color associated with it is green. When it is closed, you have trouble loving yourself and others. When it is open, you feel joy, peace, love and even unconditional love. You are able to share yourself with another and be intimate.

The fifth chakra is also called the throat chakra. It is in the throat area and the color associated with it is blue. It is associated with communication and the ability to have self-expression. When it is closed, you are not able to express yourself. When it is open you speak your truth, and you are able to ask for what you need.

The sixth chakra is also called the third eye. It is located between the eyebrows and the color associated with it is indigo. It is associated with the psychic abilities especially clairvoyance, and your ability to think, to focus, and to see the big picture. When it is closed, you don't listen to your intuition and you can be judgmental. When it is open, you have clear intuition, imagination, wisdom, and are able to think clearly, make decisions and accept yourself and others.

The seventh chakra is also called the crown chakra. It is located on the top of the head and the color associated with it is violet or white. It is about your connection to the Divine and your connection to your infinite potential. When it is closed, you have limited thinking and can't feel your connection to the Divine. When it is open, you can feel bliss, feel connected to the Universal mind, you can receive knowings, also called claircognizance, and have "aha" experiences. When it is open you can experience your infinite potential.

ASPECTS OF THE SELF

To connect with our chakras on the deepest levels, it is important to understand the different aspects of the self (Soul, Higher Self, Divine Self and Inner Child).

Soul

This aspect of self is our consciousness that came from the Divine and is our life force energy. The soul is the energy and characteristics of who we are. When we experience it, we feel peace, love or joy. When I am working with individuals and we do a soul journey, it may appear as light, or another form or image or someone may embody their soul and speak as the soul itself.

Our soul is a vast huge energy that is unconditionally loving. Before our birth, our soul creates contracts about our purpose and the lessons we need to learn in this lifetime. Those contracts are also with the people in our lives where we both agreed to play certain roles to help each other learn and grow. Our soul contracts are with our partners, parents, children, close friends and others who have an important connection with us.

Examples of soul lessons are learning to trust yourself and others, how to be more compassionate and loving to yourself and/ or others, how to have loving joyful relationships and deeper levels of intimacy or learning to trust ourselves and our decisions. Our personality self may not like what is happening in our lives, but our souls view these experiences as necessary.

When we work with our soul, we come to know our true self; the powerful magnificent being that we are. As we connect with our soul, we can access and discover our power, strength, light and love. Our intuition becomes strong and clear and we can access our inner wisdom. As we connect with the wisdom of our soul, we have lifetimes of lessons, information, resources and abilities just waiting to be tapped into. We all have a purpose for being here and a mission that is an expression of our own uniqueness. Connecting with our soul helps us to know what our purpose is here on earth and how to reach it.

We begin to access our soul by first connecting with our Higher Self.

Higher Self

The Higher Self is an aspect of us. It is the wise aspect of ourselves and the part of us that has achieved enlightenment. The Higher Self translates messages from our soul to our personality. When I work with people, they envision the Higher Self as light, an angel, a wise woman or man, a beautiful woman or handsome young man, or an animal. The Higher Self's appearance may change from meditation to meditation or it may stay the same. Also know that we may not see a visual image of this part of us, but we may be able to feel its unconditional love in our heart and body.

Divine Self or I AM Presence Self

This Self is connected to Source (Divine, God, Higher Power or Universal Consciousness). It is the Self from which our soul is born. It is the highest part of who we are and we are all connected to our own representation of Source.

Inner Child

Inside each of us is a child waiting to be heard and acknowledged. It is part of our subconscious mind and when we access the inner child we are in touch with our feelings, body, and our wants, needs and desires. The inner child can be both playful and wounded. The playful inner child within us as adults allows us to be happy, creative, play with animals, enjoy life, laugh at ourselves and all the good things you can think of; it allows us to be well adjusted adults. The wounded inner child may have been hurt, abused or traumatized by physical, mental, emotional, sexual, or spiritual abuse. An accident can also be traumatizing. This wounded part of us feels fear, sadness, anger, grief, hurt, rejection and abandonment. This is the part of us that needs attention, love and kindness so we can learn new patterns of being. Messages that diminish a child in any way and do not empower and respect a child's individuality and humanness, are inner beliefs that need to be healed.

The wounded child is the part of us that has needs and desires that may not have been met when we were children. So, as we become adults, if we have not healed and worked with this part in some way, we continue to look for those needs and desires to be met outside of us. As we heal, instead of looking to our partner or other substances like food or alcohol (anything can become a substitute), we learn to satisfy many of those needs and desires within ourselves.

INTUITION

Intuition is our ability to perceive information beyond our physical five senses. It is the information that comes from our higher parts, like our Higher Self, soul, or Divine Self and our guides and angels. We need to clear our chakras to be open to receive the guidance which can come through to us by hearing – clairaudience; seeing – clairvoyance; sensing – clairsentience; knowing – claircognizance; or being able to sense the feelings of others – empathy. The Divine is constantly sending messages to help and guide us, but we may be clogged and not able to hear.

Imagine we are a pipeline to the Divine and when the pipeline is clear the information, inspiration and energy flows freely. Now imagine a big hairball in the pipeline, this clog blocks us from receiving the information and guidance that wants to come through. The clog is really limiting beliefs and emotions that block us from receiving information we need to make better decisions. I help clients learn to trust their decisions by connecting more deeply to themselves and their intuition. When we have cleared the pipeline, we feel more confident and empowered and are able to take inspired action. Even though we refer to intuition as being part of the sixth chakra, it is more than that. It can also be part of the third chakra, such as when we have gut feelings. Sometimes we can also have a whole body experience such as when we get the chills or goosebumps all over our body. This happens when we get information that is correct and Spirit is confirming that information.

WHAT IS THE SOUL ADVENTURE PROCESS?

The Soul Adventure Process that I developed is one of the most powerful ways to manifest an amazing life. The Soul Adventures Process™ has two parts. The first part is a clearing of all your chakras, the major seven, plus others in your energetic field. This releases issues on a very deep level and helps to clear energies from this and other lifetimes that have been stored in your chakras and energetic field. It lifts the energies that have interfered with you moving forward or have been weighing you down. An example of this was a person who said she "felt like a loser" and it affected her from taking action to create success.

After the session, she noticed a big difference in how she felt about herself and her life. The issue of "feeling like a loser" was "lifted and cleared" from her energetic field. She felt more inspired and empowered to move forward towards her dreams.

The second part of the process is taking a Soul Adventure, which is a hypnotic journey to meet your soul or to work with a past life. You can journey to the realm of the soul to meet loved ones that have passed away and members of your soul group. A soul group is a group of souls that travel together in between lifetimes for eons. Some souls incarnate with you at the same time; some remain in the soul realm.

Each of us has a Council of Elders, a group of beings who are more advanced than we are. Some do not incarnate anymore and some have never incarnated. They are very high beings who guide us to our Highest and Greatest Good. They will guide us toward what challenges, lessons, and/or the mission we will have in this lifetime. By connecting with these powerful helpers, we can gain greater clarity, direction, inspiration and empowerment.

© Nanci Deutsch

ABOUT NANCI DEUTSCH, LCSW, CHT, CMT

Website www.nancideutsch.com
Email: nanci@nancideutsch.com
For a Gift: NanciDeutsch.com/chakraassessment

NANCI DEUTSCH is a Licensed Clinical Social Worker, Certified Hypnotherapist, and Certified Master Trainer. She is a Therapist, Coach, Speaker, Intuitive, Trainer and Radio Show Host who helps people live inspired and empowered lives. She has been counseling individuals, groups and couples for over 30 years. Nanci is the Founder of Inspired and Empowered Living, the Developer of the Soul Adventures Coaching Program and the Spiritual Hypnosis Training, and the Host of the *Inspired and Empowered Living* radio show on healthcafelive.com, live on Tuesdays at 6:00 pm EST.

Nanci can also be found on iHeartRadio. You can also listen to the archives of Nanci's radio show *Inspired and Empowered Living* at www.iheart.com/podcast/the-inspired-empowered-living-radio-26933237.

Nanci is available for speaking. She presents programs for therapists, has a Spiritual Hypnosis Training Program, and has seminars, workshops, and tele-classes on intuition and the soul. Visit her website for additional details.

Photo by Emily-kencairn

Lovers of Essences: Crystals, Plants & Flowers

LAURELLE RETHKE

Vibrational Healing Therapist, Personal & Spiritual Growth Consultant, Author, Teacher, Speaker and Spiritual Reverend

Over the past ten years, working with chakras has become an integral part of my life. Balancing our body's subtle energy centers is a wonderful way to ease discomforts on the mental, emotional and spiritual levels. As chakras are connected to the energy lines and organs in the body, bringing one's energy into balance affects us physically as well. When we are balanced, we are able to be healthier, more present and live in our fullest truth.

As a vibrational healing therapist, I consciously work to harmonize the chakras, align them with our midline, and balance the lower and upper chakra sets so we can manifest our dreams and live vibrantly. Working with crystals, essential oils, energy, sound, and new thought patterning, I assist clients to heal wounds and strengthen their connection to themselves, the Earth & the Divine.

In my personal life I do the same work clearing energies that are no longer serving me, centering, balancing, grounding and aligning towards the Divine. I also meditate with crystals, oils and sound, and use them individually on chakras to work on specific issues I'd like to address. Thanks to this, I am able to have a fuller understanding of how important this process can be in personal healing. I am so happy to have the experience of bringing these benefits to others and myself through this work.

CRYSTAL HEALING AND THE CHAKRAS
Laurelle Rethke

CRYSTALS

Crystals are said to hold *crystallized light consciousness*, and the longer I work with them, the more I can attest to this being true. They have a unique way of magnifying healing
and alignment through their mineral content, crystalline structure, color vibration, and scientifically measured energetic output. Acting as physical, emotional, mental & spiritual alchemists, they assist us in coming to a fuller understanding of ourselves, our place in the world, and the Divine expressing through each of us. They empower us to be our most balanced, present and connected selves.

Crystals have been used for millennia to bring healing, luck and peace, as documented in-depth throughout the *Materia Medica* written by our most ancient and revered cultures. These touchstones have been worn as amulets, used in meditation and ceremony, taken internally as elixirs or pulverized mineral medicine, and placed on the body through gridding and the art of Laying-on-of-Stones for millennia.

This chapter will briefly cover my interpretation of the Chakras, and certain stones that can be used for each chakra to bring healing and clarity. Fully healing the whole body is truly
a holistic endeavor, which includes addressing our emotions, fixed beliefs and spiritual connection. The medicine listed in this chapter are crystals, but there are many healers from the natural world... herbs, their essential oils, food, sound, flower essences, vibrational energy, color, the sacred geometry all around us, etc. Combining the tools that both excite & work best for you will bring you the fullest personal healing.

WHY CRYSTALS?

There are many reasons that can be cited on why to work with stones; from the science that's come together on the subject, to the way people feel once they've experienced a crystal healing for themselves, to recounting the endless experiences of dis-ease easing or coming to an end for people who work with them. But when it comes right down to it, I work with crystals because to me they are a physical manifestation of the Divine energies... a physical tool that empowers us to learn more about ourselves and the world around us. Rocks, crystals and minerals were the first matter to take physical form on this plane, providing the minerals needed for the waters to cleanse and plants to grow, which in turn gave birth to animal & human life. As such, they've been around a very long time, and have an ancient wisdom within them that connects us to nature and teaches us about the innate intuitive wisdom within all of us. To me, this is the most valuable component. Holding a crystal, or connecting physically to the Natural World around us allows us to know ourselves better, and in turn, connect more deeply with everyone and everything on this planet and beyond. It is my belief that living on this earth is a symbiotic relationship, and when we are in sync with the Earth and her creatures, we are most in tune with ourselves, and the Divine within us. Crystals help us to link matter to the mystery of life.

HOW CRYSTALS WORK

Looking beyond the physical science on the subject (i.e. piezoelectricity, energetic output, etc.), each crystal has its own way of expressing, just as each of us do, based on the physical properties inherent with in them. Crystals have the same minerals within them that we have in our body, and working with them through intention helps us to align our body more fully with the mineral & energetic vibration that the crystalline structure of a stone holds so strongly. This is part of how crystals can be cleansing, balancing, aligning, nurturing, grounding, activating, soothing and so much more.

How do we know which crystals will work in which way? Knowing more about the physical characteristics of a crystal are a part of how its healing energy is expressed. Once you are aware of the physical components, the more elusive symbolic healing properties are understood as simply the literal or metaphorical translation of what is physically present in each stone. This is similar to how a walnut is known to be good for your brain, because it resembles a tiny brain. This goes into the micro or 'cellular level' of how life is expressed. The physical characteristics for crystals include:

- the Crystalline Structure
- the Minerals present
- the Color of the stone
- the Location of where the crystal was found and formed
- how the stone Formed (Igneous, Metamorphic or Sedimentary)
- the Physical look and feel (aesthetics, growth pattern, weight, etc.)
- how Light refracts through the stone

There's not room in this chapter for me to address most of the above in detail, but I will share a bit about how light affects stones. You might notice I have a tendency to use stone, rock and crystal interchangeably, though these different forms of minerals can work quite differently. Stones are polished, either naturally or with lapidary tools. Rocks are not. Crystals are of a more transparent or translucent nature, and therefore more light moves through them. Light activates all stones in some way (color, etc.), but transparent or translucent crystals refract more light, and therefore vibrate with a quicker (or "higher") frequency than a stone or rock. This does not make it better to use… just different. Stones and rocks are generally a little slower moving energetically, which can feel more nurturing, stabilizing, balancing and grounding. Crystals work on the physical as well, but their tendency is to do this through assisting us with spiritual and mental shifts, or raising our vibration. It's no good to raise our vibration however, if we haven't grounded properly. We want to be able to pull those quicker frequencies into our grounded reality and balance the mystery and matter within us. Using a combination of crystals and stones balances our energies for the fullness of both physical and spiritual life.

WORKING WITH CRYSTALS

One of my favorite quotes about crystals was mentioned to me by a Muskogee Native American (which is a small part of my lineage). His wisdom holds that "the stone people get where they need to go… it just takes them a little longer to get there". There is an inherent knowledge in this culture that sees a consciousness in stones, as within all things on this earth. Whereas I might relate that crystals are a physical manifestation of the Divine energies and therefore a part of the same consciousness we are all a part of, the Indigenous cultures of the world, more fully immersed in nature on a daily basis, seem to hold a similar truth. As the first physical formations on this earth, stones hold information and mineral structures that we may access. Does this intelligence within them somehow make them energy beings of their own? They certainly emit measurable energy as we do, and biological life wouldn't exist without them. Could it be that just as animals and plants are known to have a form of consciousness within them, rocks hold a form of conscious as well? Regardless of the answer, as you work with stones you will naturally start to develop a relationship with them.

When picking stones, what matters most is which ones you are drawn to work with. While some psychics, healing therapists, and crystal experts can offer advice when selecting stones, they each have their own "filter" (or perspective) influencing them. Some have more filter, some have less. In the end, only you truly know what you need most, and what your heart and soul desires to experience. There's no need to think about it… you will be drawn to certain stones. There will be ones you feel strongly about, or that you can't leave behind. Follow this. This is part of the mystery of our own spiritual or healing journey, our own connection to the subtle energies within and around us. Following this empowers our own innate inner knowing.

Some people will feel the energy of the stones right away, or have visual images, thoughts or feelings come in (especially when placing stones on the body). Other people will not have an immediately palpable experience. Each of these responses is fine and just as it should be. It doesn't mean the stone isn't working for you, it simply could mean you're not accustomed to sensing or interpreting the subtler energies at play. No need for concern. We each receive exactly what we need. Over time, if you continue to work with the stones, you will start to feel their affects more fully as you ascertain how to interact with the subtler energies. Crystals are a great tool in helping us open to our intuitive selves.

WAYS TO WORK WITH CRYSTALS

There are as many ways to work with crystals, stones and rocks as there are people or beings who wish to connect with them. Following what feels right to you is a great place to start. Whatever you're called to do with them, crystals magnify the energy and intention you set. Some examples of the many ways to work with stones include:

- placing them around the home or on an altar, bedside, table or bookshelf
- carrying or wearing them
- making a grid with them, on the body, in the home, or around the earth

- placing them on the body for healing
- using them during meditation, sleep or journey-time
- reading with them
- using them in art

Taking a moment to connect with each crystal you wish to work with will deepen your relationship with a stone. Below is a good first exercise if you're just getting started (I also highly recommend dancing with the stone, singing to it or any other form of play):

- hold the stone and become quiet
- take a moment to connect to yourself, finding the stillness within you
- feel the support of the Earth below and the Heavens above
- take a moment to connect with the stone… say "Hi"
- With your intuitive mind, ask the stone how it would like to work with you. In turn, you can ask the stone to help you in a certain way. The Divine Intelligence within the stone (and within you) will respond in the most appropriate way to bring this intention about.

Note: *You may additionally experience a stone communicating with you through mental images, thoughts, feelings, an inner knowing, or simply a sense of stillness or peace.*

If you have a specific concern you'd like to ask a stone to assist you with, below are a few guidelines towards that goal. This will additionally further the relationship you've started with a stone, and as you become more comfortable working with the crystals, your special ways of using and connecting with them will be as easy as just playing and experimenting.

Set an Intention
Decide what you'd like to work on, which can be as broad as asking to receive the general healing or information you need at this specific time, or as specific as a certain issue that's been concerning you as of late.

See which stones call to you for this intention
Whether from your own collection of stones, or going to a shop to find new ones, pick the stones that are calling to you most with the intention you already set.

Work with the Stones
It doesn't matter how, just that you do it. Whichever method you are most called to at that time is the right method… be it meditating, placing them on your body for a crystal healing, gridding them around your home or body, carrying them or wearing them, etc. We will get called to different forms at different times. Sometimes the messages can come through when simply showing them off to friends.

CRYSTALS ON THE CHAKRAS

In Yogic antiquity there were many different chakra systems developed and used, brought forth from Sanskrit origins, with 3-12 major energy centers. The three chakra system was based on the 3 Dan Tians. In the 16th Century, a six chakra system written in Sanskrit attracted the attention of more modern scholars, and this version plus the crown chakra is what encompasses the seven chakra system used most widely in the West today. Many crystal healers add the Earth Chakra below the feet, and the Higher Chakras for all energies above the Crown. Nine is the number of completion, and this system encompasses the most comprehensive version of the Western Chakra System while also acknowledging our connection to the Earth below and the Divine above.

While it's wonderful to have a set chakra system to work with, the above information is listed because healing comes through differently every time, and I want you to feel the freedom to follow what's coming through for you in each moment… utilizing different systems at different times. I've seen very effective healings using the more yin Sacral, Heart and Third Eye chakras (the 3 dan tians), or using the more yang Root, Solar Plexus and Throat chakras, depending on the work being done. I additionally use minor chakras in the hands and feet, past life chakras, the midline of the body, and energy points positioned further below and above the body. Still the basic nine chakra system emits a strong and balanced frequency that I use most often.

When it comes to using crystals on the chakras, the simplest guide to knowing which stones to use is by color. If you follow the "rainbow bridge" to consciousness, you are already familiar with matching some of these colors to your chakras. The colors vary a little when it comes to stones, but the idea is to use red stones for the root chakra, orange stones for the sacral chakra, and so on up the "rainbow bridge". Before you have a fuller understanding of all of the stones and their uses, this is an easy way to start working with them. As you work more with the stones, they will open up more of your own intuitive wisdom, giving you the confidence you need to follow your instincts more freely and move beyond simply using the stones by color.

Chakra	Stone Color
Earth Chakra & Grounding Stones	black, browns, dark greens, dark multi-colored stones & heavy stones
Root Chakra	R: reds & black
Sacral Plexus	O: orange
Solar Plexus	Y: yellows & golds
Heart Chakra	G: greens & pinks, sometimes red
Throat Chakra	B: teals, light blue, sometimes dark blue
Third Eye	I: indigo, purple & dark blue
Crown & Above	V: ultraviolet, clear, white, purple, gold, some light blues & pastels

In general, crystal healing therapists leave stones on or around the body for anywhere between 10-40 minutes. They will often do energy work, sound healing, prayers or other therapies during.

When working with crystals on yourself, here are some guidelines:

- When using multiple crystals on the body, it is important to always place Grounding Stones first and remove them last. We must be grounded (similar to how electricity works) in order to incorporate the healing frequencies more fully into our physical reality. Also, the more grounded we are, the higher the frequencies we can access.

- Call on your guides, angels, the Divine, or any other energies that keep you protected and connected to the highest energy source while assisting you with your intentions or requests. Stay aligned to the 'highest good' for you and all beings.

- You may ask yourself, the stone or a Divine energy questions as you're working with the stones on your body to go deeper into release or healing.

- Using single terminated crystal points with the points facing towards a chakra (or a certain point on the body) will bring more attention and energy to that area. Facing the points away from the chakra will open & disperse the energy. Selenite or double terminated points may be used between chakras of the body (or in a grid) to connect the energies and allow them to flow.

- Selenite wands can be utilized to clear a room, a crystal, or a person. They align our physical bodies and connect us to Divine guidance.

- Quartz will work in any way you ask it to. As a silicate it gives and receives energy, and with no other mineral within it to influence its nature, it will assist you in the most magical way of working with you in any way that you ask.

- Close sessions with gratitude to all who assisted in the healing; from the crystals, to your guidance, to yourself for making the time to work in this way. This will assist in the integration of the work, and so much more.

- Cleanse your stones after each use if you're using them on more than one person, or if you choose to cleanse for your own personal use. (See details on cleaning stones near the end of this chapter, under 'Cleaning Crystals'.)

Most importantly, don't do anything that doesn't feel right to you. Following what feels right is the best indicator that you are fulfilling your soul's chosen journey and highest potential. If you place a stone on yourself (or someone else), and it makes you anxious or ill at ease, either ground yourself further to release the excess energy that's been generated or remove the stone. If what you're doing does feel right, and you didn't get the outcome you wanted, realize that it might take some time to get to the core issue that needs addressing. More information on this idea is listed under 'Getting to the Root Issue' in a later section of this chapter.

CRYSTALS FOR THE CHAKRAS

To follow is a bit of my view on the chakras, and some tips on crystals that can be used. There is some overlap between the Grounding, Earth & Root Chakra stones, as well as overlaps in other chakras noted throughout this section. Please remember this information is to help you get started working with the stones and is only provided as a guide for your own exploration. It is your own natural instincts of which stones to place where that will eventually bring you to your greatest healing, knowledge and wisdom.

GROUNDING STONES
Root Chakra to below the Feet

Grounding is of utmost importance. If we aren't grounded and connected to the earth's energy, then we won't be able to dump excess energy or manifest our needs as well on this physical planet. The more connected we are to the earth plane, the higher we can move energetically.

Black Tourmaline - protection, purification, strengthens energy field, deflects negativity
Hematite - strong grounding and protection, strengthens blood, removes limitations, assists addiction, increases willpower
Galena - alchemical self-transformation, reclaiming all of the self, soul retrieval and past life recall, psychic protection, strength, courage, assists detox, infection, and addiction
Smokey Quartz - connects the circuit between your energy field and the energy field of the earth in part to release stress and negativity, brings self-love and combats depression
Shiva Lingam - balances the yin & yang, raises the kundalini, connects us to All That Is
Jet - reminds us that things aren't as heavy as we think they are, absorbs negativity

EARTH CHAKRA
Below the Feet

Earth Chakra stones help us to connect more deeply to our home in this incarnation; including understanding her rhythms, wisdom, fundamental nature, and the Nature Spirits. She connects us to our previous lives and ancient wisdoms. To give attention to this area strengthens our connection to Spirit, since Earth is a physical manifestation of the Divine. When we are grounded to the Earth, life here is more connected and joyous.

Petrified Wood - steady growth, patience, a strong back & body, living by our ideals, connection to ancient wisdom & past lives, strengthens character, stabilizing, grounding
Moss Agate - connection to nature, nurturing, birthing & new beginnings, attracts abundance, balances intellect & intuition, helps release fear & stress, healing
Green Aventurine – also used at the Heart - Connects to Natures Green Ray of Love and Nature Spirits, cleansing, activating, calming, protective, it brings clarity, hope,

balancing, joy, the healing life force, being present, good luck, prosperity & shining your inner light

Serpentine - aids meditation, connects us to the Earth, activates the crown & kundalini, balances mind & emotions, retrieves memories & wisdom, detoxifies body & blood

Brown Aragonite - grounding, centering, stabilizing, patience, practicality, reliability, clears blocked lines and brings insight to the cause of issues, deep connection with Earth

ROOT CHAKRA
Perineum and the Hips

We all chose to come here. We are here on this earthly plane, in this body, at this time for a particular reason. To be grounded in this physical reality is to accept our souls' choice to incarnate on this planet and manifest our Divine Selves here while having the most basic of our needs met (i.e. family/tribe, food, shelter). This first chakra is our base structure. When we balance and stabilize this chakra, we are able to manifest our needs more readily.

Red Jasper - grounding, nurturing, soothing, restrains dangerous desires, deflects negativity

Ruby - warming, activating, activating, connects the Root & the Heart

Bloodstone - courage, circulation, purification, strength, Christ consciousness

Red Calcite - flow, vitality, finding the sacred in the mundane, regulates hormones, assist deep fears, sexual imbalances and intimacy

Garnet - strength, grounding, security, regeneration, purification, joy in physical life, clears karmic patterns and financial worries, energizing, trusting universal abundance

Spinel - revitalizes, dispels a negative outlook, transformation and new beginnings

Note: *Green Stones can soothe an overactive Root*

SACRAL CHAKRA
The lower Dan Tian, the Belly, Navel to the lower Abdomen

Creativity and Sexuality are the key words for the Sacral chakra, and they are deeply linked. This chakra is at the level of the sexual organs inside the body, so even though the genitalia are in the Root, life force creation comes from and is grown from this chakra. This energy center processes emotions & passion, leading to all types of creative pursuits, including the creation of children.

This is also the seat of the lower Dan Tian in many Eastern traditions. (Dan means the medicine of immortality, tian means field… immortal field. Dan Tian is also spelled Dan Tian or Dantians. There are 3 Dantians in our physical body, where many nerve endings come together to create the "brains" of our operation.) This chakra holds our visceral connection to the Divine entering into the body, where the "spark of life" originally occurs in a fetus as the first cells split here. The energy of the organs and meridians of the entire body collect in the lower Dan Tian, and the stomach, liver, kidney and spleen channels also pass through it. It is our "Fire in the Belly."

74

Carnelian - courage, highest goals, activates creativity and its expression, prosperity, vitality, sexuality, embracing change, overcoming fear to take action, improves lower back problems and overall health, purifies body and assists breaking bad habits

Orange Calcite - brings movement where there is stagnation, innovation, playfulness, reduces social anxiety, balances the yin/yang, assists feeling overwhelmed by creativity or sexuality, stimulates aura and physical body, assists depression, lethargy, hopelessness

Tangerine Quartz - holds the energy of the Inner Child… joyful creativity, playfulness, fearless curiosity, innocence, passion, helps overcome limitations, stimulates fresh perspectives and inspiration from the deep self plus the energy to manifest them

Orange Kyanite - Attunement & meditation, inner bridges, activates creativity, superhighway of energy through the meridians, enhances energy levels and intuition

Fire Agate - a stone of fertility and eternal youth, activating our fire and zest for life, stimulates meridians, stirs emotions, assists menopause, reconnects us to our deepest desires, etheric and physical alignment, Divine creativity, remedies dysfunctions in Root

Moonstone - attunes to the energy of the moon and all things yin, positive self-discovery, increases intuition, soothes feminine issues, detaching from the old

Note: *Blue Stones can soothe an overactive Sacral Chakra*
> **Blue Calcite** - *menstrual cramps*
> **Chrysocolla** - *feminine disorders, hormones, birth*
> **Blue Tiger Eye, Chrysocolla & Pietersite** - *sexual abuse*

•Sacral & Solar Connection (Navel)

Stones used in this location marry our creative and sexual nature to our willpower

Sunstone - attunes to the Central Sun bringing joy, creativity, benevolence, leadership, strength, manifestation & abundance, holds Divine Masculine energy, lightens depression, warms the body, increases metabolism, digestion, vitality, reproduction

SOLAR PLEXUS CHAKRA
Midway between the Navel and the base of the Sternum

Seen as our Inner Sun, the Solar Plexus is the seat of our personal empowerment and is from whence we shine. Our physical connection to Universal Intelligence, here we feel our 'gut instincts' and deepest fears. Purifying the past and digesting ideas to energize progress towards mental awareness and spiritual development, this chakra guides us through life by creating a strong sense of self, by learning to set personal boundaries, and by building willpower and self-esteem. The ability to bring change into your life and to the world is accessed within this Chakra.

Yellow Calcite - soothing, flow, recognizing and developing skills, self-confidence, balances yin/yang, assists right use of power and perceiving abundance, balances endocrine, hormones and pancreas, supports healthy blood-sugar

Pyrite - pyrite holds the energy of the Sun, burning away infection, negativity, anxiety, melancholy and fear, assist ideas, action and seeing behind the façade, protective, positive, energizing, yang, creativity, confidence, abundance, healthy sexual expression

Citrine - Attracts abundance, cleanses & breaks energy blocks, energizes
Natural - manifesting divine energy into form through intention & action, teaches being deserving of abundance, overcoming difficulty, & building stamina
Heat Treated - marries mind and will to understand power, boundaries and manifesting
Tiger Eye - balances polarities, harmonizes differing viewpoints, fortifies blood, detoxes, separates false desire from practical need, assists decisiveness and women in business
Golden Apatite - allows you to see many facets of the self, brings clarity, self-worth, creation, a sunny energy, manifestation of passions & dreams and connects to Divine Will
Amber - warmth, joy, assists in finding purpose & strength, soaks up negative energies, alleviates depression, subtle boost of energy, draws out infections, seals aura in light, helps to "lighten the load" and feel less overwhelmed, helps "phantom pain"

Note: *to calm this chakra, use light yellow, purple or violet stones*

•Solar & Heart Connection

These stones connect the Solar Plexus to the Heart. This is especially important for connecting the lower more physical needs to the higher more spiritual needs

Peridot - warmth, prosperity, releases worn out ideas and patterns, understanding our destiny, protective, assist in forgiving yourself to move on to your highest frequency
Malachite - a healed heart, absorbs negative energies within and without, releasing negative relationship patterns, protective
Prehnite - unites the heart and the will, communication with non-physical beings
Uvarovite Garnet - secures us in the knowledge of Universal Flow and abundance, instills vitality, individuality, contentment, hydration, assists solitude without loneliness, connects us to Nature, assists inflammation, detox, fever, acidosis, leukemia, frigidity

•Solar & Mind Connection
These stones work to connect our physical instincts and will to our conscious mind

Ametrine - attunes inspiration, guidance and the mind with action, clears stress, tension, blockages and programming, brings exploration, clarity, acceptance and coming into your power, strong physical healer that lends insight into dis-ease and balances yin with yan
Yellow Fluorite - balancing, organizing, discourages out-of-place growth, restructures ego and will, enhances cooperation, creativity and intellectual abilities, releases toxins

HEART CHAKRA
Middle Dan Tian, at the Heart

The first organ in our body to form, our heart is where we give and receive love, and is additionally associated with touch and all we do with our hands. A strong and muscular organ proven to emit the largest energy field, many see the heart plexus as the truest brain of the body; encompassing all forms of love, compassion, forgiveness, connection, and the ability to "follow your heart". Healing truly is centered here, for when we love and accept ourselves for the fullness of our being, then all else will fall into place. Genuinely learning to love our self – to extend the same compassion to ourselves as we might show others, to say yes and no to options in our lives that are most in alignment with serving our greatest benefit – these are powerful steps in securing a healthy heart chakra. Love truly does heal all, including us. When we are able to connect deeply to our Self, we are able to connect more deeply to others and the Divine as well. Nature additionally holds this color ray at its core. Connecting with nature and crystals can truly teach us how to love and connect more deeply with ourselves.

The heart is the center of most chakra systems and is considered the middle Dan Tian. It balances the energies from below and above, assists this circulation through the body, and allows us to fully open to the unconditional love of the Divine, and the Divine within us. This is the center where we come to fully understanding the connection of matter and the mystery.

Rose Quartz - sending out waves of love, rose quartz is a master healer that opens the heart to receive love from Yourself, the Divine and others, gently infusing love in place of anything not of love, soft emotional release of stress and worry, brings peace, acceptance, beauty and joy

Tourmaline - strengthens our energy field, connects to the Hara line and beams outward

- *Pink* - soothing, optimistic, soft emotional strength
- *Watermelon* - powerfully protects the heart, calms the mind so your higher self can radiate through, releases stress, worry, anxiety, & fear, connects to the Hara Line to bring an inner strength of character that exudes outward, pervasive pulse
- *Green* – strengthens heart field, pervasive, steady strength, surety, inner strength and surety, straight spine, brings a feeling of wellbeing

Calcite - movement and flow through stagnant energies, especially in the physical body, cleanses & amplifies energy, connects emotions & mind, positive, stimulant

- *Green* - connecting to Nature's abundance, healing the heart
- *Pink* - optical, cobaltoan and mangano - all assist in uplifting the heart, releasing fear and grief, bringing in joy, self-worth, acceptance, and unconditional love

Green Aventurine - Connecting to Natures Green Ray of Love and Nature Spirits, it brings hope, confidence, joy, & being present, regulates the heart & circulation, cell repair, regrowth, general healing, stimulates our life force & growth

Rhodochrosite - inner child & emotional healing, cleanses the subconscious & organs, aligns to play, love, joy & compassion, assists self-identity, the nervous-system and stress

Ruby - warming ruby connects our root & heart, instills peace, wellbeing, confidence, knowing you're worthy of love & an energy for life, releases trauma, aids circulation

- *w/Fuchsite* - practical yet playful energy that assists understanding others
- *w/Zoisite* - supports individuality, connection, altered states and past life healing

Emerald - high vibrational stone activating unconditional love, healing, and abundance

•Heart & Throat Connection

Used at the Throat, these stones help us voice the Heart's wisdom
Aquamarine - opening and removing blockages, isharpens intuition and opens us to the subtle energies, bringing a fine vibrational energy of beauty, clarity, calming and cooling
Amazonite - enhances communications concerning love, and to speak and live one's truth; aligns the subtle bodies; soothes emotions; dispels irritation and negativity; eliminates worries and fears; allows one to understand energetic boundaries; general health

•Heart & Mind Connection

Fluorite - balances the brain, soothes the emotions, and brings us to our most nourishing self, connects heart and mind to the intelligence of the body, realigns and restructures anything growing 'out of order'

THROAT CHAKRA
Base of the neck to the top of the Neck

Connected to truth, the throat chakra is so much more than communication. Listening is a large part of understanding ourselves and others, which assists us in communicating most effectively. Ultimately, hearing our own inner voice and speaking our truth is the benefit of a connected is considered the point of consciousness … with all of the structure of what is below it on the physical plane connected to all that is above it on the spiritual. Here is where we learn to 'have our own voice' and share it with the world.

Blue Lace Agate - cooling, soothing, nurturing, accepting and balancing, this stone combines intellect and intuition for constructive expression and communication
Turquoise - connected deeply to the energy Native Americans hold, this protective stone fortifies wellbeing in the body & spirit, allows for release and fuller soul expression, connects us to past lives, and assists moving forward in a truthful way
Blue Fluorite - clear and concise communication of one's ideas, an eye, ear, nose, throat, bones & teeth healer that restructures and can bring about a spiritual awakening
Chrysocolla - aligns the strength and gentleness of the Divine Feminine throughout you, facilitates communicating our innate intuitive wisdom, supports adrenals and stress, strengthens the inner feminine and gives her a voice
Blue Topaz - assists communicating our deepest feelings and highest truth while clearly and consciously verbalizing what you wish to manifest, allows you to see all things equally, brings body mind and spirit into union with the perfection of the Universe

Note: *Orange stones can activate an underactive throat chakra*

•Throat & Third Eye Connection

These stones work well on the Throat & the Third Eye, connecting both of their energies

Lapis - with a strong connection to Egyptian times Lapis stimulates inner vision and dreams, balances the throat chakra bringing truthful communication, empowers

Blue Calcite - filters and moves energy soothing the nerves and throat, brings inner vision and psychic ability, assists us to take responsibility for creating our reality
Sodalite - a straight-forward stone that imparts a simplicity and desire to express truths, it assists accessing subconscious & intuitive ability, and aids our 'walking' truth
Blue Tourmaline - activates, brings clarity of expression, dissolves sadness
Blue Apatite - aids self-expression and develops psychic gifts, draws off negativity, bones
Shattuckite - embracing truth, releasing spiritual fears, attunes us to highest guidance

•Throat & Crown Connection

Celestite - good for speakers, singers, musicians and artists of all kinds to channel Celestial energies through their gifts, fluent communication, connecting to the Angelic and Divine
Angelite - assisting communication with angels, it soothes an overactive or unaligned throat chakra, helps with anger, clear communication, and mending bones and joints

THIRD EYE
Upper Dan Tian, center of Forehead

The seat of wisdom, intellect and psychic development, the third eye is associated with the Pineal Gland in the center of the skull. Dr. Rick Strassman has hypothesized that the pineal gland, which maintains light sensitivity, is responsible for the production and release of DMT, an entheogen which he believes could be excreted in large quantities at the moments of birth and death. (Wikipedia)

Simply put, this is the gateway to other dimensions, higher consciousness, and the inner realms. It symbolizes the state of enlightenment, clairvoyance and precognition, and is considered by many to be the Christ Consciousness Center.

This is the spot where dualities converge. Here we unite the two hemispheres of the brain – reasoning with intuition, the linear with the abstract, wisdom with understanding, ego with spirit, the pineal & pituitary glands and yin & yang. Through letting go of attachments, expectations and distractions in the physical world, we can attain a Divine relationship with Spirit. This is the kundalini's destination, where the snake unfurls. A balanced third eye chakra represents being in your infinite potential.

Amethyst - opens intuition, clears and calms, meditative, wisdom in grief, surrender and attunement with the Divine, communion with guides, alleviates victimhood and addictive behavior, a natural sedative that balances the nervous system and oxygenates the blood
Purple Fluorite - brings you to your most nourishing state of mind and body, discourages growths, realigns thoughts, brings insight and manifestation of ideas
Azurite - expands subconscious to conscious, healing ability, letting go of anger and hurt
Cavansite - develops psychic and visual perception, clear communication with guides, brings joy, optimism to release the past & embrace the future, helps find teachers to expand consciousness, counters stress and headaches

Lepidolite - inspiration, intuition, looking within, yin, attunement to the future, ESP, moderates a rapid spiritual awakening
Charoite - being in the present moment, purifying, protective, healing

Note: *Yellow & golden stones activate the mind, sacred geometry stones bring structure*

•Third Eye & Crown Connection

Moonstone - encompassing mystery, cycles and insight, this stone attunes to the energy of the moon and all things yin, feminine and intuitive, a positive stone of self-discovery; it soothes the feminine, opens our awareness and assists us in detaching from the old
Rainbow Moonstone - brings clarity to psychic perception and emotional issues, diffuses light throughout the aura, aligns to joy, inner peace and harmony
Optical Calcites - insight, clarity, joy, movement and flow, bringing spiritual light into physical reality, seeing two sides of an issue

CROWN CHAKRA
Top of the Head and 6-12" above

The Crown Chakra is considered the point of consciousness… the gateway, or temple of heaven. Represented in Eastern traditions as the 1000 petal lotus, the flower is in its fullest and most abundant bloom; open to Divine Source's light, with all of heaven's gifts around it. This is the peak of self-realization and connection with the Infinite All That Is.

Clear Quartz - a master healer and magnifier of energies, quartz works for any issue and in any way you ask it to, it clears, cleanses, clarifies and opens all the chakras and energy pathways, works on the spiritual subtle body, connects to higher realms, expands the energy body, stimulates the nervous system, and removes adhesions
Rutilated Quartz - attunement, amplification, acceleration, awareness, manifesting
Spirit Quartz - cleansing, clearing and aligning, this crystal brings abundance, protection, connection to spirit guides, merging with our true spirit self and spiritual freedom
Amethyst - a master healer and natural sedative, it opens, purifies and transmutes, assists Divine connection and communion with guides, brings spiritual energy into the physical
Apophyllite - interdimensional light and awareness, inner peace, vision, trust, 'reiki stone'
Stellar Beam & Dogtooth - clears with high frequency light, aligns and creates doorways, interdimensional travel, Divine will, accesses higher wisdom, clears negative habits
Danburite - peace, freedom from stress, connection to higher frequencies, channeling
Datolite - higher world connection, retrieves lost information, uplifting, brings one to the present moment with emotional objectivity and a sense of purpose, releases fears of the past and the future, assists overcoming grief, indecision, and hopelessness
Shells - boundless growth, stimulates intuition, sensitivity, imagination and adaptability, brings clarity and understanding of universal order, emotional clearing and feeling safe

Scolecite - instills inner peace and tranquility, connection to higher frequencies, assist meditation and interdimensional travel, awakening the heart

UPPER CHAKRAS
6 inches or more above the Crown

These chakras open us to the highest frequencies, spiritual connection, and healing.

Ajoite - love, healing, Goddess & Angelic connection, nurturance & guidance
Coral Form Aragonite - centering, meditation, reliability, patience, practicality, insight into issues on the physical plane, stimulates higher plane communication, eases responsibility, uplifting, purifies the aura and increases inner light, clears negativity
Tremolite - higher knowledge, calm & clarity, higher mind activation, mystic rapture

•Angel & Guide Connection

Celestite - opens & clears the 3rd eye & crown for Angelic connection & communication, access to higher, connection to angel energies & higher dimensions, communication, serenity, calms & centers, clears infections & attachments, heals the eyes
Angelite - Angelic communication, gentle self-expression, serenity, expanded awareness
Seraphinite - establishes communication with angels, devas and nature spirits to bring wholeness, joy, regeneration, and a release of toxic emotions, supports spiritual healing
Prehnite - connects to the highest energy sources, heals the healer, unites heart and will

•Alignment Stones

From the heavens, through the center of your body Crown to Root, to the center of the Earth

The following stones connect and align us to the Divine energies, cleanse and straighten out channels through the main energy lines of the body, and open and connect us to the Center of the Earth through the midline of the body (a.k.a. the Hara Line). The stones assist moving the Divine Energies through us so we can connect to higher frequencies.

Selenite – a Divine lunar energy that aligns & connects us to spirit guides and our true Spirit Self, cleansing, protective, activates the light body and clears back pain
Spirit Quartz - connecting us to Spirit Guides and our true Spirit Self, this crystal brings abundance, protection, cleansing, clearing, alignment and spiritual freedom
Rutilated Quartz - an amplifier that attunes to our higher frequencies, rutile infuses us with light, enhances telepathic abilities, breaks old patterns, quickens manifestation, and accelerates expanding our awareness; sweep aura to draw off negative energies
Cacoxenite - an alignment stone that connects us to the Divine Plan of the All
Kyanite - creates an energy highway that clears the central meridian, aligns the chakras, cleanses negativity and connects you to your Guides & Angels; an attunement

stone that balances energy in the body while stimulating compassionate communication, decisions and psychic awareness, dispels anger, brings clarity.

GETTING TO THE ROOT ISSUE

A word on how sometimes getting to the root of the true issue we're addressing can be a journey. We may think it's a solar plexus issue, when really it's a blocked root or heart chakra that's creating the problem – or it can be simply how we think or feel about a core belief that needs shifting. Crystals can help in this deeper process as well.

There are crystals that assist with:

- getting to the root of an issue or disease
- aligning to the Divine Source
- shifting thoughts or perspectives, or deeply held root beliefs
- working with all of the chakras at once, or ones that work on upper, lower & middle chakras
- grounding, prosperity, manifestation, etc.

You may research these on your own or contact a qualified Crystal Healing Therapist for assistance.

If you aren't getting the outcome you are looking for, there could be competing ideologies getting in the way, or perhaps your intention isn't clear. You can also look at the alignment of your intention and what came out of it. Where does this desire come from? Is it in the highest good? Is my ego getting in the way of being clear? Is there a limiting belief I hold? Am I conflicted? Was the outcome what I needed to learn more about myself, to bring me closer to my path? Am I looking at what's hiding in the shadows, etc. Asking deeper, clearer, and absolutely honest questions (with honest answers) will help. Sometimes during this journey, it is good to seek outside assistance. A skilled therapist can often be the mirror that's needed to see ourselves more clearly. Someone who isn't currently going through your situation can have some perspective to things we are just too close to.

CLEANING CRYSTALS

Though some experts are starting to question whether stones really need energetic cleansing or not, I still find cleansing crystals to be a great tool to learn more about yourself and your relationship to the subtle energies. If you choose to cleanse, though it's all over the internet to do so, please **DO NOT soak your crystals in salt water**! Salt is one of the most cleansing items we can use, and if you use more than a pinch, it will pull some of the lovely healing minerals and color out of the stones. Soaking crystals in saltwater is just more cleansing than is generally needed and will often lessen the healing effects and beauty of the stones.

Here are some safer methods for cleansing your stones (and yourself):

- sage

- moonlight, or the sun with caution (some stones fade over time)
- selenite or Quartz Points Crystals
- water, if the crystal isn't water soluble
- burying the stone in dirt to reconnect with the Earth plane (be sure to mark where!)
- energy/intention - visualize it, or ask the crystal to cleanse

WRAP UP

All in all, crystals are one tool for connecting to ourselves and the beautiful home we live on - Earth. Connecting to Nature helps us to feel more at home here, and to feel our connection to our own Spiritual, Loving and Healing Energy that is inherent within each one of us. Crystals are powerful allies that magnify our intentions and connect us to the healing Earth energies. They open us to the subtler environment that is always all around us, and in doing this, they align us to The Divine within.

BIBLIOGRAPHY & GRATITUDE

Thank you to the Collective All for this knowledge coming more strongly into our world. Thank you to each one of my clients and students for their insight and support of me on this journey. I'd like to also thank Olivia Whiteman for the opportunity to be a part of this book, and all of the contributors for making this book a reality. In special gratitude to Phil Ristaino, Peter Alberts and Laurell Eden for their spiritual prowess and constant loving support.

Most of this chapter was written based on my experiences, study, wisdom and practical knowledge. I additionally supported this at times by consulting Judy Halls' *The Crystal Bible*, Melodys' *Love Is In The Earth*, Robert Simmons & Naisha Ahsians' *The Book of Stones*, and Joy Gardners' *Chakras* as reference guides. I recommend these books as touchstones to gain further information on how the crystals are known to work for healing the chakras. This chapter is also supported by my perusal of Wikipedia, Google Searches, and Mindat.org, plus occasional references to Travis Ogden, Frank Menusan and Lester Loving principles (in gratitude). If you are looking for more in-depth information from me, contact me for classes, or look for my upcoming crystal books, videos and CD's.

© Laurelle Rethke

ABOUT LAURELLE RETHKE

Website: www.5SenseHealing.com
Phone: 917-406-0225 (call or text) to book an appointment
Shop & Wellness Suite: The Faerie Den (on Facebook & Instagram)

LAURELLE RETHKE is a Vibrational Healing Therapist Personal & Spiritual Growth Consultant Author, Teacher, Speaker and Spiritual Reverend. Laurelle has been called a spiritual alchemist, bridge-builder & crystal maven. Working with crystals intensely since 2008, she offers Crystal Healing therapies, sells crystals to other enthusiasts, and has given classes and workshops on using stones all over NYC and the USA. As a consultant and healing therapist, she is a compassionate truth-seeker who works to get to the root of what troubles you, helping to bring in new understanding on health, healing, & spiritual alignment. She uses Crystals, Essential Oils, Source Energy, Zhineng Medical Qigong, Source Meditation, New Thought Patterning, Sound & Astrology as her main tools, and is deeply grounded in an earth-centered consciousness. Every modality she works with is intended to empower you to be your most connected and present self. She believes that deepening our relationship with the Natural World is key to connecting us to the Divine, Ourselves, and All That Is.

A Certified Master of Crystology, Floracopeia Essential Oils Teacher, and Psychology of the Body Apprentice, she additionally holds certificates in Source Awareness Meditation, Barbara Brennan style Hands of Light Healing and Astrology. She has studied Zhineng Medical Qigong, Voice, Movement, Sound & various meditation modalities with masters for many years and is a Reverend through the Universal Life Church (featured as an officiant in the award-winning documentary "Married & Counting"). Laurelle has additionally been honored with the name **Hokti Hillis Chado** by a Muskogee Carrier of the Pipe, which in the traditional tongue translates to Stone Medicine Woman. She accepts this honor with much gratitude.

Based out of her home Shop and Healing Space in Midtown Manhattan, Laurelle travels throughout the country to speak and teach workshops, and frequents as a Guest on TV, Radio & Internet Talk shows. She offers most of her services via Video Chat and facilitates Long Distance Healing Therapies. You can find out more about her and her services on her website.

MARTHA VALLEJO
Crystal Jeweler, Lithomancer and Bone Reader

I have two magical and simple ways to balance my chakras and get back into flow, quickly and easily.

First is, I go to work. I work at Aum Shanti, a metaphysical shop that also sells crystals. This makes clearing my chakras easier for me than most. I am surrounded by nature's medicine.

If I'm feeling that I need to be grounded I can go and hold on to a red, dark brown or black stone. Red Jasper, Black Onyx and Hematite are three stones that come to mind.

When I need to activate my deepest intuition and insight, I look for Lapis lazuli, Blue Kyanite or Labradorite. It's great to have choices.

Another way I clear my chakras is when I work with crystals, creating jewelry. Designing jewelry relaxes me, and there is much healing to be found in the pieces I make, not only for the people who end up with my creations, but for me as I make the pieces.

When designing a piece for clearing a specific chakra, such as making a choker to open the throat chakra so a woman can speak truthfully with more ease, creating a necklace with a hanging pendant that lays close to the heart offering a way to achieve greater compassion, or making a bracelet that allows her to be more passionate and creative by opening up the sacral chakra, I too will pick up the vibration of the stone, whether I need it or not.

I love what I do. My chapter will share with you how to wear crystals to align your chakras.

I wish you happy crystal hunting. If you are ever in NYC, drop by the store and say hello. Aum Shanti Bookshop is on 14th St between 2nd & 3rd Avenue.

USING CRYSTAL JEWELRY FOR CHAKRA WORK
Martha Vallejo

While there are many chakras throughout the energy body, I will be focusing on the primary chakras as I explore which jewelry type and placement would be most beneficial when wearing crystal jewelry to balance your chakras.

On the most basic level, if a crystal is in the presence of the bio-magnetic sheath it will work within the energy body along with the chakras. Strategic and mindful placement can help to enhance their work by bringing the power of the crystal closer to the chakra center that it has been set to work with. Also, as a rule of thumb the color of the stone is significant. This is because the work is being done through this frequency. The specific properties of the stones themselves are of a secondary consideration. As an example, when attempting to ground the energetic body any dark stone may be utilized. As another example, Sodalite is a blue stone associated with speech, and therefore connected to the throat chakra. One may want to wear a Sodalite choker to help with improving speech or fear of speaking. Likewise, if someone has an overactive throat and speaks before thinking they should wear something that is opposite on the chakra scale color-wise, perhaps a red stone to counterbalance the blue.

I present below a series of questions and answers to guide you:

HOW DO THE CRYSTALS WORK?

The mineral and person work in tandem. The jewelry doesn't do all the work for you. It is met half way. It serves as a reminder of the outcome you wish to achieve. The power is in your proactive partnership with the crystal.

HOW CAN I TELL IF I NEED IT?

A chakra imbalance can present itself in several ways and for many reasons. It could manifest physically, emotionally or even simultaneously since they are connected. An emotional upset, injury or illness could cause a chakra to not function at its fullest potential. As an example, shyness or a fear of public speaking could be the result of a "blocked" or imbalanced throat chakra since this governs how we communicate. When a throat chakra is underactive, it can physically feel as if the throat is constricting. Stuttering may also occur when trying to express oneself. An imbalance can also be overactive. An example of an overactive throat chakra manifesting emotionally could be talking too much, gossiping, and lying. Physical symptoms may appear as a sore throat or toothache to name just a few.

HOW MUCH SHOULD I WEAR?

I recommend working with one stone at a time to keep focus on where the healing needs to be done. If there are issues affecting all chakras I suggest starting with the first chakra and working up to the seventh. Another option is wearing one stone that corresponds with all chakras such as a Rainbow Moonstone or Labradorite (which contain the full spectrum of colors) and wearing it close to one's center on a long chain, or as a ring or bracelet, giving the wearer the freedom to place their hands over any chakra as needed.

CAN I WEAR TOO MUCH?

Overall, if it is comfortable and not distracting to the point where it deviates from its intended use, you have the freedom to determine what is too much.

HOW LONG SHOULD I WEAR THE JEWELRY?

I suggest wearing the mineral for at least several weeks to a month. The longer it is worn the more it becomes partnered with the person and vice versa.

CONCERNING METALS, IS THERE ANYTHING TO KEEP IN MIND?

Here are a few metals that I like to incorporate into the pieces I make:

Copper - is related to the heart chakra. In creating pieces copper is my preferred metal of choice. This metal is ruled by the planet Venus and so is filled with a loving energy. It is an excellent conductor of electricity and therefore amplifies the power being given off by the stone. Other healing properties such as assisting in circulation and alleviating aches and pains make it a favorite of mine to work with.

Silver - is related to the third eye and crown chakras and is ruled by the Moon. Because of its association with the Moon, it is imbued with the lunar properties of amplifying one's intuition and of protection. Silver is purported to never needing energetic cleansing.

Aluminum - is associated with the crown chakra. It is a projective metal, so it aids in energy being directed outward. Aluminum is ruled by Mercury and helps with communication.

Gold - is ruled by the sun. It is associated with the solar chakra which is your core and how you present yourself to the world. It aids in courage and strength.

© Martha Vallejo

CHAKRA AND JEWELRY TYPE CHART

The table below illustrates what type of jewelry would be best to wear to best serve the chakra to be worked on and what chakra primary colors balance or and what opposite colors counter balance one another.

Chakra	Jewelry Type	Primary Color	Opposite Color
Crown	Crown, tiara, forehead jewelry	Clear, white	Black, red
Third Eye	Forehead jewelry, head bands, ear cuffs, earrings	Indigo, purple	Yellow
Throat	Dangle earrings, chokers, necklace	Indigo, blue	Orange, red
Heart	Necklace, upper armbands	Green, pink	Same
Solar Plexus	Long chain necklace, mid-arm cuffs, belly jewelry	Yellow	Purple
Sacral	Bracelets, rings	Orange, red	Blue
Root	Belts, anklet	Red, black, brown	Blue

© Martha Vallejo

ABOUT MARTHA VALLEJO

Instagram: https://instagram.com/crystalpathcreations
Contact: marthavallejo@zoho.co

MARTHA VALLEJO is a crystal jeweler, lithomancer and bone reader.

Lithomancy is a divinatory art in which a selection of stones is cast and their resulting patterns are interpreted to provide insight on one's past, present and future situations

Martha's intuitive readings offer her clients the guidance to create the paths they want to take.

She has worked for years with crystals and has realized the healing benefits of working with the energies of the mineral realm.

Martha often teaches a wire wrapping workshop at Aum Shanti Spirituality Bookshop and Crystal Gallery. All crystals and materials are provided and you get to make and take two wire wrapped crystals with you. Contact Aum Shanti at (212) 260-2866 for information about upcoming classes.

Aum Shanti Spirituality Bookshop and Crystal Gallery
230 East 14th Street between 2nd & 3rd Avenue, New York City
(212) 260-2866

SHANNA MARIE
Aromatherapist and Emotional Intuitive

The feeling of being turned on and lit up is priceless. For me, it could be while watching a dragonfly flit from blade of grass to sheet of water, while shaving my shin and seeing the razor create a clean line on my soapy leg, while walking to the car holding hands with my beautiful lover or while speaking in front of a large audience. When I am present, I can rest assured that the act I am engaging in will be done well and with ease, explored sensationally, and with a sense of surrender and satisfaction.

Of course, this is not always the case. There may be instances in our lives when our resistance seems stronger than our desire, that it takes an excessive amount of effort and time for us to follow-up and follow through, to show up to commitments and even show up for ourselves. It may be because of the fear of looking bad or being judged, or self-doubt and insecurities. Whatever it is, sometimes it can feel like we do not have what it takes to do what we said by when we said we would do it. When circumstances like these creep up on me, I look at my **thoughts**. What beliefs are there? What memories am I revisiting? What am I saying to myself? I pay attention to my **emotions**. How do I feel? Where do I feel it in my body? What sensations are present? I focus on my **desires**. What am I ready to let go of? What am I ready to receive? What would I like to get out of this moment? Most importantly, I assess my **chakras**. Do I feel grounded in my body and in my environment? Am I getting pleasure out of this experience? Do I feel powerful in this situation? Can I accept this moment just as it is or that person just as they are? Am I using my voice and speaking up for myself? Can I see the blessing beyond the disguise? Can I connect with the bigger part of me, that inner being that always knows and always feels whole and complete?

This process of inquiry alone can buy us time to respond rather than react. Then once we know which energy centers in our body need tuning up, we can give them TLC using our preferred modality.

My specialty is *Reiki Aromatherapy* and it lets me combine my favorite tools for healing. I charge specific Essential Oils with specific crystals; the transportive, transformative and therapeutic effects of Essential Oils are indeed a pleasure to experience. Then I'll ask my client to inhale the oil from the bottle while I use my right hand to move energy around her body. I let intuition, my body and the Higher Power that I believe in lead as I feel and facilitate support of a particular chakra or all the main chakras for a well-rounded approach that addresses her entire being.

A LIFE WELL LIVED WITH ESSENTIAL OILS
Shanna Marie

We will be exploring how to balance energy flow in our bodies with the assistance of Essential Oils. How can we embolden our root, sacral, solar plexus, heart, throat, first eye, and crown chakras in a way that would allow us to experience ease within our current situations and elevate the quality of our life altogether? We know that chakras are energy centers that are spinning like a wheel. They move energy around as they spin and bring life force into every part of us. We have many chakras, each cell and every molecule is a chakra and each atom and every particle is a chakra. When chakras move in a synchronized manner with each other, energy flows freely and we experience a sense of centeredness and confidence. However, when some chakras are spinning sluggishly or erratically and maybe not at all, it follows that energy does not flow well. Stagnation happens or blockages show up through symptoms that may look like a form of discomfort and dis-ease, feel like emotional turmoil, and sound like rush hour at Grand Central Terminal in our heads.

I have always appreciated the intricacies of the human brain and the impeccable engineering of the human body, but more of others and not always mine. Instead of considering the body as a companion and the mind as an ally, we sometimes consider them as limiting or even antagonistic. It was not until I was in my thirties that I noticed how I significantly began to be less judgmental of myself and become more of an observer, more approving of the way my mind would process what it perceived and of my body's distinct design. I began to regard myself as a companion and a co-pilot in this adventure that I perhaps signed up for but may sometimes forget that I did. It did not and does not always feel this way, it is not all the time that I can laugh about it, but as my relationship with myself strengthened, my receptivity became more allowing and life started feeling a little lighter. I noticed how compassionate our body's systems are to us no matter what lifestyle we choose, no matter what climate we live in, and no matter what attitude, emotional conditions or patterns of thinking we take on. It is prepared to multi-task, regenerate and rejuvenate, recalibrate, procreate, eliminate, and adapt to its environment in a way that serves us best. Our bodies know exactly what to do with whatever we choose to give it or expose it to. Whatever elements we feed on or interact with will decide whether our body's functions are enhanced or disrupted, and whether or not our choices seem consistent with our intentions of being mentally and physically fit, feeling joyful in our daily experience, and having a fulfilling impact on others. Most of us share similar goals of embodying vitality and strong immunity, managing our emotions, quieting our thoughts on-demand, making a good living, and sustaining our preferred lifestyle with our loved ones. How do we achieve this when our diet is not the best, when our air is polluted, when we are frequently highly stressed and often emotionally out of whack?

This chapter shares my approach on how to experience a life well-lived in your body, where you are, with the family you were born into or the family you chose, with the work that you do, in this lifetime, and perhaps, today, in this very moment.

There are many ways to get there so let us focus on one of my favorite tools, Essential Oils. Health, wealth or happiness does not really determine the length of our life and I do not believe that we have the bona fide human capacity to prolong life. We do, however, have control over its quality— that day to day and moment to moment experience that we just string along, breath by breath and thought by thought, until we step back with awe and recognize the beautiful life we have created. What would life look like if your immune system is resilient, your emotions adjustable, and your mind is clear and in synch with your body?

WHAT ARE ESSENTIAL OILS?

Essential Oils are aromatic compounds that come from plants. I regard them as "plant blood". They are enriched with molecules that have incredible therapeutic effects on us - physically, mentally, emotionally and spiritually. Essential Oils have helped plants survive for millions of years by being their own natural defense mechanisms in the wild despite predators, the weather or other conditions. Since we humans have our own versions of "the wild" at work, at home, in our communities and in our own head, these highly concentrated plant essences can also support our bodies to afford us that unconditional presence we want while we are still alive.

Essential Oils are steam distilled or cold pressed from different parts of a plant. These processes of extracting the Essential Oils require some kind of heating, crushing or pressing action and it is no accident that they help us the most when circumstances in our lives get heated, overwhelming or when the pressure is on.

AROMATHERAPY

The therapeutic use of Essential Oils to administer support to areas of our body and aspects of our lives is also known as Aromatherapy. This modality has been used all over the world since ancient times. Essential Oils were used as gifts as valuable as gold, as antiseptics during wars, and now are very popular in spas and are becoming common ingredients in perfumes, beauty products, and household cleaners. Their ability to enhance our well-being and relieve discomfort makes them precious gifts of the Earth.

IN MEMORY OF MY SISTER MARIA "ATE LAL"

Plants and oils were a big part of my childhood. I remember my mom often talking to her orchids, putting fresh aloe vera gel on the tips of my hair, and my sister Maria rubbing coconut oil on my scalp while we watched television. It was not until after Maria transitioned into the non-physical that I deepened my study of Essential Oils. At the peak of her brief and brutal love affair with cancer, right after the doctors said her body could no longer take chemotherapy and before hospice care, my family was just desperate to give Maria any kind of relief so we purchased all sorts of Essential Oils (and crystals) from the health food stores in her neighborhood.

I knew very little about the oils then so I simply bought anything associated with the liver and pancreas, and everything that had yellow packaging to connect with her solar plexus chakra. My mom would anoint Maria's head with oils, my brothers would take turns massaging her hands and feet, and I would draw hearts around her body using the Lemon and Helichrysum roll-on Essential Oil stick. For a little while, that was enough to bring her temporary relief and we were extremely grateful. She would inhale the aroma and it would encourage her to breathe in a little deeper because she loved the scent so much. She would inhale the aroma and ask me about what was inside the bottle and how to pronounce "Helichrysum". She would inhale the aroma and it would distract her from the pain and all the tubes sticking out of her body. She would inhale the aroma and smile, say thank you, and request for more hearts. These moments when she would be present were priceless, and we would just stitch those moments along for however long or short they lasted.

I did not know at that time that I was going to do what I am doing today but the intense grief I felt lead me to this path of healing. The grief I felt after Maria crossed over was unbearable and it was Essential Oils that helped pull me through it. When the experience with the illness and the physical loss was better integrated into my life, I immersed myself in learning more about Essential Oils. Part of me will always want to keep deepening my discovery in hopes of helping other people and families who are or were in a similar path as my sister.

WAYS TO USE ESSENTIAL OILS

There are many ways to use Essential Oils. You can inhale them straight from the bottle, on a cotton ball or by using a diffuser, you can apply them topically and massage them on your skin, or add certain edible ones to your foods and beverages. Upon inhalation, application, and ingestion, we get to embody the essence of the plants inside and out. Energetically, as our own frequency synchronizes with the plants' high vibration; mentally and emotionally, as we move from panic to focus; and physiologically, as zest is restored to the tissues of our body and the intelligence of our cells take over, using these ingredients that we provide it to soothe, sedate, sanitize, expectorate, digest and more.

CUSTOMIZED ESSENTIAL OIL PRODUCTS

I enjoy creating customized roll-on Essential Oil sticks for my clients so they can conveniently carry it around in their purses or pockets. I love making products that I use on myself everyday like body soap, hand lotion, and face oil. I dilute the latter with Jojoba oil and apply the special blend all over my face (or any shaved body parts), especially in areas that move a lot and under the eyes, after every washing and before going to bed at night to keep my skin moisturized, supple and healthy-looking. Essential Oils can help you breathe better, uplift your mood, calm you down, soothe discomfort, and assist in having a restful sleep. Best of all, we can use Essential Oils to balance energy flow in our chakras.

I connect not only with people and their need for healing, but also, the plants. I regard them as our elders and I ask them for guidance every day, during my client sessions and whenever I make my Aromatherapy products. They always remind me to breathe, be open to receive, and to trust that what I am ready to share is what will help nourish others.

ESSENTIAL OILS & CHAKRAS

As I talk more about the chakras and how I use the Essential Oils to enliven balanced energy flow through, within and around them, I will be referring to sensitive circumstances that my clients and I have experienced. I hope you can identify with their situations as I keep their identities anonymous. My intention is that this shared information can offer you a better understanding of how impactful the Essential Oils can be in shifting our perception, processing moments, and managing our emotions. I have seen it with my own eyes and felt it with my own heart. We all have our own stories, challenges and concerns, yet at the core of it all, even if we may feel them in varying degrees, are collections of thoughts and emotions that shape our daily experiences, influence our choices, and ultimately create our lives. Life happens to us humans, we give meaning to everything that happens, and then what? These Essential Oils can make a difference to your mind, body, and spirit. I am inviting you to experience it for yourself.

DISCLAIMER
As an Emotional Intuitive this holistic approach resonates with me. Yet, it does not replace medical advice, it does not substitute professional care or offer a "cure," but Essential Oils have the power to elevate the quality of our lives.

ROOT CHAKRA

After my client separated from her husband, that she shared a bed with for over a decade, she moved into a new apartment. As much as she loved her new place, she also noticed how her body had difficulty adjusting to the foreign space. She went out almost every night, would seek company just for the sake of company, and would sleep at sunrise just when others were waking up. There were days when she would be in bed all day, keep her bedroom dim and not even open the windows. Part of her longed to go on vacation but also felt anxious at the thought of having to be away. She felt distracted. She did not feel grounded or "at home" in her home and in her body.

Suggestion: Vetiver [*Vetiveria zizanioides*]

Massaging Vetiver on the soles of the feet will assist you in centering and feeling rooted, planted where you are and where you choose to be when you feel like you are all over the place or that you "don't belong". It can remind you that you have the power to choose.

Release: Feelings of being disconnected, scattered, stressed and needing to escape.

Receive: Feeling connected and being present, centered and in a place of discovery.

How to Apply: Apply a couple of drops on the palm of one hand, energize it by rubbing your palms together, and massage onto the soles of each foot every morning or as needed.

Say: I AM GROUNDED

SACRAL CHAKRA

My client went on a shopping frenzy online to furnish her new property, shopping had always been fun for her but she noticed that even after she had bought everything she needed, she would still shop or look forward to the next time she had to order supplies for her business then add miscellaneous materials just to self-soothe and fill whatever void there was in her life. "What else is missing?" "Is this the best I can afford?" "Let me get the most expensive name brand since it's going on the credit card anyway." "I should get it in different colors, just in case." Her internal dialogue of why she needed this or that kept going on and on until the bills got more and more too. She was worried about all the spending and yet she kept buying until she maxed out all her credit cards. She kept looking forward to the next delivery like a kid on Christmas morning but she was not feeling fulfilled.

Suggestion: Orange [*Citrus sinensis*]

Inhaling and massaging Orange on the lower abdomen, will soothe you into stability and security whenever you feel like something is lacking in you or your life. It can remind you that you have the power to flow.

Release: Being too serious and rigid, hoarding, feeling discouraged, envious, and lethargic.

Receive: Abundance, generosity, creativity, enjoyment of life and a good humor.

How to Apply: Apply a drop on the palm of one hand, energize it by rubbing your palms together, inhale and massage onto your lower abdomen in a spiral motion, counter clockwise first then as soon as your body tells you, go clockwise. Wet one finger with the oil and anoint your navel.

Say: I AM ENOUGH

SOLAR PLEXUS CHAKRA

My client hated her body when she was growing up. She kept comparing herself to her skinnier and prettier friends, envious of her perception of their appearance. She remembered when she was in middle school, she stared at the mirror, cried, and complained to her mom, resentfully blaming her for the way she looked. She felt ashamed of her face, her body, and the way her voice sounded. A cruel script often played in her head and she would make herself throw up the food she had eaten so she could have an illusion of having control over her body. She spent more than half her life embarrassed, hiding, hurting and rejecting herself until she realized these aspects of herself made her who she was. These parts of her were all gifted to her as precious and necessary parts of her identity and story. Only then did she start owning her body and every different aspect of what makes her unique... finally embracing them, accepting and approving of them, pleasuring and enjoying them, celebrating and thanking them, adoring and sharing them, honoring and loving them. I told her to talk to herself, to write down this message and text it to herself: "I am caregiver and caretaker, the lucky lifetime lover to this beautiful, healthy, deliberately designed sacred temple." That younger version of her may still show up at times but now she knows that she is the one in charge of its security and wellbeing, and she gets to speak to it kindly the way she would have wanted someone to have spoken to her when she was at her worst.

Suggestion: Bergamot [*Citrus bergamia*]

Inhaling and massaging Bergamot on the upper abdomen will assist in comforting you, inspiring acceptance and confidence, and reminding you that you have a purpose to fulfill, a message to share, gifts to give, and stories to tell that have been assigned only to you. It can remind you that you have the power to take care of yourself.

Release: Feeling insecure and unlovable, hopelessness, low self-esteem and self-judgment.

Receive: Confidence, freedom, self-approval, feeling good enough, lovable and hopeful.

How to Apply: Apply a drop on the palm of one hand, energize it by rubbing your palms together, inhale and massage your abdomen clockwise, as if tracing your intestines, until your body tells you to stop.

Say: I AM POWER

HEART CHAKRA

Clients are not the only ones who feel pain. As I shared earlier, after my sister Maria died, there were times when I felt overwhelmed with sorrow. I retreated into my cocoon, unwilling to participate in my own life, and quite frankly, sometimes felt disappointed when I realized that I was awake again. I would get up from bed just to walk my dogs and return to the crushing weight of my blankets. I was devastated that I could not make a phone call to hear my sister's voice and listen to her stories raving about her daughters or give me the most amazing big sister advice. I missed the way she would embrace me, sit with me and just smile at me. I missed whom I got to show up as in her loving and accepting presence. I was angry at myself because I could not "save her life" or "take away" her pain. I was angry at her for "graduating" from this earthly plane ahead of me. I was angry because I could not fully be there for my mom while I was dealing with my own grief. I was angry at cancer. I was angry at her medical team. I hated the world and blamed it for every negative emotion. I took everything to heart and my body resisted it all. I coughed constantly; it felt as if I were carrying a rusty cannonball inside my chest.

Suggestion: Peppermint [*Mentha piperita*]

Inhaling and massaging Peppermint on the heart and chest area assisted in opening up my airways and letting me breathe a little fuller. It created the feeling of my chest expanding without cages and my heart lightening and coming forward as my lungs cradled it like a baby, allowing me to breathe in life the way it is and not how I need it to be. It can remind us that we have the power to let go with love.

Release: Pessimism, heaviness, anger, depression, self-loathing, brokenness and pain.

Receive: Relief, optimism, self-acceptance, feeling clear, renewed, buoyant, and strong.

How to Apply: Apply a drop on the palm of one hand, energize it by rubbing your palms together, inhale and massage onto your chest in a spiral motion, counter clockwise first then as soon as your body tells you, go clockwise.

Say: I AM COMPASSION

THROAT CHAKRA

My client noticed that her voice sometimes sounds soft and shaky in certain situations. She has gotten frustrated during several occasions when she kept quiet instead of speaking up. She has often found herself making excuses for the other people, seemingly "processing" whatever it is that she experienced with them as something she was responsible for internally resolving rather than communicating a request without reservations or expressing her insights in real time— the very moment she recognizes that there is something for her to share. It has happened to her in stores and restaurants when she did not feel completely satisfied with the service; it has happened to her over the phone where she spoke at the same time as the other person then she just let them keep going while she faded away or said "go ahead," it has happened during family gatherings when she regressed back to her younger-meeker-just-be-obedient-self while in conversation with her older relatives who have taken the liberty of evaluating how her life has turned out; it has happened with her friends that feel too familiar or talk too damn much; it has happened when others touched her or spoke to her in ways she did not want and she stayed silent; and she has also exploded with cutting verbal reactions, spewing a lot of things she regretted saying.

Suggestion: Lavender [*Lavandula angustifolia*]

Inhaling and massaging Lavender on the neck will assist you in steadying your speech and allowing you to speak clearly, coherently, boldly but kindly and freely. You have been gifted with a voice and with the freedom to express yourself. It can remind you that you have the power to communicate.

Release: Blocked communication, lying, feeling rejected, unseen, unheard, and constricted.

Receive: Open communication, relaxation, honesty, eloquence, being seen and heard.

How to Apply: Apply a drop on the palm of one hand, energize it by rubbing your palms together, inhale and massage onto your throat in an upward swiping motion then stop when your body tells you.

Say: I AM INTEGRITY

FIRST EYE CHAKRA

My client is an accomplished entrepreneur but she found herself often feeling confused, forgetful, and worried about everything. She had taken her anxiety to bed and had nightmares that caused her to have disturbed sleep and woke up feeling tired the next day. Despite her many skills, she sometimes felt like she did not know what to do with her life. With several projects all happening at once, she did not know where to begin or what to do next. She found herself in conversation questioning what her purpose really was and felt like she did not know "where it was all going."

Suggestion: Lemon Balm [*Melissa officinalis*]

Inhaling and massaging "Melissa" on the forehead will assist you in expanding your imagination, focusing and staying connected to your vision, being present to what inspires you and trusting your intuition. You have been gifted with the opportunity to experience this lifetime. It can remind you that you have the power to fulfill your dreams.

Release: Disconnectedness, confusion, blocked creativity, and discouragement.

Receive: Intuition, visions, open-mindedness, imagination, and good dreams.

How to Apply: Wet one finger with the oil, dilute it with a vegetable oil like Jojoba, and anoint your temples and pineal gland by gently stroking the sides and middle of your forehead.

Say: I AM CLARITY

CROWN CHAKRA

My client is a respected healer, she is well-known in her community and often felt in-flow with the unpredictability of life but she also had moments of feeling extremely isolated, defeated, and alone. Sometimes she felt like she was one with her inner being and sometime she felt cynical, resigned, and doubtful of the possibility of a Higher Power. She gracefully danced from one feeling to the other and maintained a successful practice anyway but she was very aware of her contrasting thoughts and experiences. Despite everyone she helped in her life, she often struggled to stay afloat internally and externally and found herself needing to remind herself that she can lean back and relax into the grace of God.

Suggestion: Frankincense [*Boswellia carterii*]

Inhaling or massaging Frankincense on the head will assist in allowing you to feel whole and complete, stable and safe where you are. It will get you present to your connection to the Universe or the God you believe in. That God that is in you, around you, and that you are a part of. You are resource to Source. It can remind you that you have the power to let the God Force work through you and overflow from you for the benefit of all.

Release: Feeling unsafe, abandoned, disconnected, distant and "in the dark."

Receive: Feeling safe, protected, loved, open, and enlightened.

How to Apply: Wet one finger with the oil and anoint your crown by lightly massaging the top of your head in a spiral motion, counter clockwise first then as soon as your body tells you, go clockwise.

Say: I AM CONNECTION

TRUST YOURSELF AND TRUST THE PLANTS

You have the option to work on a particular chakra or better yet, approach the body as the whole being that it is and glide your way from the root chakra to the crown chakra or vice versa, as you feel inspired to. It is a deeply relaxing sensual experience to allow yourself to interact with Essential Oils and surrender to the plants' healing properties. Please give your body permission to lead you through the entire chakra balancing process. Everybody is different so each person will achieve a different result with each Essential Oil. My suggestions are specific but your body will be your best guide. Consider my recommendations, but more importantly, trust yourself and trust the plants.

A lot of books like this one will talk about chakras and the different ways of creating balance within them, everything will sound convincing and may be supported with strong evidence. Enjoy them, absorb and apply them, question them, and most of all remember that they are only relevant TO YOU when YOU FEEL the effect in YOUR BODY. Do you feel good? Does your life light you up and turn you on? Do you like waking up to your life? Do you like your daily experience? When there is a moment that you do not enjoy, do you know what to do? Even when circumstances do not go your way, can you be okay? No matter what anyone else says, YOUR life has to feel good to YOU.

SOMETHING SPECIAL

We all know that nowadays we can buy Essential Oils everywhere but sometimes we need something special just for us. This is why I specialize in customizing Essential Oil blends. Feel free to contact me, if this calls to you. My website has all my contact information.

REFERENCES

- Essentially Chakra
- An Everyday Guide to Balancing Your Chakra Centers Using Essential Oils
- The Complete Book of Essential Oils & Aromatherapy by Valerie Ann Wormwood
- Introduction to Aromatherapy by Jade Shutes

ESSENTIAL OIL SAFETY

Keep Essential Oils away from your eye, nostrils, inner ears, sensitive areas and open orifices. If you are nursing or pregnant, consult your doctor before using Essential Oils.

If you have low blood sugar	Avoid Geranium Essential Oil
If you have high blood pressure	Avoid Pine, Rosemary, Sage, and Thyme Essential Oils
If you use blood thinners	Avoid Birch and Wintergreen Essential Oils
If you have seizure disorders	Avoid Basil, Chamomile, Fennel, Hysop, Rosemary, and Sage Essential Oils
If you have kidney issues	Avoid Coriander, Juniper, and Sandalwood Essential Oils
Always use a carrier oil to slow down the absorption rate and to avoid skin irritations, unless indicated as NEAT	With Cassia, Cinnamon, Oregano, and Wintergreen Essential Oils always use a carrier oil
Do not expose yourself to direct sunlight for prolonged periods of time	If you have applied any citrus Essential Oils, avoid the sun
DO NOT USE the following Essential Oils:	Bitter Almond, Boldo Leaf, Calamus, Yellow Camphor, Horseradish Jaborandi Leaf, Mugwort, Mustard Pennyroyal, Rue, Sassafras, Savin, Southernwood, Tansy, Thuja, Wormseed, and Wormwood
If you have pets	Remember that their senses are more sensitive than ours so be mindful of what you diffuse in spaces that they share with you and as a rule of thumb, if it is not safe for you, it is not safe for your pets
If you have cats and dogs	Absolutely keep pets away from Cassia, Cinnamon, Clove, Eucalyptus, Juniper, Lemon, Lavender, Melaleuca, Peppermint, Rosemary, Spruce, Thyme, and Wintergreen.

ABOUT SHANNA MARIE

Website: www.TheLovingEarth.com

SHANNA MARIE is a Spiritual Interfaith Minister and Meditation Guide who is certified in the following modalities:

- Certified Aromatherapist, New York Institute of Aromatherapy
- Certified Crystal Healer, Hibiscus Moon Crystal Academy
- Certified Reiki II Practitioner, ARE Edgar Cayce Center
- Certified Professional Cuddler, Cuddlist

She is passionate about balancing mind and body fitness, and through her brand The Loving Earth, she enjoys creating customized products using Essential Oils.

To book your sessions and place your orders, visit her website.

She is available for meditation sessions by phone, private healing sessions in person, transformational group workshops focused on shifting the mindset and self-care, educational presentations at schools, health fairs or corporate events, and officiating sacred celebrations.

Her playful presence and purposeful work have been featured in the Bronx Times, Manhattan News Network, Marie Claire, Cosmopolitan, Yahoo Style, Tech Insider, Canal Plus, The Oprah Magazine, and more.

She is also the CEO of Mind Yard New York, a Licensing and Design company that specializes in creating characters with advocacies. One of their brand's most popular properties is Your Faith Looks Familiar or YFLF [yuff-luff], featuring the NY Comic Con superstars—the YFLF Gang, superheroes who champion *Oneness Beyond Belief* and fight against the evil forces of prejudice and ignorance. Learn more at www.MindYard.info, www.YFLF.co, and www.OHMbeads.com/YFLF

ASHNI
Flower Essence Therapist and Meditation Facilitator

When working with individuals I often look for archetypal energies within the speech, mannerisms and actions of an individual (my chapter explains this further). These archetypes provide a sort of lens through which I can perceive the patterns of behavior. I then use this lens to select flower essences that will help support the individual in inviting in more positive aspects of that archetype or embracing a different archetypal energy that is in more accurate alignment with their highest good. Flower essences assist us in becoming more aware of patterns in our lives. Once we become aware, there is a space created where we can choose and create life with ease.

Chakras are centers of energy that can control and affect how energy functions within the multi field of our physical, mental, emotional and etheric bodies. Chakras like archetypes are an ancient way of defining and/or understanding the energies within our own bodily system and within the greater universe.

My chapter is intended for you to begin to make contact with the archetypal energies you embody and the ones you are interested in inviting into your life.

USING FLOWER ESSENCES AND ANCIENT ARCHTEYPAL ENERGY TO BRING AWARENESS TO THE ENERGIES GUIDING OUR LIVES

Ashni

From the center point of where we are, the present moment, we can consciously choose and create life with ease. Flower essences assist us in bringing awareness to the patterns and beliefs that create many conditions in our lives and environment. Did you know for instance that we create neural pathways in our brain by doing the same things over and over? Flower essences are alchemical water based remedies that help to bring awareness to old habits, anxiety, stress and issues of the soul.

As we grow up in this world, conditions are placed on us by our families, culture, and society. These conditions can have a wide range of effects on us and our lives. Flower essences bring awareness to the thoughts and beliefs that these conditions create. Once we become aware, there is a space created where we can make a choice. The choices we make, combined with our willingness to harness our abilities to choose, are important keys which guide our experience of life.

Archetypal energies can be experienced and perceived in almost every area of our lives. There are perhaps hundreds of Archetypes including The Celebrity, The Debutante, The Healer, The Victim, The Magician, The Teacher, The Politician and so on and so on.

The seven archetypes in this chapter that we will explore (The Priestess/Priest, The Dreamer, The Storyteller, The Caretaker, The Athlete, The Chef and The Warrior) are related to the seven energy centers known as Chakras. Chakras, like archetypes, are an ancient way of defining and/or understanding the energies within our own bodily system and within the greater universe. These seven archetypes provide a sort of lens through which one can perceive patterns of behavior. We can then use our understanding to select essences that will help support an individual in inviting in beneficial aspects of that archetype and/or embracing a different archetypal energy that is in more accurate alignment with their highest good.

Let us embark on this journey with a quiz! Here are some suggestions for how to proceed:

- You can take the quiz and choose one answer that best describes your process;
- You can choose two or three answers that best describe you;
- You can take the quiz twice. The first time choose what best describes you, the second time choose the response you want to have.

Take a few deep breaths to bring yourself into the present. When you feel ready you can begin.

Jason Long - Dandelion flower on green grass field

Archetypal Energies Quiz

1) The first thing you do when you wake up in the morning is:
   a. Pray
   b. Record your dreams
   c. Sing or talk to yourself
   d. Look out the window and listen to the sounds of nature
   e. Jump out of bed and start to work out/do yoga
   f. Eat something
   g. Get to work

2) Your preferred Environment:
   a. Mountains
   b. Caves or valleys
   c. Meadows
   d. The city
   e. The sea
   f. The jungle

3) If you could be one of the following which would you choose
   a. Priestess/Priest
   b. Planner
   c. Speaker/Vocalist
   d. Teacher
   e. Law Enforcement
   f. Cook
   g. Athlete

4) You are planning a dinner for friends. Do you:
   a. Have an inspired idea and hire caterers to help you actualize it
   b. Have a dream of an amazing dinner menu - you get up, write the dream down and create dinner based on this
   c. Call a friend to talk about your ideas or possibilities
   d. Think about each friend and make an eclectic dinner based on all their unique tastes
   e. Go through recipe books and make a gourmet meal from the best recipes you find
   f. Create a theme-based dinner and ask friends to come dressed according to the theme
   g. Go to your garden to gather vegetables and make a meal from what you find

Archetypal Energies Quiz

5. Your style of communication is:
    a. Airy- all over the place jumping from one idea or thought to another
    b. Poetic
    c. Clear and direct
    d. Responsive- tending to wait or be invited to speak or respond
    e. Strong- you often take the lead in the conversations
    f. Passionate- you tend to get into heated discussions
    g. Grounded- practical

6. Your learning style is:
    a. Interactive
    b. Visual
    c. Listening
    d. Oral- discussing what you are learning
    e. One on one
    f. Engaging all the senses
    g. Physical

7. When you have an idea you want to manifest you:
    a. Ask for guidance from a mentor or someone you admire
    b. Create a vision board or visual plan
    c. Talk to a friend or partner
    d. Try to understand what this idea is and open yourself to possibilities of how it can manifest
    e. Create a step by step action plan
    f. Feel out what needs to be done
    g. Start taking immediate action

You have completed the quiz! Now tally up your answers and read on to see what archetypes you are playing with.

ARCHETYPAL ENERGIES

CROWN CHAKRA – PRIESTESS/PRIEST ARCHETYPE

If you chose mostly A's in your answers, you are aligned with the Archetype of the Priestess/Priest and have an active and open connection to the Crown Chakra (Sahasrara or Thousand-fold). You seek inspiration from the divine to guide your actions and provide a direction for your life. The positive aspects of this choice reflect a grounded connection to Divine forces. Your motivations are guided mostly by inspiration. The shadow aspects (the ones you don't want to admit) include misuse of power and/or confusion about what power is and how to use it. You may also struggle with staying in your body with a tendency towards being airy or scattered.

Angelica is a flower essence that would be beneficial for you to work with. Angelica creates a strong bridge to divine and angelic realms. It provides protection and guidance as one explores the subtler aspects of reality.

THIRD EYE CHAKRA – DREAMER ARCHETYPE

If you chose mostly B's you are aligned with the Archetype of the Dreamer and have an active and open connect to the Third Eye Chakra (Ajna or to perceive). When in balance you are capable of actualizing big ideas or visions. You dream big, and act on your intuition or deep inner knowing with ease.

When out of balance you may be stuck in the dream phase, having difficulty bringing your ideas out of your head and into the world. You have difficulty in translating the vision you hold into action.

Mugwort is a flower essence that is a great ally for you. Mugwort can help you to understand your dreams and visions, helping you to integrate the messages you receive into your daily life. It helps the sensitive soul to find balance as it navigates the many dimensions which create your reality.

THROAT CHAKRA – STORYTELLER ARCHETYPE

If you chose mostly C's, you are connected to the Archetype of the Storyteller and have an active Throat Chakra (Vishuddha or Purification). When in balance you can communicate effectively and with clarity. The storyteller can communicate complex ideas or feelings that are received by and understood by others. Your creative ways to problem solve give you the ability to flow with ease.

Out of balance, you may find it difficult to express yourself in a way that feels authentic. It may also manifest as difficulty or inability to listen.

Calendula is a flower essence that supports warmth and receptivity in your relations with others. It helps to cultivate listening skills; this includes listening to our self and others with love and compassion.

HEART CHAKRA – CARETAKER ARCHETYPE

If you chose mostly D's, you are connected to the archetype of the Caretaker and Heart Chakra (Anahata or Unstruck). Caretakers are interested in understanding and taking care of the needs of others. You are a nurturer and cultivator of love.

When out of balance, caretakers may tend to cater to the needs of others before their own, and may find themselves often depleted or burned out. They may also have difficulties caring for themselves or others in a healthy way.

Mariposa Lily is an excellent flower essence for this archetype. It supports the soul in awakening to its inherent mothering abilities. It awakens the ability to care for oneself and for others. It opens us to the unconditional love and support that is available to all.

SOLAR PLEXUS CHAKRA – ATHLETE ARCHETYPE

If you chose mostly E's, you identify most with The Archetype of the Athlete and often function from the Solar Plexus Chakra (Manipura or Lustrous Gem). This Archetype can harness the physical forces impeccably. Athletes can identify goals and direct their energy and attention to successfully achieve them.

Out of balance, the Athlete may find themself misdirecting their energy. They may internalize emotions and often don't know what to do with all that energy.

Dandelion is a flower essence that supports the soul in embodying clarity and guides one to use energy effectively. It provides a space to find balance between giving and receiving, being and doing.

NAVEL CHAKRA – CHEF ARCHETYPE

If you got mostly F's, you are aligned with the Archetype of the Chef and are mostly connected to your Navel Chakra (Svadhisthana or "Sweetness"). You are sensual and delight in the rich flavors and textures of life. This archetype can combine different elements with ease, finding it easy to go with the flow, and find joy in participating in the co-creative process of life. Out of balance you may find it challenging to accept and flow with the unexpected. You may find yourself resisting change. There may also be a loss or lack of appetite.

California Wild Rose is a flower essence that is an excellent foundational remedy which supports the individual in embracing joy in one's work and/or creations. It helps you to enjoy the richness of the physical, emotional and mental life, creating a healthy balance in relating to yourself and others.

ROOT CHAKRA – WARRIOR ARCHETYPE

If you got mostly G's, the Archetype of The Warrior and the Root Chakra (Muladhara or Root/Support) is one you connect to. Warriors are strong, grounded and strong willed.

The balanced Warrior works for the good of all, "fighting the good fight." This relates to upholding the values and virtues that support all life.

Out of balance the Warrior may find themselves fighting without reason, withdrawing or backing down in a mechanical "fight or flight" response.

Mountain Pride is a flower essence remedy that supports the soul in understanding its strengths and how to use them to help oneself and others. It supports healthy masculine energy to both women and men. It supports us to act with integrity, or for the greater good.

I hope this information provides you with some keys to understanding yourself, and with a tool or two to refine your ability to relate to others and to life with ease. If you would like more support in aligning with, and clarifying, your true Life Essence you can contact me at lovingseeds@gmail.com

May you walk in beauty. May you walk in peace.

ARCHETYPAL ENERGIES

Chakra	Archetype	Flower Essence
Crown	Priestess/Priest	Angelica
Third Eye	Dreamer	Mugwort
Throat	Storyteller	Calendula
Heart	Caretaker	Mariposa Lily
Solar Plexus	Athlete	Dandelion
Navel	Chef	California Wild Rose
Root	Warrior	Mountain Pride

ABOUT ASHNI

Websites: sunderashni.com & minkabrooklyn.com/ashni
Contact: lovingseeds@gmail.com

ASHNI is a Flower Essence therapist, a healing channel and an educator born and raised in Brooklyn, NY.

Movement, music, healing and their expansion through meditation and love are essential keys to Ashni's being. From early experiences with death and escapades in library stacks, to discovering yoga and teachings with Buddhist monks in high school, Spirit has always piqued her curiosity and tickled her heart. From an early age, Ashni has been devoted to learning from and listening to Spirit.

After discovering OSHO in 2003 and extensive practice and training with The Meditation Module, Ashni took sannyas and became part of the facilitating team in 2005. During this time, she was also initiated into Reiki (levels I and II) and became a Reiki Master in 2010. It was during this time (2004) that she encountered flower essences for the first time. At a lecture at the old East West Books, she heard about the support that flower essences provide in aligning with our truth. She then began her apprenticeship with Linda Cohen, learning about the wide variety of flower remedies available and how they could be used to support healing of the heart and mind. Soon after, she co-created Meditation from the Source, where she utilized her experiences with OSHO Active Meditations™ and creativity to commit to exploring and experiencing life authentically and totally. She co-led 21 day cycles of Dynamic Meditation for two years, in addition to facilitating workshops and weekly meditation classes.

Leaving her Brooklyn roots to live in Costa Rica in 2011, she embarked on the Red Road Path and has recently completed her fourth year in the Moondance, from the Mexica tradition. While in Costa Rica, she also developed her line of Flower Essences, called SOULutions and received training in Zen Shiatsu from Kantu Veet Mor.

Ashni currently has a private practice at Minka. She also facilitates ceremonies, meditations, wellness services for organizations and experiences permeated with love that cultivate radical awareness, appreciation of self and overall ecstatic wellness within participants and their community, with the intention of re-cultivating a deep connection with our Earth Mother.

The
Heart
Nurturers

TIZIANA RINALDI CASTRO
Transformational Life Coach & Certified Theta Healing Practitioner

When I meet with clients for the first time I open my space from within, from where I can listen deeply, from a place of compassion, free of judgment. Often people hide and change the script of their life to make it acceptable to themselves and others. It is thus important to allow the space and time for that script to unravel, to receive the client's true story as it were, and for a breakthrough to occur. I listen carefully to the client speak and when I find an opening I offer a story in return. It may be a story from anywhere in the world.

- A passage from the Egyptian or Tibetan Book of the Dead
- A story from Perceval or from La mort d'Arthur, The Iliad, The Odyssey, Gilgamesh;
- A story from the sacred texts: *The Upanishad*, *The Bible*, *The Koran;* a fable from the farthest corner of the earth or just an episode witnessed at the corner store.
- A story, told at the right time, can either mend a hole or the exact opposite - create a fracture. In both cases it serves an equal purpose: it offers a pause and creates a bridge, and it brings us to the present time.

It is usually then, if my story is compelling enough- the correct one, that is- that the heart opens and emotions flow openly. The truth of one's feelings and the memories emerge intact, and the authentic work can begin.

My work as a Transformational Life Coach at The Resonant Self centers on *praying* your life into being, where prayer is the means to co-creating/affirming/manifesting one's own reality. In addition, I work with Archetypal psychology, Medicine Storytelling and Theta Healing, a technique particularly useful in removing blocks and false beliefs that hinder one from clearing the path to the opening of the heart chakra.

My chapter, *"Praying Your Life into Being"* explores Anahata, the chakra of the heart, the chakra directly connected to prayer. It explores and examines the healing effects of prayer, both emotional, psychological and physical, and its regenerative and transformative power.

PRAYING YOUR LIFE INTO BEING
Tiziana Rinaldi Castro

The heart Chakra is the fourth one, right at the center of the seven chakras, in the chest. It is called Anahata-in Sanskrit. It means "unhurt, unstruck, and unbeaten" and it is associated with unconditional love, compassion, and joy. Anahata connects with the physical realm of the three chakras below and with the spiritual realm of the three chakras above.

The three chakras below--the Root Chakra, the Sacral Chakra, and the Solar Plexus-preside over earthly matters, respectively grounding us on the earth (instinct, will to live, creative self-expression), connecting us to each other's bodies (interpersonal relations, creative reproduction of being), and allowing us to feel and "know" through these (will to achieve, adaptation and social patterns).

The three Chakras above--the Throat Chakra, the Third Eye, and the Crown Chakra-preside over spiritual matters, respectively allowing us to communicate and express ourselves (resonance of being), to enter in contact with the invisible forces constantly at work around us (knowledge of being), and to ease our opening towards the Source (purest being).

Anahata, its functions being self-abandonment and devotion to the being[1], sits right between the two realms, the earthly and the heavenly, a perfect bridge when it is open and thus vibrates fully.

"Res tantum cognoscitur quantum diligitur- A thing is known to the extent that it is loved". ~ Saint Augustin

What the Hindus call Anahata, different creeds throughout the world refer to with different names. In Christian Cabbala, Jesus is represented by the sacred heart; in Jewish Kabbalah, the center of the Tree of Life is associated with the heart; in Islamic mysticism, the Sufi call Sirr the innermost part of the Heart in which the Divine reveals himself[2] (to date one of the most moving and mysterious points in philosophy of religion at large) and debate at length whether love and gnosis, the last stations on the mystical path, are one superior to the other or complementary with each other. Love becomes eventually the way to gnosis: Ali Hujwiri, a great Sufi Mystic from the 11th century writes about seeing God: "We deem all torments more desirable than to be veiled from Thee. When Thy beauty is revealed to our hearts, we take no thought of affliction"(H 111; cf. A10: 120)[3]. And Junaid of Baghdad, a mystic of the 8th century had already pointed out: "Love between two is not right until the one addresses the other, 'O Thou I'" (T 2:29)[4], echoing thus the prophet Jesus, who, rephrasing Deuteronomy and Leviticus, replied to the people asking him what were the greatest commandments: "Thou shalt love the Lord thy God with all thy heart, and with all thy soul, and with all thy strength, and with all thy mind; and thy neighbour as thyself. [...] this do, and thou shalt live." (Luke 10:25-28, King James' version)

"There is a light that shines beyond the world, beyond everything, beyond all, beyond the highest heaven. This is the light that shines within your heart."
~ Upanishads

Sitting at the center of the chest, Anahata relates to the physical heart, the lungs, the arms, the hands, the thymus gland and the immune system, while energetically it relates to compassion and unconditional love.

When we are connected to Anahata and we live and operate from it in a condition of balance, we experience well-being. And though we may strive to achieve more and to improve our state, we live in gratitude and acceptance, our relationships are serene, we are prone to forgive easily and we have a gentle and kind attitude towards others.

On the other hand, when we are disconnected from Anahata, we can physically experience an unbalance in the heart itself or in our circulatory system, our blood pressure can be either too low or too high and our lungs can be affected as well. Furthermore, mentally we will be unhappy, we won't be trusting our instincts, we will be uncertain about our feelings toward our surroundings, we will feel untrustworthy and unable to relate to others as we would like. We might experience feelings of withdrawal, be cold and unattached, unresponsive to other people's needs or, on the opposite side of the spectrum, we might easily become dependent on others, have trouble setting boundaries, try to please others at the cost of our serenity and freedom. Fundamentally immature on an emotional level, on either side of the spectrum, we will resort to all kinds of manipulations in order to satisfy our needs.

Keeping Anahata open is the only way to offer an unobstructed bridge for our spirit to expand within ourselves, between our body and our mind and beyond, and live thus a balanced life. There are many ways to achieve this: yoga, meditation, psychotherapy, religious practice, art or music therapy, hypnosis, volunteer work, and many different forms of physical, cognitive, and spiritual therapy aimed at opening the chakras and realigning them so that these will be working properly again and a sense of well-being will ensue that shall benefit us and those around us.

MAKE YOUR LIFE A PRAYER

"Love thyself last: cherish those hearts that hate thee;
Corruption wins not more than honesty.
Still in thy right hand carry gentle peace,
To silence envious tongues. Be just, and fear not:
Let all the ends thou aim'st at be thy country's,
Thy God's, and truth's; then if thou fall'st, O Cromwell,
Thou fall'st a blessed martyr!"
~ William Shakespeare, Henry the VIII (3.2.521)

The practice of prayer as a successful means to co-creating/affirming/manifesting our own reality together with the Divine are the fundamental tool used in my practice.

I live, teach and work in accordance to three precepts:

1. Love thyself last,
2. Like courage fear is a state of mind,
3. Make your life a prayer.

All three of these precepts find their highest and deepest, most definitive expression in the heart. It is within the heart that we feel love, understand, or struggle with, our connection with one another, and reflect our relationship with ourselves and the world at large.

LOVE THYSELF LAST

Storytelling, in my experience as a priestess and later as a Life Coach, has always been the starting point for healing, through the emersion of a question and an answer.

I will, therefore, tell you a story. The story regards an act of disattention.

I am eight years old. I have been given a pink chick. It is the trend at this time in Italy, where I come from. Little chicks are spray-painted different colors for the joy of children, and mothers buy these poor wretched creatures with which the kid can play. In my case, it is my grandmother who brings mine home on a Thursday morning, the weekly market day, and gifts it to me. I am elated, a pink chick! She cautions me, it is a small being, I need to tend to it carefully, give it water and feed it the grains she puts in a small dish for me, and not let it out of the box. I play with the little chick for a while, stroke its little head with my index finger, and as I hold it in my hand, I enjoy its fluffiness, register the warmth of its quivering body, the thud of its little heart beating on my palm. Then it falls asleep and I put it back in the box, on its little bed of cotton wool, which my grandmother has handed me. I watch it for a while, then I go to play elsewhere and I forget all about it.

Later on, I return to the box and to my horror I realize that the chick has disappeared. I look for it and I am at once desperate and scared. Desperate that I have lost it and scared that my grandmother will get upset at me. She finally comes out and realizing that the chick is missing, she shakes her head. I was supposed to be careful, I was not, she says. I am surprised when she doesn't scold me, she is usually a very stern, even harsh woman, prone to easy punishments, sometimes she hits me. Not this time though, she turns around and goes back into the kitchen. It isn't easy to look for the chick, we live in a very large house, there are many tables, sofas, and chairs covered with cloth. Relieved by the averted threat of a beating, however, after a while I get distracted again and I begin playing with something else.

The next day I woke up and I went into the kitchen. My grandmother was there and I sat at the table waiting for my breakfast as usual. She came and put the box on the table in front of me, the dead pink chick lying in it, on its bed of cotton balls. She did not say a word, just looked at me for a moment or two, then went back to her chores.

I don't remember much of the ordeal after that, if I buried it, if my grandmother took it to dispose of it, if I cried. Only that crushed heart for the dead pink chick, and from that moment on for every small or big, crestfallen or still hopeful, vulnerable being.
It lingered on.

Nothing is mine, all is borrowed and that which I refuse to let go of, is stolen… If I remove my individual ego from the world, the world returns at peace. Things stop being what I think they are and go back to what they truly are.
~ Alejandro Jodorowsky- El Maestro y Las Magas

When I was eighteen years old I fell in love head over heels with a wonderful young man, I got married, and moved to New York with him, ready to start our new adventure together. My whole life was ahead of me, I had been accepted at New York University, I was filled with prospects, hopeful and fearless. The day before we left, my husband and I went to say goodbye to a man whom I loved dearly, the grandfather of my maternal cousins, who had been the closest grandfatherly figure I had known in my life, as both my parents' fathers had died long before I was born. Our visit together was bittersweet, my 'grandmother' Grazia had made coffee and we were amiably talking around the table about our American plans.

"I'd like to give you something for you to remember me by," my grandfather was saying, pensive. At that point I heard a fluttering of wings and turning to the window I noticed the cage containing two splendid quails, one of which was just waking up.

My grandfather loved birds and it wasn't a mystery that they loved him back. Stories went around the family about how the winged creatures would follow him around, how they had at times escorted him back home from one of his long walks in the woods, or how once, long before I was born, when he had moved from one neighborhood to another in our village, one family of birds had uprooted itself as well from a branch of a tree next to his old house, to take up residence a few days later in a nest under the eaves of the balcony of his new apartment. Nobody had marveled at the event. My grandmother had just informed him:

"The birds found you."

He had grunted and gone back about his business, he was a man of few words.

I stared at the quails for a few seconds and then returned to my coffee. My grandfather knew I was terrified of birds, especially little ones. I had been for a long time though I could not say why. Something about them. The flapping of the wings, the feathers, the sudden movement of their heads, those fixed rounded eyes, their lack of expression? I felt uneasy.

I thought them beautiful from far away and was so taken with their flying I would stare at them in awe; I would follow their arabesques in the sky with my heart pounding, touched by their freedom, exhilarated by their speed. And yet, at close range, I was paralyzed with a mix of revulsion and fear, I would shiver in tension, and often duck as if fearing an attack. The mere sight of an aviary or swallows returning to their nest under the eaves of balconies could send me into a frenzy. One of those things that just stay with you without question, and that everybody teases you for but ends up also protecting you from.

My grandfather was puzzled by my reaction to birds. To him, it was unwarranted and thus a nuisance. He noticed me looking at the cage and he got up. I sighed, what was he about to do? He went right to it, opened it and took one bird out. I thought I would die."Do you like quails, Steve?," he asked my husband.

Steve nodded, though he was uneasy, he knew about my phobia and wanted to spare me the discomfort. My grandfather came to the table and put the quail in my husband's hands. Steve opened them to receive it and immediately caressed its head with one of his thumbs. The quail closed its eyes at Steve's gentle touch and relaxed.

It was a beautiful bird. Nonetheless, I had become frozen with fear and contempt towards my grandfather; why was he torturing me? My hands clutched but I got quiet and I knew I would not say a word. A profound respect for his age and authority hindered me from rebelling. He knew that too.

He took the quail from my husband's hands and told me:

"Open your hands, Tiziana."

"Nonno, I am afraid of birds," I said with a pleading tone.

"But they don't know that sweetie," he replied, smiling with a revelatory expression.

Something inside of me cracked and hit me at once. My hands untied.

My grandfather put the bird in my open palm.

It was warm and it quivered. With anguish I waited for the terror that I thought should follow, but all I could feel was the immense smallness of the creature, the feeling of defenselessness it must have felt at that very moment in my very strong hand, its infinite loveliness in that perfect body equipped with wings, which allowed it to fly far into the sky, its incomprehensible sudden solitude, removed from its companion left in the cage by the window. Its eyes stared at me and for a moment its wings seemed about to flutter.

"The bird is scared, Tiziana."

Instinctively I covered it with my other hand, ever so gently.

Courage is not the absence of fear, but rather the judgment that something else is more important than fear
~ Ambrose Redmoon

Years later, I was sitting in an Ifà temple in Harlem, at my Godmother's feet. I had studied with her for a few seasons already and I had expressed the desire to become a priestess in the Ifà faith if the Orishas (Gods) accepted my request. My Godmother looked at me firmly and nodded.

"Give me your reasons. At least one."

She was waiting, looking right into my eyes with her piercing look, her white dreads perfectly still.

I thought I would begin a sound explanation of how dedicating my life to the Orishas would have been a way to thank them for the privilege of being alive and that service to the people would have been the most appropriate way for me to express that gratitude to the Divine, but, as I was about to open my mouth, I saw before me the dead pink chick lying in the box with its eyes closed, lost to the world because of my disattention, my delusion that it would have taken care of itself even though it had been entrusted to me for that very reason.

I feel the crushing of bones and quickly lift my foot. I can feel the softness of its plumes mixed with the sound of its little bones under the sole of my foot.

But the chick doesn't die. The chick keeps on walking. I am horrified. I keep still, my heart pounding in the chest like a ball of fire ready to explode. I see it stepping lightly, if only limping a bit, all the way back to its box. I close my eyes, bite my lips, and for the rest of the evening, I pretend that nothing has happened.

My heart exploded like a ball of fire and I could barely breathe, I traced the knot as it went up the trachea and settled in my throat. I had to swallow a few times, air, saliva, my own muffled cry before I could mutter:

"Because I don't want to forget anyone ever again."

My Godmother nodded. She deemed it a good reason.

"Make your life a prayer then," she said, and we continued on.

It was a most elementary and yet cryptic precept. I heard it that evening for the first time and I was to hear it a few more times during my apprenticeship with her at different, most poignant times. Till the last time we spoke. Her very last words to me, in fact, on her deathbed. Her legacy, her will. A daunting task.

MAKE YOUR LIFE A PRAYER – WHAT DOES IT MEAN?

To make our life a prayer – a condition sine qua non to be a priest- can be equally important for secular people whose desire is to invite the sacred into their life. Because, if we delve into the meaning of this precept, we find that ultimately its core is: to pull the sacred into our lives.

Make your life a prayer means reaching all seemingly contradictory goals are thus difficult to achieve, if we don't surrender to the heart:

- to live in the present ceaselessly and boundlessly;
- to move selflessly into the world without losing our center;
- to leave ourselves aside while entering fully into the scene;
- to detach ourselves from our own wants and needs while participating fully into human affairs.
- And, of course, last but not least, to pray, the very starting point, in fact, of this practice of bringing the sacred into our lives, from which all other steps can sprout.

Even praying, however, seemingly the least charged among the undertakings listed above, is not a simple task and needs to be learned. Unless we are called by habit or strong feelings: fear, pain, relief, or extreme gratitude, in fact, praying isn't the most natural gesture. Why?

It takes an open heart to be immersed in prayer. If done properly, fully invested in the act, praying causes and signifies an opening into the sacred, crossing the boundary of the present and the now, and sustaining the suspension within the gap between mundane and holy.

The word sacred has a very ancient root: from the Latin word sacer (archaic form sakros), to set apart, to separate, to dedicate. Its root is to be searched in the Akkadian - a Semitic language now extinct- saqāru ("to invoke the divinity"), sakāru ("to bolt," "to ban") e saqru (elevated.)

Religious feasts are a typical example of an occasion in which we enter sacred time, it is then that all together, with a common intent, we separate from the mundane and cross into "a time of eternity." As Mircea Eliade writes:

« Feasts happen in a sacred time, in eternity that is [...]. There are periodic feasts, however, -surely the most important- that show us something more: the desire to abolish the profane time already passed and to establish "a new time." In other words, the periodic feasts that end a temporary cycle and begin a new one, launching a re-generation of time». (Mircea Eliade, History of Religious Ideas, p. 410-11)

So it's prayer. Like feasts, it has the power to isolate, elevate, and thus render sacred the space and the time in which it happens. Like worshippers at a feast, the one who prays has an opportunity to transcend the present, and to enter "a time of eternity."

This is of the utmost importance. It is within that time that the heart enjoys mostly the healing effects of prayer, its regenerative and transformative power. Prayer nourishes and when the heart is nourished its chakra vibrates fully and healing is possible.

FOR WHAT DO WE PRAY? TO WHOM DO WE PRAY? PRAYER AS AN ACT OF WILL, TOWARDS HEALING OURSELVES.

Every day in my practice I help people learning how to pray, pave with them their way towards prayer. It seems a paradox that we should need help to put our hands together and ask, but it becomes clearer once we understand that prayer can mean to surrender our Higher Self to the divine within us and that it takes, therefore, an act of will to recognize our self-worth and to believe not in our ability to beg but to reach for; not to hope for but to manifest. It might take time, discipline, and method to develop the heart chakra. Prayer expands the latter and bridges our will to the sacred, and in turn, we receive bountiful and manifold gifts, the seed of healing; we begin to pray in a disciplined manner and, as the act of praying becomes less sporadic and more of a practice, the heart opens and remains open. When the heart chakra is opened it longs to receive and give love. In time, we are able and ready to connect: to ourselves fully and to others freely, without conditions.

BUT FOR WHAT DO WE PRAY? AND TO WHOM?

In Kundalini Yoga, one branch of Yoga, in which many of its Kriyā are particularly directed towards the development of the Anahata, the first Mantra to be chanted at the beginning of any meditative practice is this one:

Ong Namo. Guru Dev Namo.
It means:
Ong Namo- I bow to All-That-Is (the Subtle Divine wisdom)
Guru Dev Namo - I bow to the Divine Wisdom within myself (the Divine Teacher within).

Anyone of us who believes in the Divine has referents to whom we feel connected and in praying we might address Them. We might feel great love for the Divine we refer to and feel great respect for It and approach It from a place of great humility and prostration, but ultimately utter distance and separation. But that is only half of the Mantra -Ong Namo- I bow to All-That-is, and even in that phrase we can find ourselves (all that is). The other half calls us in the equation: I bow to the Divine Wisdom within myself. We are divine, we are teachers, we are deserving, we bow to ourselves.

If we don't find it within ourselves to love who and what we are, passionately and unconditionally, we owe it to the Divine's love for us to believe that we are worthy of it!

It takes time, it takes work, it takes method, yes!

As we pray, we understand our part in the process of praying, we realize that praying is a relationship, a covenant, a discourse, in which we play an active role and that the more we love ourselves the more we learn to love others.

We learn to discern how to speak our requests, how to voice our needs, and how to understand our part and accept our responsibility in our efforts to be agents of change in our lives.

If we pray for a relationship, for example, we meditate on the kind of relationship we desire. If we long to always be heard and understood; to be comforted and supported when in need; if our wish is to be honored and cherished by our lover at all time, and if we expect not to be betrayed, we should pray for independence and autonomy, and wish to manifest the ability to listen for and forgive ourselves, to care for and sustain ourselves, to cater to our needs and accept who we are without judgement, and never betray our integrity in any circumstance.

We can't ask to be loved without loving ourselves. It won't work, like a carpet seller who wants to peddle a moth-ridden rug.

Evolving into ourselves as we develop an open-heart chakra we become more open and yet less vulnerable. And though we long to be loved and are nurtured by our relationship with the world, we love from a place of strength and autonomy. We no longer expect to be nurtured from the outside world and so we are nurtured by it tenfold. We don't expect to be healed by others and so it is the act of loving and receiving love that heals us. We are then able to heal our wounds, to assuage the anger we might feel towards ourselves and others, strengthen our core that was weakened by suffering, dissatisfaction, mourning, loss, trauma. We experience compassion, longing for love and trust. As we learn how to cherish ourselves, we are able to love others in joy. The heart desires to love more than anything, and to be loved. It is that its natural state, be joyful and loving. And that is its strength. When we accept that we have a right to be loved as much as to love, we are more willing and able to heal our wounds, and our good disposition towards life is good medicine for others as well.

Prayer makes its transformative power manifest in many ways: the inner healing causes the outside to change as well. The world around us will appear to us unencumbered by our fears and our negative attitudes towards ourselves and others.

Once we begin feeling centered in love, recognizing our core -we are made of love and we are love- the heart will experience feelings of compassion, peace, joy. We will be open to love ourselves and others. Our life will be fundamentally modified by it: our relationships will be deepened, our commitment to life will be complete.

Our perception of the outside world becomes different. We begin telling a different story about ourselves, each other, and the world in which we live, one of compassion, love, and understanding. In the quest to live in joy, we nourish ourselves and those around us with positivity. That which appeared difficult is no longer, that which was intolerable is now bearable, even laughable, maybe. It is as if we had changed our point of view, and especially -because of the most generous gift of compassion- it is as if all things are equidistant from us and none is too close, though our heart is filled with love for all. We are rooted in ourselves and a wind cannot move us. Outside is nothingness, a mere projection of our inner fears and hopes, of our thoughts, good and bad. Everything is inside. We have given ourselves permission to love ourselves and now love fills our life. As within so without.

PRAYER AS CO-CREATION AND A TOOL FOR HEALING, AFFIRMATION, AND EMPOWERMENT. HOW IS OUR ABILITY TO PRAY CONNECTED TO OUR SELF-WORTH? -AS WITHIN SO WITHOUT-.

If the heart is closed, wounded, disconnected from the other chakras in the body, we experience discomfort and illness, loss of faith, loneliness. Praying is difficult, a discontinuous act. As a wounded pet that refuses help and might bite us, we won't go naturally towards prayer and take advantage of its healing powers, continuing instead down the spiral of discontent.

It is from the heart chakra, that we learn to listen to ourselves, to our convictions and, as in all other parts of the body, we can hold and protect the story that we are told. If the message we receive is one of little worth, we will be unprotected in the matters of love. We won't love freely but from a place of dependency, lack of self-worth and autonomy, and we will be familiar with patterns of alienation, shutting down our emotions and those of the ones we love. We might recur to emotional blackmail, drama, and all other kinds of manipulations to keep the shadow of the love we think we own and we are owned by. We shall hurt and we shall be hurt. Consequently, we will cling more tightly to our shield made of fear, self-deceit, and false beliefs about our worth, which will, in turn, nourish suffering, betrayal, and loneliness.

All these feelings naturally reside in the heart and though chakras are connected one to the other and the experience of emotional pain can be somatized everywhere in the body and felt throughout, the heart is the place where we can heal it.

Praying in a state of inner prostration, when we have abandoned all hopes of autonomy, means relinquishing the power of change and realization solely into the hands of the One to whom we are praying. Moving from our heart in a state of autonomy and freedom, of compassion, and filled with love for ourselves and others, we understand that we are agents of our change as much as graceful recipients of life's miracles. Loving outward we are loved back and we can claim what is ours and it has always been ours. That which we ask for manifests because we ask for it.

As we affirm our needs and wants we make a stand, we come forward in our will, we manifest our needs, our desires, our wishes. When that passes to be, we have received the grace of having co-created with our praying the reality that we were looking to realize.

One of the most important lessons of praying is how to accept when things that we ask to co-create don't pass to be. A grateful heart that has opened towards the source will remain centered and either re-focus on the intention or change the target graciously and gracefully.

HOW DO WE LEARN TO PRAY, HOW DO WE READY OURSELVES FOR THE TASK?

We reflect the world from the inside. As within so without. Our inner world is projected outside mirror like: our fears, our insecurities, our terrors, our feelings towards ourselves and others, our aspirations, our convictions, our ideas down to our hidden memories, our seemingly forgotten traumas. We reenact our feelings and the image and ideas that we have of ourselves and of others onto the world, and our reality is based upon them, we manifest it as such. So, a disillusioned self will find cynical friends, an angry heart will meet caustic partners, a co-dependent person with a history of abandonment will meet withdrawn, cold significant others, a person whose self-esteem is low will meet harsh, judgmental friends.

HOW DO WE CHANGE THIS PATTERN, HOW DO WE LEARN HOW TO PRAY OUR WAY OUT OF IT? WHAT WILL BRING FORTH THAT ACT OF WILL? AND HOW?

Changing the story that we tell about ourselves, and praying in the direction of praising, acknowledging whatever goodness in ourselves and our life, and thanking the Divine for it.

As we change the story we tell about ourselves, we lose the habits that have formed the framework of our daily life, and in changing the way we tell our own story to ourselves, we see the story changing before our eyes. As our story unfolds anew so does our prayer. As we compose a new prayer our story changes. The prayer that we compose changes our story.

What we have done is that we have operated "a promise to change." rather than making "a promise to change". The latter is always a daunting task: so profoundly steeped we are in our habits that moving in the direction of correcting any one of our behaviors often results in failure; after a while, believing the old story about ourselves, we tend to resume the old behavior and return, thus, to the comfortable though maddening starting point.

By throwing a curve into our own path, on the other hand, a wrench in the spoke of our wheel so to speak, we create a shock, propel ourselves forward, crack an opening in the shield behind which we hide. We force ourselves to move differently on our own turf. And now we will have to watch each step afterwards if we don't want to fall.

Changing the script of our lives will change the outcome. A new life will begin because we are no longer the same agents.

PRAYER AS SURRENDERING AND LIBERATION

Surrendering to the heart is the first call of the priesthood. The Divine speaks through it and makes Its will and beauty manifest. From that place, the precept *make your life a prayer* becomes easier to decode. As we have stated at the beginning, it means: to live in the present ceaselessly and boundlessly; to move selflessly into the world without losing one's center; to leave oneself aside while entering fully into the scene; to detach oneself from one's own wants and needs while participating fully into human affairs, and, of course, finally, to pray.

We have spoken about the power of prayer and about how its healing effects reach far, can restore our faith into the world, create beauty, strengthen the core of our commitment to life.

Yet, if the intent is not to commit to ourselves temporarily for a moment of meditation, but rather to make our life a prayer, we need to go about this in an opposite manner: rather than separating from our present to reach for the sacred, it is necessary to pull the sacred into our present at all times as we offer ourselves to the community at large. How can it be done? By accepting that the chakra of the heart always be open, that the flow of energy be rushed through constantly, and that we are consequentially exposed, touched, and possibly vulnerable. But how else will we become whole?

LOVE THYSELF LAST

Love thyself last. To achieve this, however, we will need to muster a lot of courage. It isn't easy to accept this mantra. In a society that celebrates the individual, that pampers his/her needs, and puts the ego in the forefront at all cost, stressing as just and opportune the idea of loving ourselves first and foremost as an indispensable condition to love the rest, a dictum as *love thyself last* might be unacceptable, at best confusing. When we are surrounded by public personas, politicians -and even cities and entire governments- which ego is larger than life, loving ourselves last seems abusive almost.

Exercising the priesthood, being of service to others, and living the practice of loving thyself last, on the other hand, means to "Leave the world" and enter in the Divine or enter the Divine at any given time. To be present in love, with love, and from love into the world means to be with the Divine into the world at any time.

126

It isn't so difficult when the work of loving is daily and practical, when the work of loving involves getting lost in the Divine and its work, that is the world, us, the heavens. It does

become, however, an agonizing and unsurmountable task when we think of ourselves as separated from the world. When, in other words, we perceive ourselves as the person with a measureless ego yet occupying within the world the minimal space that we strenuously defend.

The key is to understand the opposite: to love ourselves last means to comprehend how we are part of the entire world, which is immense, but how our ego is very circumscribed and measurable, in fact of minimal importance. By loving ourselves last, we have a chance to love everything first, the entire world, to be part of everything around, and within the world the Divine, and without the world the Divine again, and all that regards It, all that fills It, and all that empties It, and to be inundated with that love, to experience that love at all times, continuously.

In the great Sufi mystics' debate over whether it was gnosis or love that held the primate in understanding God, neither side won. The Divine is elusive and, ultimately, a conclusive understanding of It is at best impossible and in any case less a subject for philosophy and religion than for poetry, rapture, and meditation. But through our unconditional love for the Divine's creation we can get closer to It easily every day.

In my personal experience, an incident as seemingly insignificant as the death of a chick has dug a furrow into my heart, painfully opening the chakra to compassion and paving the way silently and surely to my commitment to the priesthood. In turn, the priesthood has helped the chakra to stay open by means of praising the Divine constantly through the work of Its many manifestations, be they the Orishas whom I worship, Mother Nature which I revere, or my fellow human beings whom I love. All of them have in turn helped me to become a better priest.

To love thyself last is a risk and a chance, an opportunity and a state of mind, a wonderful privilege and a blessed curse, and a condition sine qua non for the priesthood to be complete. It has been for me at least and I haven't regretted a single day of it this far. I haven't always been ready for it and it hasn't almost never been easy, but it was always possible if given a chance, and that is more than a lot of other endeavors in life! It gave me the opportunity to learn how to think with compassion, live a fuller life, help so many to reach within their heart to live a better life, and ultimately fulfill my Godmother's legacy, and make my life a prayer.

© Tiziana Rinaldi Castro

End Notes:

1) See, among other detailed references, Rick Richards' webpage for a quick and clear compendium of the chakras at www.rickrichards.com/chakras/Chakras2.html

2) "God created the hearts seven thousand years before the bodies and kept them in the station of proximity to Himself and He created the spirits seven thousand years before the hearts and kept them in the garden of intimate fellowship (uns) with Himself, and the consciences—the innermost part—He created seven thousand years before the spirits and kept them in the degree of union (waṣl) with Himself. Then he imprisoned the conscience in the spirit and the spirit in the heart and the heart in the body. Then He tested them and sent prophets, and then each began to seek its own station. The body occupied itself with prayer, the heart attained to love, the spirit arrived at proximity to its Lord, and the innermost part found rest in union with Him". Annemarie Schimmel, Mystical Dimensions of Islam, p. 192)

3) The Kashf Al-Mahjub: The Oldest Persian Treatise on Sufism, transl. Reynold A. Nicholson Gibb Memorial Series, no. 17. 1911 Reprint. London, 1959

4) Farid al-Din 'Attar Tadhkarat-ul-auliya or Memoirs of Saints, two vols. 1905-1907 Reprint. London and Leiden 1959

ABOUT TIZIANA RINALDI CASTRO

Website: www.theresonantself.com
Email: theresonantself@gmail.com

TIZIANA RINALDI CASTRO is a trained transformational Life Coach and a certified Theta Healing Practitioner. She began as an Olorisha of the Ifà faith, of which she has been an initiate since 1987 and an ordained priestess (Olorisha) since 1991. A published novelist and a professor of Ancient Greek literature at Montclair State University, throughout the years the different facets of her life have merged together naturally into her coaching methodology: medicine storytelling, archetypal psychology, lucid dream practice, ancestral trance, NLP (Neuro Linguisting Programming), training in transforming one's own story through re-writing it, transpersonal healing, and Make your life a Prayer- Praying Your Life into Being.

Explore together how you can transform your past, your present, and your future through medicine storytelling, archetypal psychology, rewriting your life story, transpersonal healing, and the practice of praying your life into being. Call her for a free session.

HEIDI ELIAS
Licensed Clinical Social Worker, Certified Somatic Experiencing Practitioner and Psychotherapist

As a kid I dreamed of being rescued from a chaotic and emotionally unsafe home. Psychotherapy helped me make sense of what I had endured, and taught me better ways of living. From this experience, I developed the belief that if I could emerge from the challenges of my past, then anyone could. I made it my mission to assist women who feel stuck and hopeless to overcome their limitations using psychotherapy and body work, offering hope when there appears to be none.

I believe that my ability to experience people as whole, even when they are unable to see it in themselves serves my clients best. My work enables me to lead from my heart chakra. When clients feel my empathic support and encouragement, it helps them to settle and enables us to get down to work more readily. In my private practice, I offer talk therapy in the form of Psychotherapy, as well as a mind/body therapy called Somatic Experiencing (SE).

As a Certified Somatic Experiencing Practitioner (SEP), I assist clients to go beyond talk therapy and engage their body in their healing process, in order to resolve past trauma. When talk therapy alone is not alleviating the symptoms of deeper wounds, I have found a mind/body approach to be useful. The body stores memories, so even if the conscious mind is not aware, the body remembers. We take cues from the body on what it needs and wants to do, in order to heal.

Some of the women I work with suffer from anxiety and depression. Some have survived trauma, and find themselves stuck and unable to be happy or feel good about themselves. A common practice I observe in my work is when people turn anger that was meant for someone else, against themselves. For some, the dynamics of relationships have a lasting negative imprint on their heart, which makes it difficult to feel at ease and to move on.

I assist women who find it a challenge to say "No," and who act as "people pleasers" in setting boundaries with those in their lives who take advantage of them, while simultaneously offering them skills for better living. Our work focuses on tapping into root causes for current behaviors that are hindering them from feeling good, and assisting them to make better, more self-affirming choices, thereby enhancing self-empowerment. There are a multitude of reasons why people feel blocked, and so it becomes a complicated task to sort it all out and help them find their way back to their heart.

The heart chakra is an opening to the fertile soil of Self where seeds of transformation take root and grow. Psychotherapy is the work of the heart. I feel honored that I can use my heart chakra to transform lives.

I know how difficult it can be to live freely when unresolved events of the past get in the

130

way. In my experience, people find themselves struggling with the same themes over and over again, until they are able to gain mastery over them. I also know that old coping strategies developed long ago in an attempt to survive, or in an effort to push bad memories out of awareness, usually outlive their usefulness. That is where I come in. My work provides a way out of habituated behaviors, and offers clients new ways of being.

I am truly grateful that my work offers me reason to regularly open my heart and share all that I have learned on my own path, when assisting others on their journey to take their next steps. I feel fortunate because caring about people comes easily to me.

For me, my work is an act of living my passion, because when I connect with the people that I work with, I do it from my heart. I remain truly honored to touch hearts, to lend my support and to witness deep transformation, which I consider to be vital to each individual's growth and evolution. I consider this process through the heart chakra a meaningful and sacred endeavor.

Come, come, whoever you are. Wanderer, worshiper, lover of leaving. It doesn't matter. Ours is not a Caravan of despair. Come, even if you have broken your vows a thousand times. Come, yet again, come, come.
~ Rumi

THE HEART CHAKRA AND LOVING YOURSELF
Heidi Elias, LCSW, SEP

The heart chakra, known in Sanskrit as *Anahata*, is in the center of all of the chakras. It is the 4th or middle chakra, located in the chest area, and is comprised of the heart, lungs, chest and circulatory system. *Anahata* in Sanskrit means *unstruck* and *unhurt*. Its essence is *love* in its purest form rooted in calm, balance and tranquility.

When the heart chakra is obstructed, the ability to experience joy can become stunted. At times, a heart will shut down as a result of being hurt in relationships, whether early in life, or in recent times. When the heart is blocked, it is a challenge to live with ease, and for love to flow either to or from the wounded heart.

My focus on the heart chakra enables women to love themselves. In some cases, other adjacent chakras may also be blocked. When the heart chakra is blocked, the throat chakra may also be blocked, manifesting an inability to speak up. Further, the solar plexus chakra could also be out of alignment, resulting in low self-esteem. My focus is to connect with my female clients through the heart, and to help them see the truth, in an effort to be free.

While growing up, not everyone is taught healthy coping strategies, effective interpersonal skills, or how to calm down after an upset. I teach these important life skills in my work as a Psychotherapist and Certified Somatic Experiencing Practitioner. As a result, the women I work with improve their self-esteem, gain self-confidence, and develop methods of self-regulation that ultimately resonate through the heart chakra.

As an illustration, I will share an example of my psychotherapy work with Pamela. Pamela represents a compilation of various patient issues and their struggles, in order to demonstrate the work. The name is fictitious. Like many women that I work with, Pamela had difficulty seeing the truth about her relationship and was challenged to speak up and get her needs met. Through healing old wounds and practicing self-compassion, the heart chakra remained the constant anchor for the journey back into her own heart.

Pamela is a young woman of 23 who came from a family where it was safer to hide in the shadows than to be seen. Her father, an angry, unreasonable man who teased and taunted her often, had a very bad temper and yelled loudly, which frightened Pamela. He was verbally and physically abusive, and did not show an interest in connecting to Pam while she was growing up. Any risked verbal objection to being treated badly, or expression of anger towards her father, resulted in punishment either physical or emotional, or both, and so Pam learned early on that it was safer to keep quiet.

Pamela's self-absorbed mother was neglectful and did not protect her children from their father, mostly because she was too busy ensuring her own safety and interests with regard to her husband. Pamela learned early on to remain "under the radar" in order to stay out of harm's way.

When Pamela grew up, she found that most of the people in her life were bossy and readily told her what to do, and at times she felt bullied. For most of her life, having others make her decisions worked for her, as she truly did not know her own likes or dislikes, since as a child, no one ever asked. In addition, by not making decisions, she was able to avoid the possibility of other people's criticisms. As a result, Pam never developed the skill of decision making, and she remained detached from knowing her own self.

Pam found herself in relationships with friends and associates where she was usually taking care of their needs and getting very little in return for herself. She justified this by believing it was honorable to be a good person, and tried not to think about it much. Still, these dynamics began to bother her increasingly over time, which is why she sought help.

Pamela had always secretly felt that she was destined for something greater than a life of hiding and staying small, but she would readily push those thoughts out of her mind due to her fear of success and connecting to her own power. Tapping into this "knowing" would usually surface when she was more relaxed, whether witnessing something beautiful in nature, or viewing exquisite artwork, or when hearing a moving musical piece. It was at these times that she felt more hopeful about her life and her future.

Pam described herself as having low self-esteem, depression, and anxiety. When she first came to see me, she had recently gotten out of a relationship with a man who she said had treated her well, and while he was loving and kind at first, ended up cheating on her and leaving.

We began our work simply by having a conversation, because that is what psychotherapy is — a conversation. Some of Pam's statements about her life seemed ordinary to her, but to me, they were related to her blocked chakras, with a focus on her heart chakra. As is often useful in therapy, I reflected these statements back to her in order to give her this different perspective.

I explained to Pamela that it was my hope that through our work she would feel safe to love again and would choose and find a healthy and balanced relationship and partner. We agreed that it would be ideal for her to foster her connection to her own power, as a way of strengthening her ability to know what is right for herself. Lastly, we agreed that direct communication skills would help her to effectively speak up, and say what she means in all situations.

Through our conversations about her relationship with her ex-boyfriend, Pam realized how she had downplayed and denied things that he did and said that were not nice, and she now realized they had been worth her attention. For example, he would often tell her how honest he was, and yet his actions demonstrated something else. When she attempted to address concerns with her ex-boyfriend about his behavior, he would twist her words around and label them as complaints, and then blame her for causing the trouble between them. She made excuses for him when he broke plans, was critical of her, or was excessively late.

In time, Pamela recalled that when she and I had first met, she had described her ex-boyfriend as loving and kind, and that he had treated her well. Through our conversations, she acknowledged feeling more courageous to speak the truth, and she began to challenge her own beliefs about how people treat her and how she wanted to be treated going forward, something never considered in the past. She got in touch with her anger, and for the first time felt compassion for herself for having tolerated being mistreated in her relationship for so long. Talking truthfully about her relationship in a safe and supportive environment, enabled Pam to see herself through a new lens.

I educated Pamela on the personality and profile of an Emotional Manipulator and the signs to look for when meeting new people. I pointed out that people are always telling you who they are, both verbally and non-verbally, and that it is of utmost importance to register that information. I urged Pamela to pay attention to other people's inconsistencies at the beginning of new relationships (with friends, lovers, bosses, co-workers, etc.) and to slow things down generally, in order to take time to get to know people. In time, she could then make a more informed decision.

Through an opening of her heart chakra, Pam challenged feelings of unworthiness and very old beliefs about her right to be seen and heard. She came to believe that her opinions matter, regardless of what others think. I proposed that Pam consider taking on new beliefs about deserving all that life has to offer.

Throughout our work, we utilized techniques of Somatic Experiencing (SE), with the understanding that sometimes painful implicit memories remain stuck in the body and continue to impact present time, until they are processed in the nervous system. We used body-based techniques to correct past experiences where natural reactions of fight or flight had been thwarted at the time that they had originally occurred, and in cases where there had been a shock (trauma) to the system. I also taught Pamela techniques for self-regulation which helped her calm her nervous system in and out of our sessions.

In addition, I taught Pam direct communication skills, which was vital to her being able to express what she wanted and needed. Speaking in this manner caused her to naturally command respect from the people she encountered, and helped her feel more confident. As a result of all of Pamela's hard work and determination, her self-esteem improved exceedingly, and for the first time she felt content and in control of her life.

Pamela grew to view her last relationship as a significant learning experience -- one where she gained understanding and awareness of how she behaved in relationships in the past, and then acquired the skills to make better choices through her actions going forward. She chose to use the healing process from her last relationship as a springboard to take control of matters directly concerning her. Love flowed to and from her heart chakra with ease, and Pam took pleasure in her own transformation.

As our work proceeded, Pam felt a softening in her heart chakra, connecting to the love she has for herself, by embracing the hurt child within. She was then able to turn her attention to others as well, feeling more open to possibility for real connection.

There are many paths to healing. In my work, I maintain a "whatever works" approach when assisting people to free their hearts. Because the heart yearns to realize its natural state of *Anahata*, I encourage complementary practices for opening the heart, in order to support the Psychotherapy and Somatic Experiencing processes. I believe that practices such as mindfulness, forgiveness, gratitude, service, spirituality, and love, to name a few, aid in feeling a sense of ease in life, and to becoming better than you were before.

Being mindful can be useful for opening the heart chakra because it has the power to assist you in letting go of rumination of the past and dread or fear of the future, through acceptance and being nonjudgmental. Simply put, it is living in the present moment, and allowing whatever is. Mindfulness is moment-to-moment awareness of thoughts, feelings, bodily sensations and one's environment.

Mindfulness can be practiced at any time and at any moment, as it can be as simple as a checking-in with yourself, and beginning again. All it takes is remembering to be mindful, or as the great Ram Dass said in his book of the same title, to "Be here now." (*Be Here Now*, Baba Ram Dass, 1978)

Mindfulness meditation has many health benefits: it is good for bodies and minds; it changes the brain for the better, it helps with focus; and it supports good relationships. It can also assist in connecting to one's higher or spiritual nature, as desired, which offers the potential to release the heart chakra.

I am also very aware that for some people, often for those with trauma in their history, meditation can be a challenge, because the act of settling can be too threatening. In these cases, mindfulness can be practiced in other ways, such as walking meditation, guided meditation, and so on.

Forgiveness is a way out of the pain of harbored resentment from the past. When there is a desire to open up the heart chakra, forgiving someone is the place to begin. The great author and speaker, Louise Hay, encourages us to forgive ourselves and others, because when we do not flow freely in our lives, there is usually someone whom we need to forgive. Louise is clear that forgiveness is not condoning bad behavior of people who have wronged us but instead, when we forgive another, we let them go, and in the process set ourselves free. (*You Can Heal Your Life*, Louise L. Hay, 1984, pp 76-79.)

Louise recommends imagining someone who has wounded us, as a hurt child. She suggests noticing the longing for love in their eyes, to start the process of forgiveness. In the words of Mark Twain: "Forgiveness is the fragrance that the violet sheds on the heel that has crushed it." (Samuel Langhorne Clemens, aka Mark Twain, 1835-1910)

Practicing gratitude regularly offers a shift in focus from lacking to abundance. Those who refuse to accept life's circumstances often find that they are overly self-critical and suffer a great deal. Taking the time to notice what you are grateful for is a gentle and life-affirming practice for staying humble and keeping things in perspective. Living in a state of gratitude can turn a negative outlook into one with endless possibilities.

The practice of gratitude is available to you at any time. All that is required is willingness and an awareness to change the focus. I recommend taking pauses throughout the day to notice the good and to acknowledge your gratitude to others and to yourself. Also, before drifting off to sleep at night, it can be helpful to review your day and note three to five experiences in that day that you are grateful for. Doing so relieves stress, reduces anxiety, and leaves you feeling more optimistic, by opening the heart.

Mahatma Gandhi said, "The best way to find yourself is to lose yourself in the service of others." (Mahatma Gandhi, 1869 - 1948). Doing service or something kind for someone without the promise of reward gets you out of yourself, while benefiting another. People who offer service regularly know its hidden secret -- that they receive much more than those whom they are helping. Service offers a connection to one's own heart chakra, as well as to the other person's, and it feels really good.

It has been said that the heart chakra is where the physical and spiritual meet. Balance and well-being, derived from having faith in something higher, can bring great comfort and a sense of safety to those who believe. However, faith and belief do not always come naturally to people, particularly to those who push back against the teachings of their early religious upbringing, or if something terrible happened to cause one to lose faith in something higher. There may also be other valid reasons.

For the willing, spirituality can be cultivated through willingness and intentional actions: reading spiritual books, practicing love, prayer and meditation, engaging in mind/body practices such as yoga or sacred dance, listening to music, attending spiritual groups, positive thinking and affirmations, and so on. These practices are often most effective in combination with each other for optimal impact, for example, in a morning ritual.

In my work as a Psychotherapist, any or all of these practices are areas for exploration and development to assist with talk therapy, and for opening the heart chakra. It should be noted that I believe that everyone is free to choose their own spiritual path, and that they are not bound by the religion they were born into.

A belief in something higher can offer relief and comfort to those who believe. There can be a softening and an awakening of the heart chakra, as a result. When someone believes in a Higher Power, there is an acceptance of what is and life flows more easily. There is a sense that no matter what happens, you will be *all right*. In my opinion, the age-old debate over the existence of a higher being, or which belief is right and which is wrong, is secondary to one's desire to believe, when striving for serenity or *Anahata* through a spiritual realm. Inspiration is a creative and personal process, and on a spiritual plane, the possibilities are endless.

Lastly, when you truly love others as yourself, conflict drops away. There is no longer a need to push against the crowd or an individual, as you are happy for other people's good fortune. In turn, their good fortune is also yours because you and they are one. By accepting someone else as yourself, by loving them, there is no longer the need for competition. Opening your heart and maintaining an attitude that "we are in this together," makes getting through the day a lot sweeter.

© Heidi Elias

ABOUT HEIDI ELIAS, LCSW, SEP

Website: HeidiElias.com
Contact: heidielias5@gmail.com

HEIDI ELIAS is a Licensed Clinical Social Worker and Certified Somatic Experiencing Practitioner working as a Psychotherapist in New York City for over 20 years, specializing in women's empowerment and trauma healing. Heidi remains current in new advances in clinical and mind/body practices, as they relate to healing, as well as other approaches of an esoteric nature. Heidi is an artist, a mother, and an advocate for those unable to assert their voice. She is a member of the National Association of Social Workers (NASW), The Somatic Experiencing Trauma Institute (SETI), and the United States Association for Body Psychotherapy (USABP).

DESIREE MWALIMU-BANKS
Tantra Practitioner

My journey into Anahata began with the birth of my sons. While I learned everything that I could about the science of what was taking place in my womb, I was only just beginning to understand the connection between my heart and the life inside me.

I was very fortunate to have had two home births with the support of my sons father and our community of family and friends. I was the daughter of a mother who had four natural births and I was the granddaughter of a woman who had several of her children, as the story has been told, in the woods, and on her own. I truly believe it was my ancestors strength that guided me through every step of my labor. It was not just their physical strength, but what I feel was a psychic stamina that came directly from a connection to the heart, that sustained me. My mantra throughout my labor was 'love'. I repeated this even when I was unable to utter the word entirely and it carried me through my most difficult moments.

Like many women, I compared my journey of motherhood to the legacies of motherhood in my family. My mother, whom I epitomize as a reflection of true compassion and continuous selfless service was always my bar. As a new mother, I thought that the birth of my child would immediately gift me with this sensibility-this generousness of heart; this profound love. When I gave birth, I loved my sons in ways that I could not possibly begin to comprehend; this fountain of love that seemed to flow effortlessly from my mother to all of her children. Yet my connection to this fountain felt unclear and at moments, unattainable. I didn't know how to do what she has done-and for this I felt inadequate as a mother. I learned that being a mother is also writing a new story that will empower your lineage uniquely. That I was responsible for ensuring the healthy growth of these radiant children overwhelmed me, yet I realized that it has gifted me with a profound devotion. My devotion to my sons helps me to understand that true compassion is a process that continually unfolds, like a flower in its own time. While some of us are born with a highly evolved sense of compassion, many of us have come here to learn the art and the practice of compassion; the petals of our flowers are closed in anticipation of the light that will inspire them to open. My sons were this light for me. While I gave birth to two beautiful boys, I also understand now that have given birth to a new woman in me. I am still getting to know this woman, who shadows my fears and my anxieties, and circles over my greatest joys and accomplishments-pushing me to be the best version of myself that I can be. She lives in the Anahata center of my heart and her wisdom is a flower that continues to blossom and nourish me on my journey.

NECTAR OF THE DIVINE FEMININE: THE ANCIENT BEE MOTHERS OF THE ANAHATA CHAKRA

Desiree Mwalimu-Banks

"The basis of Tantric Sadhana is always to wait for a new veil to be torn away without your spiritual qualities hardening. In nature, nothing ceases to evolve, to be infinitely transformed. To look for a stable state is to cut yourself off from reality. Everything is based on respiration. Can you breathe in for three hours? No. You breathe in and breathe out. We follow the movement of the universe, going in and out, opening and closing, expanding and contracting. All activity takes place in these two modes, and it is their perfect comprehension, their perfect integration into our practice, that allows consciousness to breathe. Never forget that consciousness breathes."
~ Daniel Odier: Tantric Quest: An Encounter With Absolute Love

The breath is an ancient song that teaches our hearts to dance. *Tantra*, is a Hindi term that means 'to loom' or 'to weave together' the inner and outer realms of perception and experience. When we think of tantra, we are often taught go to the second chakra, or Svadhistana. Located in the genitals, Svadhistana gifts us with the sense of taste and the element of water. When we look at our collective preoccupation with pleasure, we find an addiction to the sensory in the form of food, sex and substances that take us into or out of our bodies. A closer look at Svadhistana reveals a human epidemic of imbalance in this region, in which pain, fear and grief mask themselves as contemporary cultural pursuits that often leave us feeling empty and powerless. Our sensation-centric, pleasure-addicted world inspires deeper separation from and awareness of our hearts. While Svadhistana supports our right to feel and to desire; guiding us to the center of our pleasure and sensuality, it is actually, Anahata that teaches us to go beyond our perceptions of what we understand as real and tangible in our sensual landscapes, so that we may touch, taste, feel, hear and see, directly, the nature of our own perception in these realms. Anahata's presence ushers in an awareness of that part of us which begins to realize it is merely an extension of something larger; an ever-flowing, ever-changing, and all knowing space inside of each of us that leans into, and thrives under, the integrity of true love.

Anahata means "unstruck" in Sanskrit. It is the fourth chakra along the axis of the seven major energy centers in the body. Anahata is the turning point beyond the lower triangle (Muladhara, Svadhistana and Manipura) which heralds the ascent through the higher frequencies of the upper body. Anahata is the seat of balance where a divine resonance between the upper and lower triangles of the body blossom into a twelve petaled lotus. This balance is represented by a triangle that points upwards symbolizing Shiva; the solar; masculine principle, overlapping and intersecting with Shakti, represented by a downward pointing triangle, and symbolizing the feminine principle and lunar energies. The six pointed star, Anahata, reminds us of the balance that is attained when these forces are working in harmony with one another.

This is also the place where the Goddess Kundalini Shakti who has uncoiled from her abode, wrapped around Shiva's lingham at the Muladhara (root chakra), appears for the first time as a beautiful Goddess, adorned in a white. She lives in the Anahata Chakra in complete serenity. She is the Divine and Cosmic Mother who gives birth to Herself. She is the Cause. Unborn, Unceasing. Undying. The raw fiery energy of the Serpent has been transmuted into light as the nectar of love and devotion. The intelligence of Sacred Serpent is now audible and we can communicate with Her. This is the place where we hear the most sacred cosmic sound AUM, the *anahata nada*, which this Goddess embodies. The seed sound or bija is YAM. The transcendental sound of Anahata can only be accessed in the highest states of meditation. It is by the grace of Shakti that we are moved into the higher realms of existence and we are inspired to oneness and universal love of all creation. Here, spirituality is awakened through an opening of the heart. It cannot be forced. She invites us to firmly anchor ourselves in a connection to the Earth and to our own bodies. It is because we have established this connection, that we are able to fly through the wings of the heart, collapsing the boundaries imposed upon our experience through an over-identification with ego. From here, our compassion is aroused and awakened through divine, unconditional love. All of our ego-driven impulses are redirected toward selfless service, forgiveness, expansiveness, conscious awareness, and a peaceful acceptance of the brilliance of the Divine in all things.

It is important to remember there is an emphasis on firmness and soundness of mind, body and spirit in Anahata. We go forth and create because it is the heart's wisdom that establishes the balance within us to do so. The heart has the power to pierce through the transitory nature of our emotions, breaking the knot of psychic attachments and identification with the ever-changing *rasas* or various emotional states, which form the blueprints for 'fate'. Anahata symbolizes control over the emotions and the power to be the destiny-maker in one's life. Therefore, it is also the place where the *Kal-Patam* or wish fulfilling tree, lives and flourishes. When this tree begins to bear fruit in our hearts, it is said that whatever we wish or whatever we direct our thoughts toward, becomes true. The heart reminds us that it is the doorway toward immortality.

The first time I meditated on a Goddess that would lead me into a deeper study of Anahata, I smelled honey on my lips. I turned my attention inward, toward a humming sound, and found bees. When I was five years old, I was stung by a bee in my eye. I remember this eye (I still have a shiny photo circa 1982), swollen and full of wonder, taking weeks to heal. Since then, I have yet to be stung by another bee and more, to fear the sting of any bee. Years later, I realized, in many ways that this was a tiny initiation into the mysteries of the Mother Goddess which continue to unfold in my own life.

The Ancient Bee Goddess has found expression in the herstories of several matrilineal cultures around the world including that of the ancient African, Hindu, Celtic, and Aegean peoples. In Neolithic times the Bee was a symbol that was used to denote the Mother Goddess. The most famous Bee Mother icon in the West, depicts the goddess, with the head of a bee and the feet of a bird in Southern Spain. The Bee Goddess has long been revered as a potent symbol of divine feminine power. What is 'divine feminine power'? It is the power to magnetize and ultimately become what it is that you are seeking both in the seen and the unseen worlds; it is the power to lead and create with the light of one's heart; from a place of limitless joy and unapologetic pleasure in a human soul.

Throughout the cultures of the ancient world, the bee was a symbol of purity and immortality. Honey, a symbol of the nectar of life, embodied the love, beauty, sexuality, fertility, abundance, joy and peace that was exalted by the ancient priestesses that recognized, celebrate and called forth its power. Bees were worshipped as protective energies that safeguarded pregnant mothers, babies, elders and those suffering from sickness. In Ancient Kemet, Bees were connected to the establishing of royal power and sacred religious significance, embodied by the Goddess Neith (the Goddess of the arts and civilization), whose temple in the delta town of Sais in Lower Egypt, was known as per-bit, which means, 'the house of the bee'. In Kemet, honey was a symbol of resurrection and was also revered for its ability to give protection against evil spirits. Bees were regarded by the Ancients as messengers between the realms of the living and the dead. The queen bee was associated with the High Priestess, who too, functioned as a medium between dimensions, to guide women and men on their earthwalk. As such, bees are also associated with the sacred gift of prophecy. The Greek Goddess of love, Aphrodite, was worshipped at a honeycomb-shaped shrine at Mount Eryx.

Her High Priestess was called Melissa, which means 'bee', and the other virgin priestesses were known as the Melissae. The drinking of meade wine, a special drink brewed from the nectar of sacred bees, was cultivated and handed down by Priestesses to Priestesses of the Ancient Mother Goddess.

With the advent of Christianity, bees were later associated with the Virgin Mary, particularly in Eastern Europe, in an effort to popularize the Christian faith, which at that time had to compete with the ancient worship of the Goddess Auset (Isis), who's characteristics were later subsumed into the iconic attributes of the Madonna and child. In Slavic traditions, the bee is connected to The Immaculate Conception. In the Ukraine, bees are the tears of the Virgin Mary, which is again, echoes the Kemetic myth, that bees embody the Sun God, Ra, who's tears transformed into honeycombs and produced honey, upon touching the soil. In Hinduism, the bee is associated with Vishnu, Krishna, and Kama, the God of love. In ancient India, the god Indra was the namesake of the continent and the deity who separated heaven and earth, who is said to have received honey as his first food.

The Indian Bee goddess Bhramari Devi, received her name from the word Bramari, meaning 'bees' in Hindi. Bhramari Devi dwells inside Anahata and emits the buzzing sound of Bees, called 'Bhramaran' which serves as the origin for the yogic 'Brahmari breath'. In Vedic chanting, this sound of a bee humming was emulated, representing the essential sound of the universe.

We tend to think that wisdom comes from the head, but the Bee Goddesses who live on in the myths of world cultures, remind us to honor the eye of wisdom that lives in the heart. It is always the heart that leads the head and not the other way around.

The Ancient Bee Goddesses teach us:

- – Wisdom
- – The path toward immortality
- – Psychic communication and mediumship
- – Our connection to the Mother Goddess
- – Cooperation
- – Fertility
- – Sexuality
- – Reincarnation
- – The essence of Divine Feminine Power
- – Wealth
- – Abundance
- – Diligence
- – The power of giving and receiving
- – Seeking and savoring the sweetness in life
- – Watching our psychic trees bear fruit
- – LOVE

May our journey into the psychic treasures of Anahata be empowered and illuminated by the divine eyes of wisdom embodied by the Ancient BeeMothers, who's nectar feeds the world.
© Desiree Mwalimu-Banks

BIBLIOGRAPHY

Ransome, Hilda. *The Sacred Bee in Ancient Times & Folklore*. Mineola: Dover Publications, 2004.

Kritsky, Gene. *The Tears of Re: Beekeeping in Ancient Egypt*. New York: Oxford University Press, 2015.

Buxton, Simon. The Shamanic *Way of the Bee: Ancient Wisdom & Healing Practices of the Bee Masters*. Rochester: Destiny Books, 2004.

Sjoo, Monia and Mor, Barbara. *The Cosmic Mother*. New York: Harper Collins, 1987

Iles, Linda. "Priestesses of the Bee". *Isis Lotus of Alexandria*. 2010. March 2017. https://mirrorofisis.freeyellow.com/id576.html.

Photo by Anthony Rossbach

143

ABOUT DESIREE MWALIMU-BANKS

Blog: bywayofblog.com/stories/#/desiree
Contact: themuseandtheloom@gmail.com

DESIREE MWALIMU-BANKS is a New York City-based artist, writer, mother, educator, tarot divination expert, Reiki and Tantra practitioner, who is joyfully devoted to being of service through her work. She brings a passion for the sacred feminine and the narratives of women in the African Diaspora to her work. Desiree loves working with women from all backgrounds in returning to a knowledge of the divine feminine and an embodiment of the Goddess in the modern world. She loves to host workshops, and moon gatherings, that focus on connecting women to each other through ritual, movement, astrology, and the study of archetypal energies sacred to women's journeys. Desiree supports women in using pleasure, creativity, and radical self-expression as paths to personal transformation and spiritual empowerment.

Desiree has served as a guest lecturer for the Manhattanville Purchase College Undergraduate Interfaith Studies Division. She was a presenter for "Relax, Relate, Release", a Brooklyn-based, annual women's health and wellness expo in 2013, and co-presenter for the 'Alchemy of Sex & Spirit', a workshop for the Caribbean Cultural Center Roots & Stars Salon Series in 2012. Her article 'Tantric Love' was published in Heart & Soul Magazine's July/August 2013 issue, and she was a contributing writer for the 2014 debut of Sensheant Magazine which explores women's relationships to sex and sexuality. She has most recently contributed to the Spirituality section of Teen Vogue.com in 2016. She is a resident diviner for both Urban Asanas Yoga Studio's Breath & Beats events and the Kings County Distillery in Brooklyn, NY.

Desiree lives in the Boogie Down Bronx with her sons, her husband and her Smith Corona Electric 76 typewriter. She works across several boroughs in New York City.

NOELLE LAUREN
Certified Reiki and Crystal-Healing Practitioner

When a client comes in, making them feel safe and at ease is my number one priority. I want the session to be driven solely by the energy and the spirits around us. I start by burning herbs, particularly sage. This cleansing ritual from the Native Americans dates back for centuries. This is called smudging. Not only is burning sage one of the oldest, but it is one of the purest forms of cleansing. Interestingly enough, the Latin form of sage, 'Salvia,' stems from the word 'to heal.' This protects the client and the healer as well, as one calls on help from the spirits and the ancestors during the session.

I remember one of my very first sessions. I was working on a client and she had a major blockage with her solar plexus chakra; the solar plexus is the one most connected to your personal power and confidence. I always have lived my life with conviction and have known what I wanted out of life. It wasn't until I was brought to my path to heal, that I started questioning where I was going. I will get into that story later in my chapter.

I didn't embrace the fact I was put on this earth to be a healer. Because of this, my solar plexus was weakened which left me susceptible to outside energies when I first started healing. After this client's session, I had severe stomach pains. At the time, I did not see the connection. Other than that, I felt like the session went well, and my client could not have been happier. She walked out of the session feeling relaxed after releasing so much bottled up energy.

A few weeks later I was working with one of my Shamanic teachers and one of her first lessons was to express how, as a healer, we must protect ourselves from energies which we release from our clients. If we are very strong healers, we tend to pull a great amount of bad energy from our client. This is very good for our client, but not for the healer if we do not take the steps to shield ourselves from these energies. I shared with her the story of my stomach pains after working on a client. "This is a good thing. You are able to unblock and pull the energy out of your client. You already have a natural gift. You just need to learn how to channel the energy and protect yourself." She continued to explain how important it is to ask for guidance from the elements, as well as incorporating many other shamanic rituals and ceremonies. I learned a lot from her. And I thank her for I am a better healer because of her teachings.

A BLOCKED HEART
Noelle Lauren

The Heart Chakra, which is Anahata in Sanskrit, is pronounced "ahn-ah-ha-ta". The literal translation of Anahata is "unhurt, unstuck, or unbeaten." It is located at the center of the chest, at the level where your heart is. It controls not only your heart, but also your lungs and shoulders. It is the center from where love and joy come out. When this chakra is blocked, or closed off, it interferes with free-flowing energy which allows us to be fully open to love, and to be loved as well, thus experiencing pure joy and happiness. What causes this clog of energy throughout our chakra system? This chakra is so valuable and essential to our emotional state of being. When our emotions are thrown off course, it can lead us down a path of utter sadness, anger, and even sometimes severe loneliness. Feelings of being unwanted or rejected, as well as holding on to resentment, can not only lead to mental issues, but can also manifest to physical pain throughout the body as well.

I had a very true personal experience with my Heart Chakra…

Back some years ago I was dealing with physical pain in my chest. I started having severe pains that would come on out of nowhere. I had to think to myself, what was happening in my life to cause this. First it would happen every so often, and as time went on it started to get worse. The pain never came during a stressful situation. So, I thought, this can't be stress related. I've always been one to hate the word "stress." Things happen in our lives for us to work through and evolve. Feelings and emotions occur as a reminder that we need to work on something within ourselves. I thought perhaps it was pain coming from a car accident I was in years back. So, I started seeing an acupuncturist. Acupuncture had always been the cure to any physical pain I had in the past. I am one who always looked towards the Eastern medicine way of curing anything, but as my sessions progressed, I was not feeling any sort of relief. The pains were coming more frequently. At that point, I thought it might be time to see a cardiologist. The doctors looked at me as if I was crazy. You are too young to be here. Your heart is fine, it's just stress. After several tests and dollars later, everything came back negative. Is that it? Then why do I feel this way?

I thought to myself, I know what to do. I did some research and booked a solo trip to Costa Rica. After a few days, settling in, and taking time to reflect on everything that was happening, I met with my healer. I remember the moment I laid down, I started to shake and I was scared. Fear was rushing through my body like fire that couldn't be extinguished. At this moment, I had nothing to fear. I was in the presence of someone, who had me; I was taken care of. Her touch calmed me at times, but an hour session felt as if it was going to go on forever. I wept and roared. All this energy which I was keeping inside of me poured out like a waterfall. At that moment, I knew, I was holding on to so much of my past, and it was eating me up inside. It was causing me not only emotional but physical pain as well.

146

After our session, we sat for several minutes. She made me some herbal concoction that was a mix of healing plants from the forest. I went from an explosion of pain to requiescence. She explained to me that I was holding on to my past and it was causing a major block in my heart chakra, causing this immense physical pain. She explained that in many shamanic cultures, those who were meant to be healers often fall prey to many ailments, one being physical pain. "You are meant to heal; you just need to face that this is what you have been called for. You are holding on to the person you have been for many years, but you need to accept what you have been called on to do." We spent several days together during my trip, and she taught me many things. One thing touched very close to my heart. "You will find that many people will come to you with this issue. You yourself came to me because of a blockage in this area without you even knowing it. Come back to this and use this as a teaching tool to help you better yourself as a healer going forward. Do not hold on to so much. You need to take what happens, be grateful of its presence and let it go. This will forever be your teacher."

Our left side holds on to our past experiences, both painful and joyful. Your left side is what responds to our environment. Your right side of your body is what represents the future. When there is stagnant energy, happening to either side of your body, it is because you are either holding on to things of the past or worried so much about what hasn't happened yet and dwelling in the future. To have a clear open heart chakra, we must stay centered and present. We are to live our life with a forgiving and open heart.

What activates and balances your heart chakra? Here are some healing remedies to keep your heart chakra healthy.

REIKI

I remember when I first started learning to do reiki. There was an extraordinary moment that happened in class. Our reiki master was having us practice distance healing with other students in the class. I remember feeling doubtful about myself and my healing abilities for a second during that moment before it was my turn to begin. Within seconds of when I started sending reiki out, I felt the pull in energy from the other student. My hands were guiding me to send reiki in the direction of her heart chakra. The pull was so strong that it was as if someone had held my hands down to keep sending energy in the direction of her heart. After several moments, I closed my eyes and started to see colors of green. Now at this time I didn't know if this was the color of her heart chakra or the color of healing. After the session finished, our master went around the room and asked each student who was acting as the "client" or one being healed their experience. Now mind you, the student who I was practicing on had her eyes closed throughout the whole session. Not once did she move or fidget. I thought whatever energy I was sending toward her, was clearly not strong enough to do anything. When our master got to us, she began to cry. "I felt my heart fly open," she began to speak with a shakiness in her voice, "as if after all these years of trauma, someone finally was able to find the right key to unlock it."

Reiki is one of the best healing techniques to lift and understand your emotions and to release trauma.

HEART OPENING MANTRAS

You can chant this while riding the train, or as a sitting or dancing meditation, or as you sit up from bed in the morning. There are no rules for this mantra.

Chant: Ong So Hung
Translation:
Ong – Creative Consciousness
So Hung – I am that
Chant twelve times

The mantra below helps to heal the energy of yourself, or those around you who you would wish to heal.

Chant: Ra Ma Da Sa Sa Say So Sung
(Yogi Bhajan)

Translation:
Ra - Sun
Ma - Moon
Daa - Earth
Saa - Impersonal Infinity
Saa Say - Totality of Infinity
So - Personal sense of merger and identity
Sung - The Infinite, vibrating and real

When your chakra is in balance you feel benevolence towards others including yourself. You go through your day with an understanding of, and kindness to, everyone you meet. There is no judgement in your heart. You are free to go through your day without condition. You are love, you are bliss.

METTA MEDITATION

I leave you with my interpretation of a heart opening meditation I use often in my workshops. It is called Metta, which mean "loving kindness" in Pali and is often used by those who practice Buddhist meditation.

To start this meditation, find a comfortable seat. Allow your spine to be straight and begin to focus on your breath.

Metta is first practiced toward oneself. In Buddhist teachings it is said that we are not able to practice compassion or love to others if we do not cultivate loving kindness towards ourselves.

After you have found the rhythm of your breath, put your hand on your heart. And repeat the following phrase:

"May I be filled with peace, may I be happy, may I be healthy, may I live with ease, free from pain, and with forgiveness in my heart."

Continue this several times until you start to fall deeper into the practice. At this point you should start to feel an overwhelming amount of warmth radiate through your body. As you fall deeper into this state of pure self-love, you can now direct your attention to sending this loving kindness to someone who you hold very dear to you. Take your hands and rest them, palms up on your knees or thighs. Picture them sitting across from you. And repeat the following:

"May you be filled with peace, may you be happy, may you be healthy, may you live with ease, free from pain, and with forgiveness in your heart."

As you say these phrases allow words and heartfelt energy to sink in deeper. As you continue this meditation, you can bring to mind anyone else in your life. You can even send this out to those who may be challenging you in your life. It will help in practicing acceptance and forgiveness.

And as you bring the meditation practice to a close, put your hand back on your heart and close with telling yourself, "I love you."

LIVE HARMONIOUSLY

Energy is contagious. For us to live in this world harmoniously, it is our mission to keep ourselves taken care of so we can send forth the strongest positive energy possible to those around us.

TAKE CARE OF YOURSELF

Here are a few things you can do:

Essential Oils:	Rose, Neroli, Rosemary, Lavender, Ylang Ylang, Frankincense
Crystals:	Rose Quartz, Peridot, Aventurine, Rhodonite, Emerald, Jade
Sound Healing:	Binaural Beats, Tibetan singing bowls
Herbs:	Cayenne, Jasmine, Lavender, Marjoram, Sage, Thyme, Cilantro, Parsley Herbs are another way to stimulate, energize or trigger the heart chakra. Herbs can be used in cooking or steeped in a tea. It is best to use fresh organic herbs, leaves or roots since the healing is the most beneficial.
Nature:	Spending time in nature. Retreats and trips. Practicing mediation in the park. Here you can find yourself and release any negative emotion.
Yoga:	Yin Yoga and Restorative Yoga
Volunteering:	A blockage of the heart chakra can sometimes make it hard to give out. But this is the most meaningful act of kindness one can give. Charity allows you to open yourself to others and creates an atmosphere where you can show selflessness. One of the major driving forces for feeding the heart chakra is selflessness.

ABOUT NOELLE LAUREN

Website: healinginthecity.com and gofundme.com/mindfulschoolsnyc
Contact: Noelle@healinginthecity.com, or contact form on her website

NOELLE LAUREN, a certified Reiki and crystal-healing practitioner, has been studying the art of healing science since childhood. Noelle is a visionary. She sees the possibility for positive growth in every client she meets. It is her life's passion to assist others in their journey toward mindfulness and emotional resilience. She uses shamanic healing rituals, energy-work, sound and aromatherapy to help her clients find ultimate healing.

Spiritual wellness techniques comes second nature to Noelle, who was raised by her grandmother and introduced to holistic therapies at the formidable age of five. Since then, she has made a conscious effort to live the best life possible. She believes wholeheartedly that those ideologies can be instilled in society's youth as well. As the Ambassador of the 501(C)(3) nonprofit organization Project Happiness, Noelle works closely with fellow New Yorkers, teaching not only children, but people of all ages, how to peacefully combat their own personal struggles.

Through various methods such as meditation/mindfulness therapies, yoga, dance/movement and counseling, Noelle assists in expanding lives. She can move with you through emotional blockages, teach you to let go of false restrictions set by life's uncontrollable events, and help you to gain access to the only force that can ever truly be controlled—your own happiness

For more about her work with NYC Schools, visit her gofundme page.

Project Happiness is a 501(C)(3) nonprofit organization dedicated to empowering people with the resources to create greater happiness within themselves and the world. Their vision is all about using mindfulness and positive exercises to promote happiness and overall better quality of life. After years of holding community circles, workshops and events, she joined the team of ambassadors around the globe and was named the Official Regional Ambassador of New York for Project Happiness.

Photo by Chris Petrow

The Storyteller

ANTHONY JAMES CANELO
Master Herbalist, Author and Inventor

My healing path began at the heart. I was twenty-one years old. I had been living with neuralgia on my arms, chest, and throat for four years. I had tried every avenue of natural and mainstream medicine available to me. Certain avenues of natural medicine did help; fasting, meditation, and aerobic exercise in particular. Other natural remedies did not work. Most of mainstream medicine was ineffective. I was often misdiagnosed. After four years of cleansing, dieting, exercising, and other physical-healing avenues, I began to realize that the final portion of my physical pain was being determined by my overall emotional state. I suppose I was destined to learn how to live from the heart.

Without going into detail, it was a challenging and worthwhile phase. It made me who I am and at the end of it I was finally able to breathe a lot better. Later, I met many people going through similar physical and emotional challenges. It seems life has a way of bringing you people who struggle with the same issues you have had or are currently working through. These were the people who came to visit me at my wellness center.

Today I live pain free and have learned to be especially mindful of matters that pertain to the heart. I have started a medicinal vaporizer company. The idea is to help people open up their lungs with healing, herb-based vapor. So far I appear to be one the one benefitting most from my work.

I believe it is impossible to love anyone, or anything, more than you love yourself. I also believe it is impossible to receive any more love than you will allow for yourself. Over and again, this seems to be a lesson I am meant to learn.

My chapter is a story from a book I published called, "The Secret One." It is called, "The Old Man and the Orchard." It focuses mainly on the fourth (heart) chakra, encapsulating patience, over greed and ultimate giving.

Visit Amazon.com for more stories and books I've written.

THE OLD MAN AND THE ORCHARD
Anthony Canelo - an excerpt from his book 'The Secret One'

In an ancient valley, in a round house, in front of an old banana orchard, lived an old, wise man. He sat alone in his lemonwood chair, listening for his visitors to arrive. On arrival, his new visitor, with fluttering eyes and a flashy, broad grin, took an eager seat in front of this old, wise man. The old wise man imparted a polite greeting to him, then instructed him as to the rules of the game that they were going to play.

When the rules were made clear, they focused in stillness and quiet for a brief time.

The young visitor began to perspire from his forehead.

The old wise man looked beyond the young man, waiting completely still.

In the wise man's outstretched palm, there was a large, polished, black diamond.

It was for the taking, provided that the young man was deft enough to snatch it out of his gentle, wrinkled palm. If so, the large diamond and the orchard would be his forever.

In the blink of an eye, the wise man's palm collapsed, retracting swiftly into his pocket. The game was over. The young man, though sullen, made his polite exit with a smile and was not seen again.

Though time had ravaged the edifice of this old wise man, his super-keen reflexes were beyond reckoning.

There came many visitors to his humble home. All of them were eager to acquire the orchard, hoping to grasp a heavy, shiny piece of forever in the process. There were those virtuous guests of the home, and then there were those manipulative, clever folk who visited him. None could steal the black diamond from his palm.

There came one day a wise, young warrior on horseback, from an unknown territory in the west, who circled the ancient valley four times prior to receiving word of the bizarre orchard lottery.

In the moment he understood, this man unsaddled himself beside a quiet river to contemplate such an incredible opportunity within his dreams.

When six days had passed, the young man on horseback approached the round home. He tied his horse to a large maple tree. He entered the old man's home in a calculated and polite fashion.

The young man had understood the rules of the game several days prior to the old man's instructing him from his seat. In the moments that the old man spoke, the young man hit upon a stunning and unique observation: the wise man could not see. He was blind.

158

This he noticed because the old man always seemed to gaze beyond him, never in his eye. Then, within the last moments of instruction, the young man cleverly disrobed. He understood that the old wise man reacted not from visual impulse but from an auditory impulse.

So the young man—completely nude, engaged in the sweet and timeless art of concentration—sat there with the old wise man. The old man looked beyond him, unmoved. Five hours passed, and nobody moved. In the next five hours the young warrior's wrist rotated upward ever so slowly and ever so quietly. The setting sun brought dazzling color and hue through the room. The window in the wall brought a gentle wind over the old man.

The singing of birds, the laughter of children—these things did not go by unnoticed or unappreciated.

Many hours into the night did the young man sit with this old and wise man. When the morning dew began to form on the young man's eyelashes, his hand was relaxed and open and his arm was halfway extended toward the shiny, black diamond. Several more long hours passed.

At noon, lunch was served to the small children. The understated poise of the old man went unchanged.

By four o'clock, the young man's palm began to cast a light shadow over the old man's palm. All the time, the young man was getting closer and closer and closer.

At dawn, in a moment of profound peace, the young man's hand was nearly on the diamond. Then the old man lifted his chin, procured the black diamond from his left palm with his right two fingers, and placed it into the young man's outstretched hand.

The old and wise man said, "I have observed within you the character, patience, and mind of a true wise man. You are a man who is fit to tend to the duties of my beloved orchard. You are a man who can patiently watch the beautiful ripening of our fruit so far into spring. Bless you and your family on this immortal and enchanted evening! My diamond and my land now are yours!"

Then the smiling old man sat back in his chair, wiped a few tears from his clear, blue eyes, and vanished into the great unknown.

Photo by Donald Teel

160

ABOUT ANTHONY JAMES CANELO, CNHP, MH

Website: 5to1formulas.com

ANTHONY JAMES CANELO is a master herbalist, author and inventor. His books are available on Amazon.com. Anthony is an inventor. You can learn more about 5:1 Formula on his company's website.

5:1 Formulas - Aromatherapeutic Vaporizer Technology
Age Old Herbalism: All New Technology

The
Holistic
Practitioners

MUNIRA MERCHANT
B.S.A.M. (Ayurvedacharya)

I grew up in India totally embracing ancient Indian traditions for healing.
But, I supplemented the traditions of my family by attending medical school.

I am a doctor of Ayurveda, a five thousand year old medical tradition that originated in Northern India from one of the ancient texts of the Vedic tradition. The meaning of the word is *life knowledge* from the words *ayur* for life and *veda* for knowledge. And after my name I list the credential B.S.A.M (Bachelor of Shudha Ayurvedic Medicine).

I'm very proud of these credentials because it is these extensive years of study, training and practical requirements that provided me with the knowledge and tools I use today to help my clients to get back into chakra alignment.

Many people in the western world think they understand what an Ayurveda physician is but what it really involves to become one is really unknown to most.

We receive the same medical school training as allopathic physicians, yet we serve our patients with a more personal and holistic approach, aiming to strengthen the body's ability to heal itself and stay healthy.

Yes, I've dissected a cadaver, and took all the courses in anatomy, chemistry and biology so that I could really understand the human body. My training, however, also included learning how essential oils, gemstones, chanting and yoga poses can supplement healing as well.

When I meet a client, I have the knowledge to analyze what dosha (body type--Pitta, Vatta, Kaffa), he or she has and proceed from there in advising the best course of action for their particular Prakruti (constitution). I can give recipes as well as teach an individual how to best prepare and cook the recommendations I make to get their health to thrive. I can share specific yoga poses that a person should do, and just as important, what shouldn't be done. I can suggest gemstones that a person would want to have around their home, office and on the body to shift energy to vibrate on a higher level, and when best to take a break from that crystal and work with the energy of another jewel.

Most crucial for health, is knowing you have a partner who cares about your success in maintaining a healthy mind and body. That is why I offer a boutique Ayurveda service that provides a client access to me via email and texting.

I wish you much success in balancing your chakras.

SHEERSHASANA - HEADSTAND

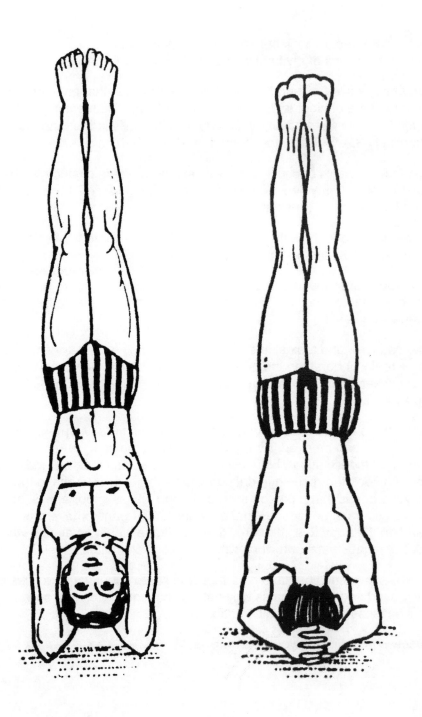

CHAKRA BALANCING, SHEERSHASANA, USTRASANA
Munira Merchant, B.S.A.M.

Chakras are invisible wheels in the body. They spin at a very high speed creating vacuum centers that draw life force energy from surrounding universes. Each chakra then gives this energy to its surrounding area including skin, muscles, glands, organs and so on as well as to the psychological, emotional and spiritual part of our being. Any blockage in the chakra will create weakness or some condition in that particular area. And therefore, along with ongoing treatment, chakra cleansing will be very beneficial.

There are different methods of cleansing or balancing chakras. But not all cleansing work with every chakra or every individual. Just opening the chakra is not enough; it should stay open in its normal state, it should not remain underactive.

According to Ayurveda, one's Prakruti (constitution) is the determining factor for any treatment. Which of the three dosha energies (Vata, Pitta, or Kapha) is aggravated and is creating vikruti (disorder) should be considered. Before cleansing a chakra, I first determine Prakruti to find whether one or more dosha are involved. People with a high Vata energy can't concentrate properly and are restless. In such situations, I don't use visualization or meditation; massaging with particular oils or gemstones are more useful. Clients with high Pitta, having blockage of Manipura chakra (the solar plexus), respond very well to meditation on the other hand. I also get very good results with gemstones.

Some of my female clients, who complain of not being able to express themselves properly, get very good results in opening their Vishuddha chakra (the throat chakra) with the use of Aquamarine gemstone. Aquamarine gemstone has many benefits and is also anti-aging. I use Aquamarine for Ayurvedic anti-aging facials too.

Yoga postures prove wonderful in opening chakras. Some chakras are very tough to open, like the Anahata chakra (the Heart chakra). Anahata is the connection between physical energy and spiritual energy. It is part of both. Many times, after multiple attempts, it still remains underactive. For this, I feel the best is to try yoga postures. For balancing the Anahata chakra, Ushtrasana (camel pose) is excellent. Also, young clients who have depression problems feel better doing Sheershasana (head stand) to energize Sahasrara (the Crown chakra) along with their treatment. Point to be noted here is that yoga asanas should be learned properly before attempting them.

The first three chakras (the root, sacral and solar plexus) are physical in nature and respond to food very well when it comes to energizing and balancing them. Clients who suffer from knee pain come to me for Janu Basti, a procedure in which knees are bathed in warm Ayurvedic oil, which gives relief and improves mobility. Legs and joint problems are associated with the root chakra. I advise them to eat root vegetables growing deep within the earth like potatoes, sweet potatoes, beets, carrots, onions and garlic. And for Manipura, the golden bright chakra, can be best energized with golden milk, a milk based beverage mixed with spices and fresh turmeric.
© Munira Merchant

Photo by Anne Edgar

168

THE BENEFITS OF GEMSTONES FOR HEALING
Munira Merchant, B.S.A.M.

Gemstones have been used for ages for beautifying jewelry, but according to ayurveda and astrology they are not merely for jewelry use. They can be used for healing certain conditions. Real gemstones have prabhava. Prabhava means 'specific effect' in Sanskrit.

Gemstones can have a direct effect over doshas and the subtle energies, and thereby influence both physical and mental health. They also can clear your aura and stimulate kundalini energy. Knowing the healing property of a gemstone may be helpful when decision what jewelry to wear.

When gemstone jewelry is being worn for a specific purpose and benefits, certain things should be kept in the mind:

- the Prakruti (constitution) of the individual
- the metal in which it is set (it should be two carats or more)
- most important, there should be skin contact with the gem. Therefore the pendants and the rings should be open so that the gem can touch the skin.

An important point should be noted that with all its benefits, any gemstone must not be used as sole treatment for any disease or condition

Here are some very popular gemstones and the chakras they are associated with.

Diamond	Activates Ajna (6th chakra) and Sahasrara (7th chakra)
Moonstone	Has a very good cleansing effect on Ajna (6th chakra) and Sahasrara (7th chakra)
Blue Sapphire	Stimulates Vishuddha (5th chakra)
Emerald	Opens Anahata (4th chakra)
Yellow Topaz	Activates Manipura (3rd chakra)
Coral	Very powerful stone to open Swadhisthana (2nd chakra)
Ruby	Stimulates Muladhara (1st chakra)
Garnet	Activates Muladhara (1st chakra)

© Munira Merchant

Here are some very popular gemstones and the therapeutic effects they have.

Gemstone	Benefits	Setting
Diamond	Strengthens the uterus, pacifies Vata and Pitta, and brings out creativeness.	Should be set in white metal, preferably in white gold.
Moonstone	Is neutral in energy. Pacifies both Vata and Pitta. Its calming effect is good for menorrhagia, fever and asthma.	Should be set in silver to pacify Pitta and in gold to pacify Vata.
Sapphire	Has calming effect on emotions and brings peace of mind. Is cold in energy.	Should be set in silver for Pitta individuals. Should be set in gold for Vata and Kapha individuals, as gold is a hot metal.
Emerald	Has a good effect on the mind. It calms irritability, anger and aggressiveness and promotes intelligence. Being a cold energy, it pacifies Pitta.	Should be set in a cool metal like silver.
Yellow Topaz	Is warm in energy. Balances Vata and gives strength. Is beneficial in diabetes and all wasting diseases.	Should be set in gold, as gold tonifies.
Coral	Is very good for Pitta disorders like acidity, sour mouth and acid reflux. Is an aphrodisiac for males. Gives vigor.	Should be set in silver.
Ruby	Has the fire element and so it is hot in energy. Pacifies Vata and Kapha. Helps remove weakness of body and mind, and gives strength.	When set in gold, can be very tonifying.
Garnet	Is a less expensive stone than ruby, yet has many qualities of ruby and so it can be used as a substitute.	Should be set in gold.

© Munira Merchant

ABOUT MUNIRA MERCHANT, B.S.A.M.

Website: ayurvedawellnessusa.com
Contact: dr.munira2012@gmail.com or 347-283-9764

MUNIRA MERCHANT is an Ayurvedic Vaidya (physician) from India. She is also an Ayurvedic cosmetologist. She uses ancient Ayurvedic techniques such as pulse reading, aura reading, advice on self-healing through individualized diet, gentle detoxification, life style modifications, stress management, daily and seasonal routines, yoga and meditation. These modalities are helpful in conditions like arthritis, neck, lower back, knee and musculoskeletal pain, digestive disorders, allergies, asthma, sinusitis, skin ailments, weight problems, stress, anxiety, memory problems, hair loss and more.

Dr. Munira's knowledge and experience in Ayurveda always leaves her clients, (whether it's helping someone who can't move her neck, or someone who has trouble sleeping), feeling grateful and always leaves her feeling happy she can be of help.

She has been practicing and teaching Ayurveda for about thirty years, first in India and now in New York.

A personal Ayurvedic consultation with Dr. Munira includes:

- Prakruti (identifying body constitution)
- Vikriti (finding disorder)
- Guidance (to diet, lifestyle, gentle detox, stress management, daily & seasonal routines, therapeutic yoga, and more.)

The menu of services she provides is extensive and customized. Visit her website to learn more.

ALICIA ARMITSTEAD
Chiropractor & Certified Master in Nutrition Response Testing

I'll never forget the first time I worked with chakra energy. It was with Sarah, a 34-year-old woman. I had been working with her for about six weeks on dietary and lifestyle changes and designing a clinical nutrition program to help her. She was reporting a little improvement, but not the progress I was expecting.

In my healing work, as a Chiropractor, I use muscle testing as a tool to help identify what nutritional support the body needs to heal. Using muscle testing I screen for heavy metals, heavy chemicals, immune stressors like bacteria, viruses, fungus, and parasites and food sensitivities using homeopathic vials (see bio). Any of those things can cause an imbalance in the body; in Sarah's case, depression and anxiety.

I knew that healing can be compromised at times with patients if the emotional aspect is not addressed. So, this time instead of muscle testing the organs, with Sarah's permission, I decided to muscle test the chakras and see what would happen. I had seen pendulums used in testing chakras, so I thought if pendulums can pick up imbalances maybe muscle testing can too. I put my hand on each of the seven energy centers just a half-inch off the body to see what would happen. To my surprise the body responded! Up to this point, I knew what chakras were from a very superficial point: energy centers in the body each correlating with certain emotions. The red one had to do with feeling safe, the orange one had to do with our sexuality and so forth. Her heart and crown chakras felt weak. With the crown chakra weak I decided to talk to Sarah about a daily spiritual practice and see if she would be open to meditate to let go of negative thinking and practice self-love, even if only for 15 minutes. Another exercise I gave her was to think of ten things to be grateful for each day. It could be the same ten things each day so long as she spent time in gratitude to help open the heart chakra.

I delved into learning all I could about the chakras. It was fascinating to learn that chakras were not energy centers just in the front of the body but four-dimensional balls of energy that could also be addressed on the sides and the back of the body. I started developing protocols for muscle testing on each chakra.

It was wonderful to watch Sarah over the next couple of weeks become happier. Using tools to help open up her chakras to help her emotionally really empowered her.

I appreciate that through my nutrition work I can now help people physically detox and now emotionally detox as well. It is wonderful!

PEERING THROUGH CHAKRA LENSES
Alicia Armitstead, D.C.

I've spent a lot of time reading about how colors affect the chakras and it made sense to me that each chakra had a specific color depending on its frequency because that's what color is according to physics. Color is all light but at different wavelengths or frequencies. Red has the longest wavelength or slowest frequency, and purple has the shortest wavelength or fastest frequency. It is these different wavelengths that give each chakra different characteristics. It made sense to me that the more spiritual chakras (sixth and seventh) had faster frequencies and therefore a higher vibration. Using color, for example, if you wanted to open up the throat chakra, you could paint a room blue, wear a blue shirt or even better, a blue necklace or scarf right on the throat, or light a blue candle. From a very scientific standpoint I saw using color at a certain frequency being picked up from the eyes, then going into the brain and the brain stimulating the body to open up a chakra.

CHAKRA GLASSES

It was this concept that made me start using chakra (eye) glasses. Chakra glasses look like regular sunglasses but they have different colored lenses and depending on the chakra you want to open up, you wear those specific colored glasses to stimulate the brain to open up that chakra. In my research there were a few companies that made them, so I ordered them and started testing them but they weren't giving me the results I expected. So I started muscle testing very specific wavelengths of color to find what exact color would be best at opening up each chakra and this led me to develop my own chakra glasses that could open up a chakra within 60 seconds of wearing. That's all it took, 60 seconds! But it wasn't permanent and it never will be because energy is always shifting so patients wanted their own pair to keep using between appointments and so I realized the need for making them available to the public.

When going out to the public with the chakra glasses, people would try on the glasses of their choice as opposed to the ones I muscle tested them for in my office and it was always fun to watch people's reactions. A lot of times the person would be attracted intuitively to the color they needed and try that one on. They would try other colors too but I could always see a bigger smile on their face with the color that they actually needed and only after they were trying on the glasses and interested would I explain muscle testing and confirm what they needed afterwards. People are attracted to the glasses because they are fun and cool but I know I am helping people's energy shift and open up for the better.

People also like to wear them longer than 60 seconds so I started making them with UV protection to be like sunglasses. I personally wear my Third Eye glasses as sunglasses.

MUSCLE TESTING, AFFIRMATIONS AND CHAKRAS

Using muscle testing with chakras also allowed me to muscle test patients for very specific affirmations that they can use to open up the chakras.

Muscle testing is based on quantum physics. E=mc2. So if energy equals mass times the speed of light squared then anything with mass has energy and we are using that energy and muscle testing to get a response from the body. This response allows us to know what energy is disrupting the body and make very specific lifestyle and supplement recommendations for that person based on the muscle testing.

Muscle testing works by a practitioner, like a chiropractor, applying a pressure on any muscle in the body. It is easiest to use an arm. As the practitioner applies pressure to the arm the patient resists by applying the same amount of pressure back so the arm is nice and strong. Then the practitioner applies a little pressure to each organ with the other hand. As pressure is applied, let's say to the liver, and if there is a problem in the liver, the body won't like the pressure. It will send a signal to the brain and the brain will want to protect the liver, so that if I apply pressure to the liver AND the patient's arm at the same time the arm goes weak (meaning the patient can no longer resist the pressure I am applying) because the body doesn't care about the arm, it wants to protect the liver.

The question is: why the weakness in the arm when pushing on the liver? To answer this question, the practitioner uses homeopathic vials to screen for stressors. The practitioner screens for heavy metals, heavy chemicals, food sensitivities and immune stressors by placing the vials on the body, one group at a time. Once the vials are placed on the body the arm and liver are pushed again by the practitioner and if the weak arm now goes strong, that change in muscle testing is because one of the vials is resonating with the liver, as the body can pick up on the energy through the glass. Just like when sunlight has come through the windows on a hot day, when you get into a car, it will be sweltering hot. On the same line, the energy waves from the vials go through glass and if they match an energy wave in the liver then that match takes stress off of the nervous system so now the weak arm gets strong.

Because muscle testing is quantum physics, energy based, we can use words to muscle test too because each word has a specific wavelength that the body picks up on through the ears. Once the ears hear the words they can make a patient's arm stay strong or go weak. So I would muscle test the chakras and if the heart and root chakras were weak I would then muscle test again in a specific way to find out which one was the priority. For more information, read David Hawkins' book, *Power vs. Force*.

Let's say the heart is priority and when you study the heart chakra you know some of the affirmations used are "I am love", "Let love in and fear out", "I am open to love", "I deeply and completely love and accept myself", etc. So when I muscle test the weak heart chakra and say these affirmations, sometimes they would work and sometimes they wouldn't and so I would start saying other affirmations for other chakras and keep going until I found the right one. And in the above example of the root and heart chakra sometimes I would find an affirmation that connected the two such as, "I am safe to be open to love" because the root chakra has to do with feeling safe and you can't create love until you feel safe enough to do it. Once the patient said this affirmation three times I would then go back and muscle test all chakras and sometimes I would find that it not only helped the heart chakra but the root chakra was now strong too. Sometimes the root chakra was still weak and the patient needed another affirmation to strengthen it. So they would leave the office with two different affirmations to work on.

Affirmations can be used just by saying it a few times a day to open up the energy. A good way to remember is by saying it every time you see the clock change an hour or maybe a reminder that pops up on your phone, or sticky notes up on the bathroom mirror. The usages are endless. But one of the most powerful uses is to use the affirmation in tapping.

TAPPING (EMOTIONAL FREEDOM TECHNIQUE) AND CHAKRAS

Tapping, also known as Emotional Freedom Technique, taps acupuncture points to stimulate energy to shift in the body. In acupuncture this energy is known as qi. It was developed by Gary Craig. When doing the tapping the patient says statements to help the energy shift. It benefits the patients to have their chakras muscle tested first as to what statements to have them say. Patients who have done this reported greater results!

MUSCLE TESTING, EXERCISING AND CHAKRAS

I have developed very specific ways of using exercise to open up the chakras and help patients on their healing journey. Exercise has to be very specific and you can't recommend the same exercise program to everyone. If you under train you don't get the benefits and if you over train you put the body in even more stress. Knowing exercise is a great stress management tool, I wondered if the reason it helped with stress is because it helped open up the chakras. So to find out I would test a patient's chakras before and after exercise and see if it would strengthen the weak chakras and it did! I took all the information I was collecting from testing patients to find what exercises were best. I then took the exercises and developed an exercise class to open up the chakras. People got the physical benefits of a workout while maximizing the emotional benefits too with these specific exercises in a specific sequence.

Here is an example of an exercise for each chakra you can do at home! Some of them are yoga poses you may not be familiar with so look them up first so you know how to do it. Do as many as you would like to feel like you are getting a good workout. Start at the root chakra and working your way up to the crown chakra and then ending with the root chakra to help you feel grounded again after opening up the higher chakras.

- Root chakra – squats
- Sacral chakra – cat-cow pose
- Solar plexus chakra – sit-ups
- Heart chakra – push-ups

- Throat chakra – fish pose
- Third eye chakra – child's pose while massaging forehead onto floor
- Crown chakra – tripod headstand

MUSCLES TESTING, ESSENTIALS AND CHAKRAS

The last tool I have delved into using muscle testing and chakras is essential oils. There is a lot of information on essential oils and chakras but every resource seems to recommend a different oil for every chakra so I used muscle testing to figure out what tested the best for each chakra and narrow it down to only one oil instead of a list of oils per chakra. But the first step was to find the highest-grade essential oil company. There are many brands out there and my research led me to a company called doTERRA and I love using their oils! Here is the list of the best oil for each chakra:

- Root chakra – Balance – a blend of spruce, rosewood, blue tansy, and frankincense
- Sacral chakra – Deep Blue – blend of wintergreen, camphor, peppermint, blue tansy, chamomile, helichrysum, osmanthus
- Solar plexus chakra – Lemon
- Heart chakra – Elevation – a blend of lavender, Hawaiian sandalwood, tangerine, Melissa flower, ylang ylang, elemi resin, osmathus and lemon myrtle leaf
- Throat chakra – Bergamot
- Third eye chakra – Lavender
- Crown chakra – Serenity – a blend of marjoram, Roman chamomile, ylang ylang, Hawaiian sandalwood and vanilla

These tools (muscle testing, chakra eye glasses, affirmations, tapping, exercising and essential oils) have enabled me to better support my clients. I invite you to visit my office and get a first-hand experience on what muscle testing combined with one or more of these tools can do for you.

© Alicia Armitstead

ABOUT ALICIA ARMITSTEAD, D.C.

Website: www.healingartsnyc.com
Contact: 866-585-5999

ALICIA ARMITSTEAD suffered as a child from asthma and at the age of 16, after years of medication and hospital visits and the asthma getting worse, she sought out alternative forms of medicine. She found Dr. Freddie Ulan who is the founder of Nutrition Response Testing, and after following the program she hasn't used her inhaler since.

Before opening the practice Healing Arts Chiropractic & Nutrition Response Testing® in 2006, she earned her Bachelor's of Science and Doctor of Chiropractic degrees from the University of Bridgeport and University of Bridgeport Chiropractic College.

She is one of only a handful of practitioners in New York City to be certified as a Master in Nutrition Response Testing®.

For a visual demonstration of muscle testing, you can view her video on YouTube at https://youtu.be/eYb6_w5nusc.

MONICA BENNETT
Certified LifeSuccess Consultant, Reflexologist, Naturopath and Nia Dancer

My life has taken me on a journey of self-discovery for life, love, and truth. I was born to parents who were both holocaust survivors. My childhood years were filled with uncertainty and fear, which led to many unhappy and disappointing results. I knew in my heart and soul that there must be a better way.

So, after years of study and applying the principles of the laws of the universe, the answers were revealing themselves to me. Everything is energy. The frequency and vibrations in our bodies are known as the chakras or energy centers. By balancing our chakras, we heal our minds, bodies, emotions and spirit. When we align our energy to divine intelligence of the universe we can tap into profound health and vitality. It is through the chakra system that we connect to this wisdom of source energy. Balancing the chakras is what I do for myself and my clients.

REFLEXOLOGY AND THE ROOT CHAKRA
Monica Bennett, N.D.

Reflexology is a direct way to communicate with your connection to the earth. Our feet touch the ground every time we walk. How we treat our feet will affect every part of our body and every part of our body will impact our feet and the root chakra. During my study of Naturopathy, I became fascinated by this modality of Reflexology and decided to pursue it as a practice. There is evidence that reflexology was used as long as 5,000 years ago in China, Egypt, and India. There is evidence that reflexology has also been used over the centuries in the Western world as well, but it has only recently taken off in the early nineteenth century in America, thanks to the efforts of Dr. William Fitzgerald.

This pioneer and popularizer of the "zone therapy" inspired the physiotherapist Eunice Ingham whose patient and painstaking research led to the detailed maps of the feet which is used today. She divided the body into ten energy zones, five on each side of the spine, running from the big toe (zone 1) up through the head. They run longitudinally; they pass through the body, from front to back. All the organs, muscles, and functions of the body lie in one or more of these zones, and their corresponding reflexes are found in the same zones on the feet and the hands. Each zone is a channel for the life force, known as "chi" to the Chinese, "prana" to the Hindus, and any obstruction or blockage in that energy flow affects the organs or functions within it, leading to dis-ease.

We can balance all our chakras or energy centers through reflexology, however the root chakra is the first to feel the healing effects. Our feet, like the roots of a plant, connect us to the earth. When we feel grounded and safe in the world our root chakra is strong and our feet and legs reflect this strength in our bodies. Just like a strong healthy plant, the soil must supply the nutrients to feed the root. Our self-care must feed our roots to maintain healthy feet.

Our bodies are a manifestation of our mind. Our body is our temple, and we want to take the best possible care of it. Our thoughts impact how we feel and these feelings express themselves through our body as vibrations. In order for our mind to communicate efficiently with our body we must keep the lines of communication open.

The root chakra, representing itself as the color red, is vital for our stability and health, which provide a means of facilitating these pathways to stay open. Each foot contains 26 bones, 20 muscles and 114 ligaments as well as over 7,000 nerve endings, making them very sensitive and responsive to the sensory input of reflexology. There are four types of tissues that are what you can call the "super highway" of communication or energy exchanges that indicate if the body is in alignment or if there is a gap.

These tissues are the:

1) connective tissue or fascia.
2) muscular tissue
3) nerve tissue
4) epithelial tissue.

If there is an impingement like scarring, trauma or adhesions, etc. in the tissue, there will be communication barriers and your root chakra will be out of balance.

All the systems of the body can be worked on. The digestive, circulatory, lymphatic, reproductive, endocrine, nervous and immune systems all respond to pressure points on the feet or the hands. Obstructions, according to modern reflexologists, are caused by crystalline - calcium deposits on the delicate nerve endings, due to congestion, inflammation, or tension in the nerve pathways. Pressure on the reflexes, which encompass minute nerve complexes, break down these deposits, and free the pathways. Again, by applying pressure to the reflex points, the reflexologist eventually releases blocked energy, restoring a clear flow throughout the body. This is the first step (no pun intended) toward restoring balance and the first step in the healing process. When your feet and your root chakra are balanced, you will feel powerful and with a sense of belonging. From your soles to your soul you give yourself the gift of health.

© Monica Bennett

Chakra Reflexology Points on the Foot

Chakra		Glands/Organs
7		Pineal Gland Pituitary Gland or None
6		Pituitary and/or Pineal Gland
5		Thyroid Gland
4		Thymus Gland/ Heart/Lung
3		Digestive System Glands
2		Ovaries/Testies
1		Adrenals

Right foot

eyes
brain heart brain
eyes
ears
ears
shoulder
shoulder
lung
lung
stomach
stomach
gall bladder
spleen
liver
pancreas
pancreas
kidney
kidney
large intestine
large intestine
small intestine
small intestine

Left foot

bladder

Chakra Colors

7 Crown - Violet
6 Brow - Dark Blue
5 Throat - Cyan
4 Heart - Green
3 Solar Plexus - Yellow
2 Sacral - Orange
1 Base - Red

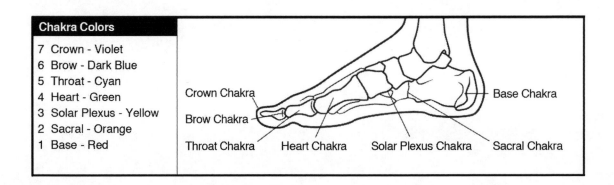

Crown Chakra
Base Chakra
Brow Chakra
Throat Chakra   Heart Chakra   Solar Plexus Chakra   Sacral Chakra

182

ABOUT MONICA BENNETT, N.D.

Website: www.monicabennett.biz
Contact: positivemonica@yahoo.com or 516-297-0672

MONICA BENNETT is a Certified Life Coach and owner of Positive Mind LLC. She has taken extensive training and workshops with many masters, such as Carolyn Myss, Cheryl Richardson, Deepak Chopra, Anthony Robbins, Wayne Dyer, Christian Northrop, Louise Hay, and most recently been working with Bob Proctor from the movie and book "The Secret". She became a certified LifeSuccess Consultant under his mentorship.

Monica earned a bachelor's degree in Naturopathy in 2000 from Clayton College, and in 2009 completed her Doctorates degree.

She received her certificate in reflexology from The Open Center in Manhattan and continues training and learning new procedures in this practice.

She is a biodynamic gardener and has since sold her horticultural business which she operated for 23 years.

She also is a certified Nia (Neuromuscular Integrative Action) dancer; a dance fusion of martial arts, healing arts, dance and spiritual self-healing.

She also has studied the Silva Method, The Sedona Method, Psycho-Cybernetics, NLP, Cognitive Behavior Therapy and many other techniques to enhance and change the patterns of the mind to erase the negative influences that we have been programmed to believe.

The
Dance
Groover

MARIA GUTIERREZ
NYC Groove Director

Movement is my way of aligning the subtle energy body or the chakras. I was blessed to discover healing through movement in my late twenties. After a long and painful period of undiagnosed immune disease, it was confirmed that I had Lyme disease for over three years without treatment.

The after-effects left me physically, emotionally and spiritually bankrupt. Doctors claimed that my symptoms were not curable but could be relieved by pain and sleep meds.

Trusting my intuition, I knew I could and would completely recover from the residual damage done.

Sometimes, the worst scenarios end up saving us! I had to dig deep and change everything. First, I needed to move. I needed Joy. Being a dancer since I was three, I decided to go back to my first love! Leaning into the pain and moving through it helped me release and realign.

This was all intuitive, as I had no knowledge of the chakra or energy system at the time. This experience allowed me to focus on my true connection with self and surroundings, to feel authentically and honor my body and spirit in ways I didn't know existed. To thine own self be true. No matter what! We can heal.

It takes truth and time, but I am living proof that it can and will happen if we allow it!

MOVEMENT IS MAGIC!
Maria Gutierrez

There is magic in the movement and the music. As far back as our primitive sisters and brothers, movement, dance and music were used to call in the gods. Tribes moving as one to a rhythm in ceremonies, or individuals dancing to ignite emotions or memories stored in their bodies which can then be released are powerful and proven forms of therapy. These acts engage our personal power, our collective consciousness and the innate intelligence that exists in every cell of our magnificent selves.

The chakras are activated in the most natural and instinctive way when we move our bodies authentically and freely. Although many believe there are a different number of chakras ranging from seven to twelve to an infinite amount, engaging them in movement requires no definition or thought.

There are no exact definitions, limits or words that matter in this area because everything is simply energy. Energy cannot be truly described in human terms. It cannot be created or destroyed. It can only be moved and transformed, which can then be cleared to allow healing on a deep and cellular level within our bodies and soul.

When we engage the energy inside of ourselves the magic begins.

Each chakra influences a certain superpower from connecting us to Gaia (the earth mother) and her insurmountable power to our own creativity, sexuality, love, voice, intuition and most of all Spirit.

In our search for industry, knowledge, and technology we have moved away from this innate intelligence.

It is why many of us feel lonely, lost, sad, distracted, etc…

We were not meant to live in our minds alone, believing every thought as fact, and acting on every impulse without processing them through our bodies and our chakra system.

EXERCISES FOR THE SEVEN MAIN CHAKRAS

Whether it be in movement, dance or meditation, energy must move through us or it will stay stuck and cause instability of thought, actions and eventually illness. For simplicity, we will work with doing exercises for the seven main chakras. Do them in the comfort of your own sacred space. Envision the chakra colors as you move. It will create a beautiful experience, as well as help the activation of energy in that area.

1. ROOT CHAKRA

Let's start from the ground up! This chakra is associated with survival instincts and trust. It is also associated with our relationship to our mother Gaia in particular.

Movements and music which are tribal and grounding feel great when working with this chakra. Relaxing the upper body and bending the knees will bring our awareness to below our feet. Walking, stomping and dancing with deep breaths into the lower belly brings clearing and activation to our root body. If we can experience this outside and barefoot, it will also add grounding help from Gaia and help restore chi.

Envision the color Red.

2. ABDOMINAL CHAKRA

The Abdominal Chakra is associated with pleasure, food, sex and reproduction and birth.

This could bring about the birth of a new project and creativity, not necessarily children. Slower sensual music with movement in the hips, (belly dancing & Latin dance such as salsa), sparks this chakra into action. Figure 8 hip motions combined with awareness and breathing into the hips is another wonderful way to flow the second chakra energy.

Envision the color Orange.

3. SOLAR PLEXUS CHAKRA

The Solar Plexus Chakra is associated with personal power, freedom of self and authenticity.

Any movement using the ribcage such as hip hop or chest rolls work. An exercise that I love for this area is sitting comfortably, grounded into our hips, while stretching our arms out to the side and reaching our left arm as far left as possible, engaging the ribcage and breathing deeply into the solar plexus. These same movements should then be repeated on the right side of the body.

Envision the color Yellow.

4. HEART CHAKRA

The Heart Chakra is associated with our relationships to others, emotions and love.

Some of my favorite dances and moves involve this chakra. Very slow jazzy music that allows us to create circles with our chest feels absolutely delicious. The slower the better! Do not rush here! Take deep breaths into the heart, releasing stuck or sluggish energy, while moving the thoracic spine in gentle motion. Another amazing movement to help release this area is spreading your arms and imagining they are wings. Pretend to fly and while moving your arms take deep breaths into the heart.

Envision the color Green.

5. THROAT CHAKRA

The Throat Chakra is associated with expression, listening and receiving all forms of expression aside from spoken word, such as art, writing, music and dance. We focus on listening here because to express the truth within, we must also listen and receive the messages that spirit has for us. All the greatest artists speak of the work coming through them. This is the flow of the fifth chakra. Movement in this area involves voice, singing, humming and Ohm. Using our breath to elongate our ohms sends the vibration throughout our bodies and the universe.

Envision the color Sky Blue.

6. THIRD EYE CHAKRA

Third Eye Chakra is associated with the spirit.

Seeing within and the spiritual truth behind it all.

The third-eye involves intuition, ESP and a knowing that cannot be put into mere words. When we work with opening the third eye, we wish to maintain a sense of stability in our bodies. Otherwise we could experience light headedness, out of body sensations and feel disoriented. This movement is very necessary for grounding.

Let's begin by planting our feet firmly on the ground. Bring your awareness to the space below your feet. (This may also be done seated) Use the slowest music possible with no lyrics. Close your eyes and start by circling the head counter clockwise, slowly, from smaller to larger circles. While adding breath, as you release blockages in this area please be aware of your center and remain grounded.

Bring your chin down to your chest, raise your head back up, and then tilt back as far as is comfortable.

The slower the better…

Envision the color Indigo.

7. THE CROWN CHAKRA

The Crown Chakra is associated with Spirit, our relationship to the universe, God, or a Power greater than us.

The movement that best activates this chakra is free-style dance. No specific music, dance or movement can be recommended here. This chakra frees the movement of your soul. It may be different every day. It's a freedom to move from the deepest parts of ourselves, releasing and connecting to whatever music calls you. You may feel self-conscious at first but listen to how your body is asking you to move. The innate

intelligence of the body to connect with the soul to heal happens here. Breathe and enjoy! Create pleasure in your movement.

Envision the color Amethyst.

Now that we have explored the individual chakras, remember that your body is trying to express messages from your soul, your emotions and constantly asking to release stuck energy.

These energies can make us feel tired, sluggish and even create illness.

The good news is that we can also heal our bodies, minds and spirit by allowing them the freedom to express/release these trapped energies.

I would like to share some of my favorite movement modalities with you but I also encourage you to find your own.

For me, Dance is #1! Yoga, swimming and walking are also favorites of mine and are simple. EveryBODY can do them.

Move, Live and LOVE

© Maria Gutierrez

ABOUT MARIA GUTIERREZ

Website: www.experiencegroove.nyc

MARIA GUTIERREZ is a Cuban-born girl from a family of professional Rhumba and Mambo dancers, and knows the power of music and dance. She has been a dance instructor for over 15 years and LOVES helping people find joy through dance. She began teaching dance fitness ten years ago and found out exactly how terrified people are to move their own bodies. Maria started researching ways to help her students relax and actually enjoy the process. Luckily she found GROOVE!!! She immediately connected with this movement. It was exactly what she was looking for; authentic dance for EVERYbody! She has been able to help hundreds of people benefit from this simple way of moving.

Today, she is a NYC Groove Director sharing its mission of elevating consciousness through free-flowing expressive movement.

The Meditation Guides & The Yogis

DENISE GALON
Owner of both Head Massage NYC and Divine Wellness, and Indian Champissage Practitioner

Life can be a bit overwhelming at times, and you need to remember to stop and regain your composure and balance. I do that with daily relaxation and breathing.

In 2011, I had an accident where a cashier at a supermarket pushed me over into another empty cashier's station. It was not intentional, but she was rushing, as she was the only cashier working with a long line and nearing the end of the day. The accident ruptured eight discs in my neck and spine, tore three meniscus, and damaged the ulnar nerve in my left arm, leaving my fingers numb. The injuries made it impossible to sit, stand, walk and climb. Each day was a struggle to just get out of bed or use the restroom. When this happened I cried and cursed, only making the pain worse. My meditation practice became void and I became bitter. How could this have happened to me ruining my life?

I am a doctor, specializing in Ayurvedic treatments. As a holistic doctor, I didn't want surgery or Western drugs. I kept intense pain away with acupuncture, chiropractic care, and herbs. But it was on the days I meditated that the pain lessened, and recovery happened. When I had my last MRIs, the technician asked me how I was able to walk with such intense injuries. Relaxation and breathing, I answered, and he laughed. But it's true.

When we allow the mind to control our emotions, everything intensifies. Ayurveda literally means "wisdom of life" and that wisdom comes from the universe only when thoughts quieten. When that voice inside you finally gives up, only then can true spirit be heard.

The fall of 2017 was one of the worst periods of my life: I was exhausted, the accident and the upcoming court case had murdered my sleep! I was not meditating regularly; allowing trauma to control me, and my pain grew worse. Losing the court case did not help: how could they be so cruel! Poor me! I sat and tried to figure out what happened.

A good friend reminded me that we are always in control of ourselves. That as a great healer, I can heal myself, if I want. As a doctor of herbology and metaphysics, I know this to be true and immediately went back to my chakra meditation practice. I listened to my own *Relaxation and Breathing* CD, which I recorded in 2013.

In just a few months, my pain was considerably less, even though the tests still show the injuries. I no longer let these destructive outside forces control me. When you allow the creative energy of the Universe guide you, you have the power to heal, to create, to give, to flow, to do whatever you desire.

At this time, I do my chakra meditation daily. If I have a late start and don't do it, things just happen in a not so good manner. I then sit down, close my eyes and do a mini version to get back on track. If I wake and can't move, I visualize the chakra colors and tone the chakra sound to get out of pain.

I truly believe meditation is the key to life. You have the power to heal anything. Just do it. Don't judge, go for it. If you need help to get started, go to my website www.divinewellness.com and download my *Relaxation & Breathing* CD. In no time, you will go with the flow and life will be bliss. *Om shanti shanti shanti Om.*

CHAKRA MEDITATION
Denise Galon

In 1978 I had the good fortune to meet two men who would forever change my life: Andy Anselmo, a doctor of metaphysics, and John Albert Harris, his partner. Both of these great men became my mentors and led me into a life where I was able to transcend my past, with meditation.

I had been a dancer/singer on Broadway, lost my voice and injured my right knee, which left me out of work and very bitter. You see, I was a victim, allowing that energy to overtake me thereby continuing the victimization that I grew up with, proving that I couldn't escape my upbringing, no matter how hard I tried.

A girlfriend of mine witnessed my demise and ordered me to become her stage manager for a production of "Miss Julie" which was the first theatrical production to be held at The Singer's Forum Foundation, a non-profit studio for singers. Did I mention the job didn't pay a dime? But it got me out of bed ... helping to whip these non-actor/singers into shape.

While I was setting up for rehearsals, etc., I overheard some of the vocal classes. John Albert Harris was praising a vocalist with comments reserved only for great singers. I couldn't believe it. How could someone praise someone who couldn't stay on pitch? But guess what? A week later they could stay on pitch, and a month later they were actually good.

I stayed around, because I really had nothing else to do, and witnessed miracles every day. It was intoxicating and mystifying. Andy Anselmo was very elusive and only spoke with me after he saw me perform. He said, "Fix your teeth and lose weight and you will be a big star." I didn't hear the positive, only the bad teeth and fat comment, which I resented. After all, I had a very critical mother and here was more criticism. If I was open spiritually at that point, I may have very well become the brightest star on Broadway.

The Universe had other plans for me. John offered me classes to help pay for all the work I did. I had a crack in my voice, where only air came out on about five notes in the passaggio, the break of the voice from chest to head voice. John would say, "Wonderful," and I would think "Bullshit". You see, it's hard to break a pattern. One day, I had a bad cold and John said, "Wonderful," and I said "It sucks." He then said, "When you give up the negative thinking, you will improve faster." What?! Me negative? I was just being honest!

Andy also had revealing words for me after I fell down and sprained my ankle. He pointed at my forehead and said, "Change your thinking, change your life." I didn't understand what thinking had to do with the pothole in the street where I fell. I was very unaware at that time.

John began every class he taught with meditation. He called it relaxation, to get people centered so that they were freer to express themselves in their singing. After the meditation, he had breathing exercises to warm up the body and the voice, peacefully, naturally and joyously. Singing is one of the hardest art forms, because you need to be healthy and happy to express your soul. The meditation helped to get rid of the ego, the striving, the worry or thought of being good; you just were.

John didn't talk about any hocus pocus, he got even the most nervous, worried person into a state of deep relaxation, so they were able to express their soul from whatever vocal level they were, even the beginners. I remember that some of the best (most touching) performances came from the recitals of a class called "Singing for People Who Think They Can't." And, when I didn't do my meditation prior to a performance, it was just glib. So, I began to meditate on my own, every day and guess what … my life did indeed change – no more a victim!

John and Andy had me read Joel Goldsmith, Unity, Dr. Barker and many other metaphysical writings. And one day, in my quest for beauty and truth, I found many other people of like mind at a fair called *The New Life Expo*, created by Mark Becker in New York City. People were opening up to me, constantly teaching and guiding my metaphysical studies. I then received my doctorate in Metaphysics in 2002.

This was an amazing world where life was charmed. Phyllis Diller taught me scripted visualization manifestation. After all, she created herself, a woman comedian in a man's field. Joe Vitale taught me abundance manifestations, Louise Hay affirmations, and many, many other gifted people from whom I still learn. They taught me how to manifest my career as an opera singer where I went on to win competitions and sing all over the world.

In 1996, I met another important teacher, Narendra Mehta. He taught me about the chakras. I had studied traditional Chinese medicine to keep myself healthy as a singer. I later learned that Ayurveda (wisdom of life) came before Chinese medicine. The Chinese monks studied with the Indian monks because they recovered sooner from their wounds and returned quicker back to battle. That is how acupuncture was born from Ayurvedic marma and chakra stimulation. All are energy medicine.

I studied Indian Head Massage with Narendra and his wife Kundan. This was a long-practiced modality, mostly done at home by a mother or grandmother to relieve tension and promote healthy hair growth. Narendra's mother rebalanced him at age one, after he was blinded by acid drops at a hospital where they took him for an eye infection. Narendra had head massage whenever he was stressed by the blindness, and when he went to London to study to be a doctor, he was craving the head massage, but the school of thought of Western massage was not to touch the head, as you might cause a brain seizure. This was when Narendra decided to bring head massage to the West. Narendra returned to India, as an Osteopathic Doctor. He took a head massage from every venue he could find for eight years, and developed his Champissage™ technique from what he thought was the best of the best. He also added massage of the shoulders, arms, neck and face to the traditional head massage because computers had entered the home and people had major stress in those areas. He brought his technique to London in 1982, had success, but still felt something was missing to make it a complete modality. He then studied Ayurveda and found by adding balance to the upper chakras, the entire body fell into alignment. His technique was solidified.

We met at a convention in London. I was there performing an opera, and I didn't perform well because of some insomnia and jet lag. Narendra did a very brief treatment on me, asking if I wanted to be stimulated or relaxed. No massage therapist had ever asked me that; they just did what they did. I told him about my stress and sleeplessness and after five minutes, I was nodding in the chair. He had overwhelmed me with the subtle chakra rebalancing. I could barely walk out of the Expo and had one of the best sleeps of my life. I returned the next day for the stimulating treatment. He and I soon became great friends.

Narendra and his wife tricked me into learning the Champissage™ Therapy, for which I am glad, as practicing and teaching it has been a great joy in my life. This is an amazing treatment, for when you balance the chakras, you also get a benefit of chakra balancing yourself. This was so much more rewarding than the singing, as I was always looking for the next project in that life. The healing modality was complete satisfaction for me, seeing the benefit of the work and the difference made helping people to heal themselves.

I became voracious in my studies about chakras, learning different ways to activate and balance them by feeling, energizing, breathing, visualizing, etc. with many Vedic masters. I found Narendra's method to be quite simple and complete.

One day, leading a meditation class, I found myself combining John's relaxation method with chakra balancing. It was a wonderful meditation class and each time I led it the meditation became deeper and more profound. I taught these classes for several years before I lost my space, which led me to record a guided session. That recording has four segments: first a visualization; second a relaxation; third chakra energizing; and, fourth Pranayama breathing exercises. You may do all (about 45 minutes) or just listen to the relaxation to help with sleep, or do the breathing exercises to make your body stronger and healthier, etc. I even like to listen when I have had a challenging day.

John taught me to relax the mind first, and then go through the body releasing tension out through your hands and feet into the floor back to mother earth, grounding you. Then he pulled white light, or he sometimes called it creative energy, through the body again starting at the top of the head.

Narendra had me visualize each of the chakra colors when balancing them. He would say visualize and breathe in the color sky blue and exhale the sound *Ham* to balance the throat chakra. I asked him if he remembered or knew what color was, being blind. His response was no, but the universe knows, and he reminded me that we do not give or receive energy, just open the door for the patient or client to balance themselves. He was brilliant!

THE CHAKRAS

Let's talk about the chakras. You have hundreds throughout the body and some extending up out of the body. We are just going to concern ourselves with the seven main ones going up and extending through the spine, starting at the base of the spine up to the top of the head.

I find it interesting that throughout holistic medicine this pattern is the mainstay for healing. The spine is the base of chiropracty and in Chinese medicine the governing meridians start at the groin and meet at the lips, with the rear meridian passing up over the head. In Ayurveda, the chakras are depicted as energy vortices with a Vedic symbol surrounded by geometry, flowers and color. There are also sounds to balance these seven chakras.

I believe these chakras develop each year in a child, starting from fetal to age one for the first chakra, age one to two for the second chakra, etc. all the way up to age seven, when the chakras are finally fully formed. They usually say the child's blueprint is set by age seven. If someone is chronically having throat issues, I say go back to age 4-5 and see if there was a trauma at that time, like a move, a divorce, etc., work it and meditate and balance it. There are so many tools to work with like essential oils, colors, crystals, sounds, therapy, etc. Work with what works for you. Don't be afraid to try something new.

I like sending the color and the sound with one hand on the heart, as you must always love yourself before you can send love to another, and one hand on the chakra. Close your eyes and breathe in the chakra color and either tone or exhale the sound. Do this three times and then switch your hands and do three more times. Healing is accomplished in odd numbers in Ayurveda. I find three to be perfect.

Since I like to start at the top of the head, let's start there … with the three higher chakras.

The seventh chakra, the *Sahasrara* is located at the crown of the head and harmonizes with the pineal plexus. This is the master chakra, interpreting information from the other chakras opening your link to the Universe. In Sanskrit, the name means 1,000 petal lotus. When you balance and open this chakra, your brain and whole system receives endless energy and Universal communication. When this chakra is out of balance ego takes over, leaving you unsatisfied and depressed, allowing fear and anxiety to take over. This chakra color is violet or gold and the sound is *Om*. Its element is Spirit, and is balanced by crystals of Amethyst or Sapphire, and the essential oils of Lavender and Frankincense.

The sixth chakra, *Ajna* also known as the "third eye" located in the center of the forehead, harmonizes with the cavernous plexus. It is where memory and imagination is created. When this chakra is out of balance headaches, insomnia and nightmares may occur. Clairvoyance can be attained when this chakra is open. This chakra color is indigo and the sound is *Om*. Its element is the Mind, and is balanced by crystals of Lapis Lazuli or Angelite, and the essential oils of Lemon and Rosemary.

The fifth chakra, *Vishuddha* located at the base of the throat, controls the voice and harmonizes with the laryngeal plexus. When the throat chakra is out of balance communication and expression is stifled and over time leads to chronic illnesses like asthma, sore throats and fear related stress. Truth can freely be expressed when this chakra is in balance. This chakra color is blue and the sound is *Ham*. Its element is Ether, and is balanced by crystals of Turquoise or Aquamarine, and the essential oils of English Chamomile and Myrrh.

The fourth chakra, *Anahata* is the bridge between the higher and lower chakras and located in the chest/heart. It rules the lungs and the heart and harmonizes with the cardiac plexus. This chakra must be in balance to express love and charity to the world. When in balance you have an endless supply of energy and joy, and when out of balance you become withdrawn, needy and insincere. This chakra color is green or pink and the sound is *Yam*. Its element is Air, and is balanced by crystals of Rose Quartz or Jade, and the essential oils of Bergamot and Rose.

THE LOWER CHAKRAS

The third chakra, *Manipura* located about 2" above the navel in the stomach and harmonizes the solar plexus. This area is where Prana is stored and responsible for digestion and energy. In balance, harmony of the emotional body (ego) with the spiritual takes place creating vitality and calmness. Out of balance, you become over dominant, insensitive, despondent, overweight and egotistical. This chakra color is yellow and the sound is *Ram*. Its element is Fire, and is balanced by crystals of Citrine or Amber, and the essential oils of Juniper and Neroli.

The second chakra, *Svadhishthana* located in the lower abdomen, harmonizes with the prostatic plexus. This chakra is responsible for circulation, bladder, kidney and reproductive health. In balance, sexual energy and creativity flows freely, allowing you to express kindness. Out of balance, you are unable to express your feelings adequately and life becomes infertile and unproductive, aging you. This chakra color is orange and the sound is *Vam*. Its element is Water, and is balanced by crystals of Carnelian or Chrysoprase, and the essential oils of Sandalwood and Jasmine.

And, the first chakra, *Muladhara* located at the base of the pelvis/coccyx, harmonizes with the sacral plexus and is where Kundalini is stored. In Ayurvedic Yoga and meditation this cosmic energy can be released, moving up through all the chakras ending at the crown chakra bringing illumination. This chakra is responsible for elimination of liquid and solids and grounds us to the earth. When this chakra is out of balance, you feel ungrounded, untrusting, become focused on material possessions, and have trouble holding on to money. In balance, you are connected with nature and trust in the flow of life. This chakra color is red and the sound is *Lam*. Its element is Earth, and is balanced by crystals of Hematite or Ruby, and the essential oils of Myrrh and Patchouli.

Examine what may be off in your life and focus your meditation on balancing those chakras to find your bliss. Enjoy working with the chakras and meditate daily to keep your physical, mental and subtle energy in balance. I believe it is the key to a long healthy, joyous life.

My teachers live in my *Relax and Breathe* recording. This recording is suitable for beginners and experienced meditators alike.

© Denise Galon

ABOUT DENISE GALON, PHD, LCICI, CMT, RA, D.AYUR

Website: headmassagenyc.com and divinewellness.com
Contact: divadtg@aol.com or 917-400-8110
Meditation Recording: *Relax and Breathe* is available on her websites

DENISE GALON has a doctorate in Metaphysics and Herbal Sciences. She is also a Certified Massage Therapist and experienced in Iridology, Sound Therapy, Aromatherapy, Ayurvedic Nutrition and Medicine, Chinese Energetic Medicine, Touch For Health Kinesthetic Healing, Chinese Herbology, Philippine Psychic Surgery, Pranic Healing, and is a Medical Intuitive.

Dr. Galon draws an exclusive clientele for face lifts, detox treatments, herbal and essential oil treatments with a base in Ayurveda and Asian Medicine.

As a holistic healing expert, Denise has gathered the best equipment used for diagnostic treatments and products sold for home treatments and gifts. Denise hosts a variety of classes and certification courses in NYC on alternative methods and remedies for stress and illness such as Essential Oil Training, Face Yoga, Mehta Face-Lift Massage, Kansa Vatki Foot Massage, and Champissage™ Indian Head Massage.

Dr. Galon brought these Ayurvedic treatments into the USA London Center of Indian Champissage and is the only instructor certified to teach all their modalities.

Her office is based in NYC
Address: Divine Wellness NYC / Head Massage NYC
          305 2nd Ave, Suite 4 - New York, NY 10003

Her *Relax and Breathe* recording is suitable for beginners and experienced meditators alike and can be purchased on either one of her websites.

RITA LONDON
Kundalini Yoga and Meditation Instructor, and Energy and Sound Healer

As a Kundalini yoga and meditation instructor, energy and sound healer, I help people to relax, clear blocks and balance their energies so they can express who they are with greater ease and joy.

While breath is an essential component of my Kundalini yoga work with clients, sessions also combine yoga postures, meditation, Reiki and other energy techniques and sound healing. I create the conditions for the natural intelligence of the body to induce self-healing and transformation.

In a typical session, I design a program of breath work and yoga that specifically address what someone is working on (for example, feeling blocked, emotional fatigue, fear, grief, or simply wanting overall well-being or greater spiritual connection). After a private yoga session, the client lies on a massage table where I use different energy techniques to balance the chakras and further stimulate the flow of energy. Each session ends with a "gong sound healing" to deepen the relaxation experience and enhance and seal in the energy work. The gong's vibrations create a complex synthesis of overtones that the human mind cannot categorize. As a result, the sound cuts through and releases subconscious blocks, leaving one feeling deeply relaxed and rejuvenated.

I design unique home practices that support each individual's needs and goals. A routine of even 10 minutes daily brings tremendous benefits. It is said that it takes 40 days to change a habit and 120 days to confirm a new habit. Doing a practice for 40 days consecutively helps to shift our habitual patterns and alters our behavior from the recesses of our subconscious.

BREATHING YOUR WAY TO WELLNESS, VITALITY AND JOY. KUNDALINI YOGA & MEDITATION
Rita London

An ancient Kundalini sage once said, "When short of wisdom, breathe." Thousands of years ago yogis discovered that the rhythm and depth of the breath can impact energy states of wellness, emotion and consciousness.

Most of us don't think about breathing; it is what we do automatically. But breath is key to our health and well-being. In Kundalini yoga, breath is fundamental to shifting states of being. There are many different breathing techniques that work holistically or focus on a specific chakra. These breathing practices can promote health and vitality, improve mood, calm the mind, increase focus, release subconscious blocks and create a deeper sense of connectedness with oneself and the cosmos.

When we learn to direct our breath we can begin to master our mind, emotions, energy and our lives. This is because our breath is intricately connected to our emotions and thoughts. We can change habitual patterns with fast-acting breathing techniques that can move stuck energies, allowing them to flow more freely and help us to power through our fears and obstacles.

WHAT IS KUNDALINI?

Kundalini yoga is an ancient healing practice that is highly effective in coping with today's modern stresses and challenges. This yoga form integrates intensive breathing techniques with movement, meditation, mantra (sacred words repeated to raise one's vibration) and mudra (hand positions) to move energy through the chakras to release blocks, create self-healing and a flow of spirit to enhance intuitive awareness.

In Kundalini yoga, the spine is considered the spiritual center. Kundalini means "like a coiled serpent," referring to energy that rests at the base of the spine. As the dormant energy flows freely through all of the chakras, an awakening of consciousness occurs.

Yogi Bhajan, a master of Kundalini, brought this practice from India to America in 1969. Until that time, Kundalini was a secret practice that over thousands of years had been passed on and taught to a select few. In the late 60's, Yogi Bhajan had a vision that people living in the Aquarian Age (beginning in 2011) would have stresses so challenging that people would suffer intense stress, fatigue, depression and confusion. He felt it was his mission to break the silence and share the powerful healing tools of Kundalini yoga with people in the West. Yogi Bhajan left numerous materials on Kundalini yoga including books, lectures, videos and most importantly, teachers.

MY STORY

My first Kundalini class was an instant game changer. Suffering from post-traumatic stress syndrome, I had lived much of my life on "high alert." Though I was high functioning, I often suffered from generalized anxiety. After I took my first Kundalini yoga class, I experienced a profound calm and felt energized and happy. I was intrigued.

As I continued to practice weekly, I noticed that negative mental patterns began to dissolve, as fears, doubts and anxieties lessened dramatically. I began to inhabit my mind and body differently. I no longer ignored the gentle whisperings of my soul and allowed my intuition to guide me. New energies were flowing through me that filled me with joy, confidence and a divine loving presence. I felt a greater compassion for myself and others. Eventually, I decided to leave my job to become a Kundalini yoga and meditation instructor so that I could share this life-changing practice with others, After a few years of consistent daily practice, I was able to wean myself off of anti-anxiety medication, which I had been taking for 15 years.

Living a conscious life is life-long journey. I have learned that we are all natural healers and with the right tools can set the conditions for our own self-healing. I am deeply grateful for this beautiful practice and the opportunity to help others to live their best life.

TWO KUNDALINI GIFTS FOR YOU.

1. Stress Relieving Meditation

This simple breathing technique will help you feel relaxed and refreshed.

Sit comfortably in a meditation pose on a chair or on a yoga mat with your spine straight, your chin tucked in, and your chest lifted.

Place hands in Gyan mudra (index finger and thumb touching) or any other comfortable mudra.

Close your eyes and focus on your breathing.

Breathe in through your nose for eight equal sniffs.

Exhale through the nose in one powerful breath.

Continue this breathing pattern for 3- 11 minutes.

To End

Inhale deeply and hold for 5-10 seconds. Exhale. Inhale deeply and hold the breath for 15-20 seconds, while rolling the shoulders. Exhale sharply. Inhale deeply while rolling the shoulders as fast as you can. Exhale, relax your shoulders, and rest.

2. Sat Kriya

Sat Kriya is an essential practice of Kundalini Yoga. Its main purpose is to activate, control and balance the energy of the lower three chakras—the root, the sacral and the solar plexus energy centers. Using the mantra Sat Naam, Sat Kriya strengthens the pelvic floor, rejuvenates the entire sexual system, removes energetic imbalances, as well as aiding with mild depression.

It is best for beginners to start with three minutes repeated every day for 40 days. With practice it can be practiced for up to 62 minutes.

Sit comfortably on your heels with your back straight.

Lift your arms straight up with your elbows hugging your ears. Interlace your fingers together, except for the index fingers, which should point straight up. For women the left thumb crosses over the right thumb and for men the right thumb crosses over the left thumb.

Start to chant the mantra Sat Naam.

Once you have a rhythm going, begin to pull in your navel and lower belly toward your spine as you chant Sat. Relax the belly as you chant Nam.

Continue for three minutes (or more, as you become more experienced.)

To End

Inhale deeply and pull the Root Lock (squeeze the pelvic floor and tighten your buttocks.) Feel the energy moving up the back, past the shoulders to the top of your head (your seventh chakra). Exhale keeping the arms in place and release the lock. Inhale again. Afterward, rest for twice as long as you have practiced Sat Kriya.

© Rita London

ABOUT RITA LONDON

Website: www.ritalondon.com

RITA LONDON is a certified Kundalini Yoga and Meditation instructor, Reiki Master and sound healer with an extensive background in modern dance and creative arts education. She is passionate about sharing the healing benefits of Kundalini Yoga and Meditation with others and showing how it can be easily integrated into everyday life.

For more information or to book an appointment, please visit her website.

LAKSHMI VOELKER
Founder, Get Fit Where You Sit

In 1982, I met Michael Reed Gach, the founder of The Acupressure Institute in Berkeley, California. Back in the day, I took many workshops with him; from Jin Shin Acupressure,
to the application of acupressure, to various yoga postures/asanas.

I was fascinated with his work, so I read his book Acu-Yoga: Self Help Techniques to Relieve Tension. It became my teaching tool for many decades to come. I savored every page, every word, every picture of how to apply the points and meridians of acupressure to every yoga asana!

I noticed how this application increased the circulation of the life energy. This was the beginning of many two to four hour workshops and classes containing Acu-Yoga (the marriage of acupressure and yoga: two ancient arts of healing).

I had t-shirts designed with the chakras on them for myself and my students. I created workbooks and hung colored pictures of the chakras and their meaning in the studios where I taught Acu-Yoga.

I noticed the color of clothes my students were wearing to class as well as what color unitard I pulled each day out of my closet. We put the appropriate crystal in our pockets or bras of whatever we needed to work on in our lives, like a yellow citron crystal to feel empowered again, or we would wear a ruby red t-shirt to feel grounded. Some of us wore the same color day after day and others of us mixed and matched! These observations took us out of dull and sometimes boring habitual colors of black and brown, or even white, which I know contain all the colors of the spectrum, but we were all about color and healing!

CHAKRA EXERCISES & AFFIRMATIONS TO BALANCE & HEAL PRACTICED ON A CHAIR
Lakshmi Voelker

The chakras are centers of energy in the astral body. Six of them are located along the spine; the seventh is located at the crown of the head. All of them are depicted to have a certain number of petals of the Lotus flower, a sound vibration, a color and a gemstone, to name a few differentiating aspects.

The first chakra (the root chakra) is considered a lower chakra, while the seventh chakra (the crown chakra) is considered a higher chakra. We cannot see the chakras for they are subtle energy fields within our bodies.

The following are some chakra exercises and affirmations to balance and heal our internal energies practiced on a chair.

FIRST CHAKRA: MULADHARA CHAKRA

Sit at the front edge of your chair, lean back, placing your hands beside you on the seat of the chair. Lift your buttocks up and back down, gently. Repeat six more times visualizing the color *RED*.

Crystal: Ruby and Garnet

Association: Security and survival. Finding your purpose in life.

Growing roots and grounding.

Affirmation: "I open to receive the gift of life."

SECOND CHAKRA: SWADHISTHANA CHAKRA - Crystal: Coral

Identity, creativity and sexuality.

Flowing with change.

"I am a unique manifestation of energy in physical form. I dance in harmony with the rhythm of that energy."

Make fists with your hands and place them into your groin area. Press in and breathe deeply for 30 seconds while visualizing the color *ORANGE*.

THIRD CHAKRA: MANIPURA CHAKRA - Crystal: Topaz

The power center of the body. Finding our will, purpose and action.

"I open to the fullness of my power. I have within me the power to create, sustain and transform."

Place your hands on your knees and arch and curl your spine (forward and backward). Do these movements six more times while visualizing the color *YELLOW*.

FOURTH CHAKRA: ANAHATA CHAKRA - Crystal: Emerald

Love and compassion. Living in our hearts, from our hearts.

"I open to the depth of love that dwells within me. I am love, I receive love, and I give love."

Stretch your arms out to your sides and back. Raise your chest up and out. Bring your palms together in front of you, curving the spine. Repeat six more times while visualizing the color *GREEN*.

FIFTH CHAKRA: VISSUDHA CHAKRA - Crystal: Sapphire

Center of expression. Communicating our hearts to the world.

"I open to the Universal Truth within me. I receive it. I share it."

Turn your head slowly side to side eight times, then up and down eight times while visualizing the color *BLUE*

SIXTH CHAKRA: AJNA CHAKRA - Crystal: Lapis

The center of meditation, contemplation, visualization, affirmation, intellect and intuition.

"I open to the wisdom that dwells within me. I open to my guidance."

Sit tall in the Sitting Mountain pose, place your palms behind you on your chair with your fingers pointing away from you. Focus on the high seam Dristi and breathe deeply, focusing on the Third Eye space between your eyebrows. Continue for as long as you want while visualizing the color *INDIGO*.

SEVENTH CHAKRA: SAHASRARA CHAKRA - Crystal: Moon stone

Governs Universal Consciousness. Enlightenment, our connection with all that is.

Connecting to the Divine Power

"I am one with all."

Sit in the Sitting Mountain pose with your back against the back of the chair. Place the backs of your hands on your lap with the palms facing up and the thumb and pointer finger touching. Close your eyes and focus on your breath for a few minutes while focusing on the color *VIOLET*.

Finish by focusing on a healing white light surrounding your body and mind.

ABOUT LAKSHMI VOELKER

Website: getfitwhereyousit.com

LAKSHMI VOELKER, E-RYT 500, C-IAYT, YACEP, AY Ambassador and creator of Lakshmi Voelker Chair Yoga™, has more than 50 years of experience in yoga and the fitness industry specializing in office, senior, and adaptive/disabled fitness. She developed Lakshmi Voelker Chair Yoga™ in 1982, Lakshmi Voelker Chair Yoga: The Sitting Mountain Series in 1990, and the DVD Get Fit Where You Sit in 2007. Lakshmi has certified more than 1,700 teachers nationally and internationally, including healthcare professionals at the Mayo Clinic and the New York City Department of Education. She regularly runs trainings at Kripalu, The Open Center, YogaWorks, Discovery Yoga, and Texas State University. She also offers online teacher trainings worldwide.

BRENDA YARNOLD
Chair Yoga Teacher

Having a strong spiritual connection transcends everything else. Once we have connection with Spirit, everything falls into place. For me, one of the ways I connect with Source is by focusing on the crown chakra "Sahasrara," the divine connection to love and wisdom. Sahasrara is described as the 1,000-petalled lotus flower and resides right at the top of the head.

I work daily with chakras, spinning vortexes of energy, both in my yoga studio, "Bella Buddha," with my senior students, and in my role as Director of Lakshmi Voelker Chair Yoga (LVCY) Teacher Training.

AT BELLA BUDDHA

I like to show my yoga students how to connect with the Divine Spirit within them. We often begin class with a short reading from a spiritual book and an associated affirmation. I repeat the affirmation out loud, inviting my students to repeat it to themselves silently with (or without) a corresponding mudra (hand gesture) that "seals" the intention, such as Anjali Mudra, which means "divine offering," or simply stated as "placing hands in prayer."

I then ask my students to notice what kind of energy they are experiencing; what kind of energy are they carrying with them today, how does this energy feel in the body? We then set intentions. An intention is simply something you wish to create for yourself. It could be a new way of relating with your partner, it could be a new way of interacting with others, it could be a way you would like to feel. We set the intention as if it were already true: "I am calm and at ease throughout my day," "I am friendly when meeting strangers," "I can choose to be at peace." Once they set their intention, I invite them to feel in their bodies what it would feel like physically if their intention were true. From here, we bring awareness to the crown chakra, "Sahasrara," because it relates to pure consciousness and is associated with transcending our limitations. I have the students imagining a white or golden light emanating from the top of their head up into the heavens, feeling God's power and love draw down through that light and into their being making everything true and real and good. And we sit with this.

DURING AN LVCY TEACHER TRAINING WEEK

The LVCY teacher training program has a module that covers the chakras. There is such a relaxing, beautiful shift in the room that we usually follow this module by taking a short break that involves upbeat music and moving.

216

THE YOGI WITH THE CHAIR
Brenda Yarnold

I love to teach Lakshmi Voelker Chair Yoga (LVCY). I love everything about it from its emotional gifts to its physical gifts.

As I sit in my chair waiting for my class for seniors to begin, I notice the room and the people in it. It warms my heart to see the community being built and honored amongst the students; watching the more experienced students "mentor" the newbies reinforces that it is indeed important to lead by example in creating a safe, welcoming, and judgment-free space for others and showing that we are all responsible as a group in achieving this outcome. Meeting adult daughters who are desperately trying to find ways to help their aging mothers regain just a little bit of their prior confidence and self-esteem humbles me.

LVCY makes yoga accessible to everyone through levels of flexibility. With "levels of flexibility," we honor the uniqueness, needs, and situation of every individual. No pose is ever the same on everybody, and this could be for a variety of reasons: genetics, health issues, or injuries. With levels of flexibility, we can adapt any asana (yoga postures) for any person regardless of age, physical challenges or health reasons, even if you are unable to get down onto the mat. LVCY makes your entire yoga practice accessible from the safety of a chair: any chair, anywhere.

Most of my students are seniors, and a good percentage of them are going through challenges, some of which are hefty:

PHYSICAL CHALLENGES:	EMOTIONAL CHALLENGES:
<ul><li>knee replacement surgery</li><li>inability to get down to the floor</li><li>nerve conditions</li><li>shoulder impingement</li><li>arthritis</li><li>simply getting older</li><li>breast cancer survivors</li><li>fibromyalgia</li><li>recovering from physical injuries</li></ul>	<ul><li>losing a spouse</li><li>losing a child to cancer</li><li>watching grandchildren try to survive in today's difficult world</li><li>fear of losing mobility</li><li>fear of loss</li></ul>

Sun
Salutation
Yoga
Sequence

YOGA ASANAS & ALIGNING YOUR CHAKRA

Yoga is wonderful as its poses (asanas) may seem to work on a physical level, but many of the poses have emotional and spiritual connections as well. In fact, many poses specifically work with aligning the chakras.

To balance your chakras, or spinning vortexes of energy, you may consider integrating the following into your practice. When in the asana, focus on the associated chakra and its meaning and how it relates to you.

Blocked Chakra	Asana	Associated Body Parts
Root Chakra (Muladhara)	Seated Tree Pose (Vrksasana)	Base of the spine, legs, feet,
Sacral (Svadhisthana)	Seated Goddess Pose (Deviasana)	Hips, sacrum, lower back,
Solar Plexus (Manipura)	Seated Boat Pose (Navasana)	Spleen, pancreas,
Heart (Anahata)	Seated Camel Pose (Ustrasana)	Heart
Throat (Vishuddha)	Seated Cat Pose (Chakravakasana)	Throat
Third Eye (Ajna)	Seated Child's Pose (Balasana)	Area between the eye
Crown (Sahasrara)	Seated Corpse Pose (Savasana)	Top of the head

When I see my senior students privately, I see them as holistic beings and because I get to know my students on a more intimate level, I am able to offer them poses that best benefit their wellbeing and align their chakras on a chair.

As a yoga educator, I believe in the concept of yoga as a union between Spirit and life as we experience it here on Earth. I make an effort to find out about my students as whole beings: their spiritual lives and how that affects them physically. I ask myself "How can I be of service and empower my students as they move through their challenges?"

Yoga Bhajan has said, "Why in old age are we frustrated? Because there is not a lot of wisdom for us to share. The only value in old age is wisdom. So, in your life train your mind with the knowledge of perfect harmony in every relationship. Communicate freely and learn from everything the art of living. This, the highest art of this planet, must be mastered so that you can live realized." Bhajan, Yogi, *The Teachings of Yogi Bhajan: The Power of the Spoken Word* (1977) printed in Michigan by Sheridan Books.

LVCY empowers its teachers and students to bring their authentic and unique selves to the chair. No matter what's going on with you, be it physical or emotional, there's always room for you on the chair. No one is immune from past hurts, suffering, set-backs, or loss, and LVCY understands this and teaches a multitude of ways to bring yourself up from the mire and darkness and into the light. Whatever your gifts are, bring them to the chair

We have a teacher training offering 25 CEU's (continuing education units) every year:

- New York Open Center, NY, NY (March and August);
- Kripalu Center for Health and Healing, Stockbridge, MA (June and October);
- The Discovery Yoga Center, St. Augustine, FL (September);
- YogaWorks, Costa Mesa, CA (March)
- 1440 Multi-University in Santa Cruz, CA

© Brenda Yarnold

ABOUT BRENDA YARNOLD, MA, E-RYT 200, E-LVCYTT

Website: www.bellabuddhayoga.com
Contact: 732-749-0729

BRENDA YARNOLD is a yoga instructor, the owner of Bella Buddha, a yoga and fitness studio in Belmar, NJ that caters to the beginner, to intermediate-level students and children and seniors.

She is also a senior teacher and the Director of Lakshmi Voelker Chair Yoga.

Brenda Yarnold has always desired to help others, particularly those who feel challenged in their bodies from illness, weight, age, or other issues. She is trained in functional anatomy and is currently working toward her 300-hour yoga therapy certification. Brenda has a compassionate, non-judgmental training style and her programs are challenging, yet fun.

As a yoga educator, she believes in the concept of yoga as a union between Spirit and life as we experience it here on Earth. She makes an effort to find out about her students as whole beings: their spiritual lives and how that affects them physically.

She likes to show her yoga students how to connect with the Divine Spirit within them. Often, she begins class with a short reading from a spiritual book and an associated mantra. She repeats the mantra out loud, inviting her students to repeat it to themselves silently with (or without) a corresponding mudra (hand gesture) that "seals" the intention, such as Anjali Mudra, which means "divine offering," or simply stated as "placing hands in prayer."

Lakshmi Voelker Chair Yoga Teacher Training (LVCYTT) / Certification

All Scheduled Training Dates:

getfitwhereyousit.com/about_Lakshmi_Voelker_fitness_exercise.html

New York Open Center - Lakshmi Voelker Teacher Training
www.opencenter.org/chair-yoga-teacher-training

Kripalu - Lakshmi Voelker Teacher Training
kripalu.org/presenters-programs/lakshmi-voelker-chair-yoga-teacher-training-module-1
kripalu.org/presenters-programs/presenters/brenda-yarnold

The
Doctor &
Nutritional
Intuitives &
Visionaries

KAZ MIRZA
Physician, Co-Founder of CHAD'S

Cancer. Heart Attacks. Alzheimer's. Diabetes. Stroke. What do these diseases all have in common? Certainly, all of them bring pain and suffering to the afflicted individual and their family, but medically speaking, these diseases are all chronic in their development. As opposed to acute, meaning less than six months to affliction, chronic diseases take at least six months to develop, often years, and are insidious in progression until the diagnosis occurs. Heart disease has been the #1 killer of men and women for the last 100 years, and remains so. Cancer is claiming lives at a rate alarmingly close to heart disease, with lung cancer the most common cancer among both men and women, due to the smoking epidemic. Breast and prostate cancers are the most common among women and men, respectively. Diabetes is one of the most common diseases in the United States with rates now more common among children than ever before. Type 2 diabetes is directly attributable to the standard American diet, and uncontrolled diabetes can lead to blindness, limb amputations, and cardiovascular disease. Alzheimer's disease progressively deteriorates the mind until loved ones are no longer recognizable, directions to home are no longer remembered, and times and places become unknown. There is currently no medical treatment for Alzheimer's disease in the market. A stroke can result in immediate death, or paralysis. Like heart attacks, the timing of stroke treatment can save the patient's life. These are examples of diseases that are very different in name, presentation, and processes, but perhaps the most important commonality among them is that these diseases are all preventable!

It is my job as a purveyor of medical knowledge to find natural cures because that is the best and most powerful way to heal. In my clinic I am dedicated to natural health, the maintaining of that health and healing patients with chronic diseases.

I think it is no coincidence that foods that heal your heart are often plant based and green in color and that the color green is associated with the heart chakra. I believe one of the best ways to balance your heart chakra as well as all of your chakras is through your diet. My chapter shares the benefits of whole foods and plant-based diets.

.

WHOLE FOODS, PLANT BASED DIETS AND THE HEART CHAKRA
Kaz Mirza, MD

"Let food be thy medicine, and medicine be thy food."
~ Hippocrates, the father of modern medicine

Many things in our lives are completely out of our control, however the choice to age gracefully without pain and suffering is in our hands. Cheeseburger or veggie burger? Eggs or oatmeal? Milk or non-dairy? Chicken or broccoli? We face decisions at every meal. All foods are certainly not created equal, and eating the best nutrition has more profound effects on health than drugs or surgery can ever provide. Do not let the current medical industry fool you. I've completed medical studies, including the US medical exams, worked in American hospitals, treated and advised patients, and managed the care of my father's heart disease for years, so I'm very familiar with the treatment options. The modern industry, IN MY OPINION, is counter to nature in many ways due to mega-profit generating private corporations, and as a result absolutely no nutrition is taught in medical school.

Now, the original Latin meaning of the word physician is based on the word physica, or "things relating to nature." It is my job as a purveyor of medical knowledge to cure the natural way because that is the best and most powerful way to heal. If all foods are not created equal, then which foods are bad and which foods are good for us? First, we must understand the underlying cause of chronic disease to answer this question. Let's take the #1 killer of both men and women, heart disease. LDL cholesterol builds up in the walls of the arteries, becomes oxidized, inflamed, and in the presence of hypertension can easily protrude and occlude the arteries that sustain our heart and life. Heart attacks can be deadly or debilitating if not treated right away. The symptoms include crushing chest pain, pain radiating to the left arm, and in women the pain can radiate to the neck. Sweating and shortness of breath can also accompany these symptoms.

The natural way to prevent and reverse chronic diseases, including heart disease, is to eat foods with no cholesterol or saturated fat which gets converted to cholesterol in the body. In nature, cholesterol is only found in animals. Our body creates all the cholesterol we need in the liver, without the need for any exogenous intake. The next step is to eat foods rich in antioxidant content. Oxidation occurs as a byproduct of energy production, and must be neutralized to prevent oxidative damage which can accelerate arterial blockage and aging. Inflammation is the next step in the process, and inflammation contributes to many chronic diseases in addition to the cancer, heart disease, Alzheimer's, diabetes, and stroke I've mentioned so far. If you suffer from arthritis, constipation, inflammatory bowel disease like Crohn's disease, or eczema then you will want to eat a diet rich in anti-inflammatory foods. There is mounting research about having healthy gut bacteria. Antibiotics and animal based diets tend to destroy good bacteria and promote the growth of bad bacteria in the gut, which leads to many uncomfortable bowel, skin and other chronic diseases. The last step to the progression of heart disease is blood pressure. Even this can be controlled by diet more safely and effectively than drugs.

So what should you not eat? Meat, fish, eggs, dairy, excessive salt, sugar, and processed foods should be promptly and immediately eliminated from your diet. Meat includes red meat, chicken, and fish. If it has a face or a mother, don't eat it. Perhaps that sounds extreme to you, to which I would respond, having your chest, or your loved one's, chest cavity cut open with the heart exposed, sounds far more extreme to me. That's what happens in coronary bypass graft surgery. These dietary restrictions will not cause any lack of essential vitamins, minerals, or nutrients, and works for everyone from children to elderly, from sick patients to triathletes.

What should you eat? The most comprehensive and reliable medical research recommends a strict adherence to a vegan diet. The more strictly you adhere, the least likely you are to experience life-ending and life-debilitating chronic diseases. A whole food, plant based diet is the way to reverse heart disease, many cancers, Alzheimer's, diabetes, stroke, bowel disease, skin disease, and even depression at their root cause. Disease can literally be turned off with adherence to this diet. I would require patients suffering from chronic disease to substitute animal protein with plant protein including beans and lentils. Heart patients report within weeks of being on this diet having less chest pain and more energy, and take less or even stop needing medications*. Patients often lose weight and lower their cholesterol, increase their antioxidant content, reduce inflammatory markers, and drop their blood pressure. These are real vital statistics for life, and an individual should know these numbers for their personal health management.

*Please consult your medical health practitioner before starting any new diet regime.

© Kaz Mirza, MD

ABOUT KAZ (DR. KAZ) MIRZA

Contact: chadscenter@gmail.com

DR. KAZ MIRZA was introduced to natural medicine at a very young age - his parents are both Indian and practiced Aryuveda. His family noted that he could be a good doctor and steered him in that direction since childhood. It was during his MD years, that Dr. Kaz began his focus on taking a natural approach to helping patients get out of the medical system, drugs, and surgeries.

Dr. Kaz is dedicated to changing your life by teaching you exactly how to live a long and healthy one. He can provide further guidance and support to you in his clinic.

Dr. Kaz along with his father founded CHAD'S. CHAD'S stands for Cancer, Heart, Alzheimer's, Diabetes, and Stroke and is a registered non-profit organization with the mission of preventing these diseases.

CHAD'S offers a program designed to deliver the fastest results for weight loss, lowering blood sugar, lowering blood pressure, lowering cholesterol, and doing it all 100% naturally.

STELLA PRESTON
Nutritionist and Health Coach

Working as a health coach professional, my own personal care is vital because without a balanced system whereby my energies are functioning at optimal level, I am unable to give others the care that they require.

Today, I find that I am highly intuitive about my emotional and physical state of being. This was not the case many years ago. I suffered the most incredible stress imaginable.

I sometimes look back and wonder how I managed to get out of bed. By the end of the day, I would collapse on my couch. It was a given that there was a stagnant flow of energy in my chakras. My healing came about when I focused on what I was eating and practiced yoga to open them. Since I refuse to take any medication to relieve stress, I used specific food choices to enhance my moods. I focused on cooking. I prepared my food with positive intention and ate slowly, being in the present moment.

To this day, I pay attention to my energy level making changes whenever I feel out of balance and assessing my emotional and physical state frequently.

A few years ago, I learned how toxic certain cookware could be. I replaced my cookware to eliminate toxins in my food. I started with only one medium size Titanium 316 pot a friend had lent me. Today I have an entire set. I'd be happy to share more information about this cookware with anyone who is interested.

I was trained in a number of modalities (Reiki, aromatherapy, nutrition, reflexology, many forms of bodywork therapies, herbal remedies, Bach Flower remedies, etc.) in my holistic medicine training, and all modality training starts with the understanding of chakras and blocked energies.

It is the starting point of any modality used to support the balancing of a person's core and in helping clients arrive at optimal health. Yet it was my own personal struggles that got me into chakra healing as a modality of its own.

My chapter has a wealth of information on understanding better how what one eats affects a person's chakra. I would love to help you figure out how chakras can benefit you, and if I can be of any help, please feel to reach out to me.

BALANCE YOUR CHAKRAS WITH FOOD
Stella Preston

Though the medical community has a fair understanding of the physical body and its complex systems that support life on a cellular level, doctors receive insufficient support to explore areas concerning energies that cannot be measured scientifically. Modern medicine has shown little investigative interest in the function of the biofield, also called the aura, a magnetic energy system that surrounds the physical body. This outside energy field is multi-layered and is connected to several wheels or energy power centers called chakras; they are spread out along the spine from head to foot and are power stations that are vital to physical health.

There are about 200 chakras in the body; however, seven major chakras vertically aligned along the spine as port of energy from which energy flow is carried by the Meridians, a network system of transportation, to associated organs in the body (Eden). There are 12 primary Meridians that act as transmitters of energy from the chakras to the vital organs of the physical body. To better understand the mutually symbiotic relationship between the aura, the chakras, and the meridians, one can consider this analogy; the aura is energy body also known as the biofield that surrounds the physical body. The chakras on the other hand are like the vital organs inside the body, and the Meridians are like the blood arterial system that transport oxygenated blood to the vital organs. Each chakra corresponds to a specific vital organ or parts of the body to control the energy level of that organ. When energy level is weak in a particular organ, this creates an environment for disease in that specific area. It is important that we pay attention to the healing of our energy bodies just as much as we do with our physical bodies. The physical and energy bodies have a co-dependent relationship. Prolonged tension, stress, or blockage originating from a specific chakra will manifest itself into symptoms or diseases. The chakras are bridges connecting our consciousness to our physical forms.

UNDERSTANDING THE FUNCTIONS OF CHAKRAS

What are the functions of the chakras? The chakras are basically energy systems much like the different systems of the physical body. They provide energy forces that sustain and maintain the workings of the vital organs and are connected to different state of well-being. The chakras affect our emotions, thoughts, and physical health while the reverse is also true; our emotional state, thoughts, and physical health can also affect the chakras hence affect our overall state of well-being. Because both bodies are interconnected much like the nucleus and mitochondria of a cell, there is a constant flux of change in our Aura or biofield energy. Every part of our being is made up of matter-energy just like the Universe. The laws of energy dictate that energy changes form depending upon its surroundings. For example, our Universe is made up of matter that constantly changes depending on surrounding influences. Given that chakras are energy forces, and meridians are the transport of such energy, the energy level of our chakras and flow of energy by our Meridians either support or deplete our physical, emotional, mental and spiritual health.

When one balances the chakras, a healthy environment is created for a healthy state of being in the physical form. But, to first balance these energy power centers, it is vital that one has a clear understanding of their functions and role in the physical body. The primary seven chakras transmit universal energy to and from the body through the meridians to "feed" vital organs. The energy flow being transported by the meridians is called qi/ki/prana. Each chakra controls energy flow to and from a specific vital organ. Thus, it is important to have an understanding of the overall functions and the resulting consequences of weak or strong essence of the seven major chakras.

FUNCTIONS AND ESSENCES OF THE SEVEN MAJOR CHAKRAS

As previously noted, the Meridians are pathways in the body which help energy to flow from the chakras to major systems in our bodies; this transfer of life-energy keeps these systems functioning at optimal levels. When the energy flow called qi, ki or prana is interrupted by imbalances in the body, energy flow is disrupted much like clogged arteries carrying oxygenated blood to various parts of the body. When impeding the chakra energy power centers and/or the meridians become "clogged" enabling energy flow to the systems of the body, an opportunistic environment for diseases flourishes thus creating a pathway for illnesses.

The Seven Major Chakras

While the meridians are responsible for the flow of life-energy, the seven chakras connect directly to vital organs located in different areas of the body. To address any imbalances, there are a number of therapies that can be used to balance our chakras. Nutrition is one that is often overlooked; when nutrition is used to balance our chakras, we are feeding both the energy body and physical body which support an environment for a strong spiritual connection with the universe.

Chakra	Locations on Body	Corresponding Body Organs
1st Root	At front – genital area and coccyx (tailbone) at base of spine.	Genitals, gateway to birth, kidneys, and spine.
2nd Sacral	Lower abdomen 2" below the naval and at 1st lumbar vertebra on spinal area.	Bladder, ovaries in women, kidneys, gall bladder, bowel, and spleen in men.
3rd Solar Plexus	Above naval area below center of breastbone and 8th thoracic vertebra.	Intestines, adrenals, pancreas, liver bladder, stomach, and upper spine.
4th Heart	Center of breastbone and 1st thoracic vertebra under shoulder blades.	Heart, lungs, thymus, and circulation.
5th Throat	At base of neck at hallow collarbone area and 3rd cervical vertebra in back.	Bronchial tubes, vocal cords, respiratory system, thyroid, mouth, tongue, and esophagus, ears, nose, and throat.
6th Third-Eye	At forehead between eyes and back at 1st cervical spinal area.	Eyes, pituitary and pineal glands, and brain
7th Crown	On top of head slightly to the back.	Spinal cord and brain stem

There are a number of considerations necessary to maintain vibrantly functioning chakras.

Food meets a basic biological need. So, that can be a good starting point. Also, because the physical and energy bodies are inter-connected, changes to the physical body with proper nutrition can affect the energy body simultaneously. All that said, eating nutritious foods is only one act in a chain of many. You can eat wholesome foods in a variety of colors, but if the cookware you use exposes you to high levels of chemical toxicity, the benefits of the nutrients in your food will be counterbalanced by the ill-effects of the chemicals you absorb with the food. If you get organic vegetables and yet watch them with chlorinated water instead of non-alkaline water, you are ingesting chemicals that can have a negative impact on your physical body.

In addition, keeping the body well hydrated with adequate clean alkaline water is beneficial for optimal health. Of course, sufficiently masticating your food, making deliberate food choices, listening to your body and abstaining from over eating or too much drinking, being present, and cooking with positive intentions are all ways of feeding your body purposely to balance the chakras.

These factors often get little consideration. I cook for friends with the intention that I will love them with my cooking. So I tell myself that I will cook with love in my heart. The thoughts with which I begin my cooking come from my energy body and vibrate into the food. Intention is just as important as the ingredients.

To control certain aspects of your life and the personal challenges we all face, it is necessary to embark on a lifestyle change that heals blockages in all areas of our energy and physical bodies.

When one is aware of specific organs and their corresponding chakras, certain types of foods can be consumed to release blockages and strengthen specific energy centers. This will address the symptoms at their origin and thereby create an environment for healing and promoting a healthier function of an entire system. When one area is out of sync, it compromises other areas in the physical and energy bodies.

WAYS TO MAINTAIN VIBRANTLY FUNCTIONING CHAKRAS

There are several ways to heal your chakras with food. One way is to intuitively locate a specific chakra imbalance and then use specific foods to balance that chakra. A second way to is to tune up all seven major chakras by eating foods on a rotating basis or by consuming a wide variety of foods daily – enough to benefit several chakras per day. Another way is to identify the emotional issues and physical symptoms and match them with the chakra and its corresponding foods. In other words, unblock chakras with nutrition by identifying energy stagnation manifested by physical symptoms or emotional issues and then consume specific foods that will remove the stagnation.

BALANCING CHAKRAS WITH NUTRITION

Balancing chakras with nutrition is perhaps like feeding two birds with one scone. You feed the physical body while also balancing the energy body.

For example, the root chakra located at the coccyx (tail bone) is concerned with feeling grounded in the physical world whereby one possesses a strong foundation and sense of security. Insecurities of any kind might suggest that this chakra is weak or closed. Therefore, one would benefit from eating tomatoes, strawberries, raspberries, beets, and root veggies such as turnip, pumpkins, garlic, rutabagas, and pomegranate to name a few.

The root chakra also controls the birth pathway and genitals, and sex organs. In many cultures, pomegranates are considered an aphrodisiac representing fertility and abundance (Dr. Axe - draxe.com, "7 Incredible Pomegranate Seeds Benefits," #3 is life-saving.) Therefore, pomegranates would be an excellent food to consume if symptoms of blockage involve the reproductive system.

Also if you are having lower back pains or money issues, as well as survival instinct and needs it would be advised to eat foods that are red in color as that is the color of the Root Chakra.

The chakras are a network of energy centers and when one is out of the balance, it creates a domino effect causing all of them to be imbalanced.

As for the Crown Chakra, there are no foods associated with it. This is because the food that balances the crown chakra is of a different matter: oxygen and sunshine.

I remember the last time my Crown Chakra was full of energy. I experienced an ethereal type of existence. I had been on Purium's 10-Day Transformation Program. It did lots to balance my crown chakra. I felt as if I were functioning at the highest level of consciousness. I performed tasks that remained undone for years in that period of time.

Disclaimer: The Transformation Program is intended for use only by healthy adults. You should consult your physician or other health care professional before starting this or any other nutritional supplemental program to determine if it is right for your needs. And if you experience at any time discomfort, distress or any other symptom, please discontinue using the products immediately and consult a physician.

Still today, I think with greater clarity when I eat optimally. I feel more spiritually connected to the Universe when I eat just enough to sustain my physical body. One lesson learned as I look back at my young self is that before one can repair any imbalances in the body, one must be intuitively in tuned with what depletes and restores one's life energy.

234

FOOD FOR YOUR CHAKRAS

Root Chakra (red)

Psychological Issues	Some Physical Imbalances
Loneliness/insecurities/ depression/indecisiveness/ feeling ungrounded/phobias.	Fatigue/obesity/sciatica constipation/Leukemia/lower extremities/varicose veins/diarrhea/sexual dysfunctions.
Chakra Balancing Foods	
Red apples/beets/ tomatoes/paprika/cayenne/strawberries/raspberries/pomegranates/ root vegetables: sweet potatoes; carrots; turnips.	

Sacral (orange)

Psychological Issues	Some Physical Imbalances
Eating disorders/addictions/low self-confidence/ low libido/dependency issues.	Sexual dysfunctions/uterine problems/alcoholism/ drug use/allergies/eating disorder.
Chakra Balancing Foods	
Carrots/mango/oranges/orange peppers/peaches/apricots/sweet potatoes/ nuts & seeds: flax, almonds, cinnamon, lots of water as sacral is associated with water.	

Solar Plexus (yellow)

Psychological Issues	Some Physical Imbalances
Lack of memory/insomnia eating disorders/fearful sugar addiction lack of concentration.	Digestive/intestinal disorders/food allergies/ulcers, hepatitis/diabetes/hypoglycemia/obesity/ eczema/acne/stress-related skin conditions
Chakra Balancing Foods	
Bananas/pineapple/corn/lemon/yellow curry/ complex carbs: oats brown rice/spelt/rye/farrobeans/vegetables and sprouted grains	

Heart (green)

Psychological Issues	Some Physical Imbalances
Apathetic/distrustful/detached/ unforgiving/hopelessness/ faithlessness.	Pneumonia/upper-back pain/asthma/breast problems/respiratory problems/premature aging/upper-back pain.

Chakra Balancing Foods - Greens such as kale/broccoli/ Spinach/chard/dandelion greens/parsley/celery/cucumber/zucchini/matcha green tea/ avocado/lime/mint/peas/spirulina/green apples.

Throat (blue/black)

Psychological Issues	Some Physical Imbalances
Nervousness/anxiety/fearful/ADD/ poor coping skills/feelings of isolation.	Nasal/sinus problems/sore throat/jaw pain/TMJ/Voice loss/thyroid problems/teeth and gum problems.

Chakra Balancing Foods
Blueberries/blackberries/coconut/water/herbal teas/ raw honey/lemon and fruit that grow on trees such as apples, pears, and plums

Third-Eye (indigo)

Psychological Issues	Some Physical Imbalances
Headaches/migraines/nightmares/seizures/ neurological disorders/ learning difficulties.	Eye problems/glaucoma/ear problems/hearing difficulties/ spinal conditions/scalp/hair issues.

Chakra Balancing Foods
Purple grapes/purple kale/blueberries/purple cabbage/eggplant/purple carrots/cacao

Crown (white/violet)

Psychological Issues	Some Physical Imbalances
Depression/confusion/loss of faith/disconnected feelings/dementia/epilepsy/schizophrenia.	Light sensitivity/headaches/dementia/ autoimmune disorders/neurological disorders.

Chakra Balancing Foods
Fasting and detoxing are most essential for crown balancing.

ABOUT STELLA PRESTON

Website: www.beonhealthy.com
Contact: smp3808@gmail.com

STELLA PRESTON is a Health Coach in New York City. She began her holistic career in Australia earning a post-graduate diploma in Remedial Therapies/holistic practices at the Australasian College of Natural Therapies and additional training at the Nature Care College of Naturopathic & Traditional Medicine. Upon completing her studies, she practiced as a Natural Remedial Therapist/practitioner to help clients foster conditions that help alleviate their symptoms of dis-ease and promote well-being on all levels.

Upon her return to the United States after nearly 12 years living overseas, she continued her training with The Institute for Integrative Nutrition as a Certified Holistic Health Counselor. She has continued to search for traditional remedies from around the world to incorporate into her practice.

Working with her, you will learn to tackle your well-being by utilizing multiple modalities instead of pharmaceutical drugs to address any types of discomfort.

ASHLEY SPERBER
Holistic Health Coach, Nutritionist, Chef and Aromatherapist

I was first introduced to chakras by learning that mine were closed, from a stranger on the street in Manhattan. Even as an expert New Yorker, I may have found this unsolicited insight to be unnerving, but that wasn't the case. Through the act of something I call "divine intervention," I became receptive to a message I didn't know I needed to hear. Operating at a high functioning pace disabled me from reflecting inward, surveying my true needs, and assessing if they're even met. I think many of us choose to ignore who or what has failed us, especially when we ourselves are the culprit. It wasn't until a complete stranger informed me of my own personal limitations that I was ready to experience growth and all it had to offer

Working with the chakras has brought me healing in ways that I didn't know were possible or necessary. Immersing myself in their wisdom helped me understand the beliefs and agreements that are so deeply ingrained in the woman I identify myself to be. Applying the ancient techniques of opening and balancing each energy center has provided me with blissful pride and self-worth. The shifts didn't happen overnight. Nothing was comfortable, easy or fun, but no expedition to self-discovery should be. Facing ourselves, for all of us, is terrifying, and that's why many won't do it. I wanted to change that. With my own personal journey as the inspiration, I committed to ushering others into their own life of liberation

I completed certifications in several healing modalities that were each esteemed for their ability to enhance, or "raise the vibration" of the chakras. In 2015, I started a health coaching practice in New York, which has allowed me to support others in their transformation. As a health coach, it is my responsibility to identify and address patterned behaviors that are rooted into the belief system we subscribe to. My clients come to me because they aspire to get into better health, but they don't realize that their self-inflicted holding pattern is what prevents them from getting there.

Over the years, I have developed a proficiency in recognizing chakra imbalances when they reveal themselves as character "flaws" or ailments. Almost all of my clients have root imbalances, because that chakra is responsible for how we relate to the physical self. When the root is healed, the client recognizes their self-worth. Once that value has been instilled, they feel deserving and able to commit to a balanced lifestyle.

NOURISH YOUR CHAKRAS
Ashley Sperber

Chakras are energy centers located in the body, regarded for their impact on our physical, emotional and spiritual well-being. Dozens of varying chakras exist in each of us, however, in this chapter we will only visit the primary seven. Each center is a vortex; a swirling current of energy that sustains its own pace and direction. We can raise the frequency and improve the condition of each chakra through several activities, but few are as fun as eating!

There are a few different approaches to nourishing each chakra through diet. One school of thought is called "eating the rainbow", in which color therapy is applied. Each chakra is associated with a specific pigmentation, beginning with red at the base and ending with violet at the crown. The concept behind this ideology is that surrounding yourself with (and in this case, consuming) colors in correspondence with each chakra, will enhance their abilities. For this reason, I have provided the colorful foods that are traditionally paired with each one. Alternatively, I practice a different method which is action based, as opposed to color based. In every segment, I will briefly describe the properties of each chakra, and how they are illustrated and supported through representational foods.

Before getting started, I would like to briefly emphasize the importance of what "nourishment" truly entails. When we think of nourishment we think of food, because that is what feeds us when we are hungry, yet we seldom pay mind to what satisfies us through other means. As humans, we have a need and desire to connect, love, learn and expand. Food does not provide us with any of those abilities; experience does. As I discuss the nutritional needs of each chakra throughout this chapter, please take note of the emotional nourishment that is also necessary to fully support that part of the body and soul.

ROOT CHAKRA

The first chakra, or the "root," is the foundation of the system and it's located at the base of the spine. Because the root fundamentally supports the infrastructure of this sequence, its healthy development and strength is required to maintain balance in the individual. These energy centers are so interdependent that if one of them is imbalanced, preceding or succeeding chakras will be influenced.

The health of the root is highlighted in this chapter because it governs our relationship with food. In fact, an imbalance of the root can result in eating disorders- both compulsive and deprivational. This chakra is responsible for how we establish our physical identity and observe self-preservation. When we have a poor relationship with ourselves, it is demonstrated through the traits and characteristics we possess. Limited desire and/or ability to uphold proper nutrition, fitness regimens, or self-care practices are all indications of an imbalanced root. From a nutrition standpoint, there must be a tremendous emphasis on developing the root before focusing on any other area of the body. Only after we have implemented mindful eating can we build upon the framework of our bodies.

An imbalanced root chakra will emotionally result in fear and will physically result in eating disorders, constipation, or joint pain. The root chakra's element is Earth, its energy state is solid, and its purpose is to ground us. Because of these factors, the food group that is recommended to signify and support the root is protein. Proteins are the building blocks from which we, ourselves, are established upon. Because the root chakra is anatomically associated with the adrenal glands, individuals will experience fatigue and lethargy when they are not grounded.

There are several different sources of protein that support the root chakra, but the most common is from land animals. When purchasing meat, always look for "grass fed beef and dairy" and "free range chicken and eggs" (or "wild caught seafood" for sea animals). In lieu of animal protein, plant based proteins, such as legumes, nuts and seeds can be supplemented for any conscientious vegans. In fact, conflicting evidence suggests that consuming animals inhibits us from attaining expanded consciousness. I suggest making a sound choice based off your own personal belief system and nutrition requirements.

In addition to protein, root vegetables are also recommended due to their connotation. Beets, parsnips, turnips, carrots, rutabaga, yams/sweet potatoes, radishes, ginger, turmeric, garlic and onions are wonderful examples of vegetables that are buried deep in the Earth, retaining all of the soil's minerals and beneficial microbes. These foods signify grounding in a literal sense because they spend their entire existence beneath the surface.

When sourcing produce, it is ideal to consume organically grown fruits and vegetables in order to avoid hormone disruption, immunodeficiencies and carcinogens. The detrimental effects of pesticides have been critically analyzed; however, genetically modified foods are still under scrutiny. Glyphosate, aka "round-up", is the most widely used pesticide that is now responsible for sterilizing our microbiome. Our gut biomes are also sterilized via antibiotics administered to conventionally raised animals. Without active colonies in our gut, we risk suffering from inflammation, depression, weight gain, insomnia, and several health imbalances that are subject to terminal illness. Choosing organic, local vendors is the safest, most viable option in sourcing your food responsibly. The food we put into our bodies, becomes our bodies, so don't settle for less!

Eat the rainbow (red): red apples, cherries, pomegranate, red peppers, watermelon, strawberries, raspberries, cranberries, goji berries, hot peppers, tomatoes, beets, radishes and kidney beans.

SACRAL CHAKRA

The sacral chakra is located about 3 inches below the navel, and is commonly identified as the "womb". This area of the body governs our desires- both emotion based and sex oriented. When we are imbalanced in the second chakra, we emotionally face guilt and the undying need for self-gratification. Physically, we suffer from infertility, sexual dysfunction, bladder infections, lower back pain and poor circulation. The sacral chakra's element is water and its purpose is to create fluidity in the body. In order to facilitate a flow of energy throughout our cells, nourishing liquids are the designated food group assigned to the sacral.

The glands that are associated with this chakra are the gonads, which means that we operate from a place of nurturance. Nurturance wholly encompasses this area of the body, which is creation. Fundamentally, we create life with our gonads, through the exchange of fluids. It is here that we learn of the significant correlation between our sexuality and emotions. We first plant a seed with our sexuality, and when that seed blossoms into a being, we then bestow that blessing with abundant love, care and protection. Recently, human beings have over complicated this process, resulting in both sexual and emotional dysfunction. As with any chakra, an emotional block, manifests into a physical ailment. When emotions are poorly managed, one might find themselves to be sexually deviant, or conversely, undeserving of intimacy. Desire can be a very confusing feeling to apprehend, especially if one hasn't explored the basis of their emotional ties. All too often, we are consumed by the fast paced lifestyle surrounding us, as opposed to what resides within us. We look for these distractions at times, because it's easier than coping with the storm beneath the surface.

Stagnation in the body can be a result of these erratic behaviors. Denying the body's need for physical contact or the soul's need to express itself will undoubtedly cause mayhem in this chakra. Consuming liquids is a metaphor just as much as it is a literal action. Remain in motion. Honor a feeling as it comes, and let it flow freely through you. Don't block it; embrace it. Understand its purpose, and then set it free. Do not attach yourself to it; it does not define you. We spend so much time avoiding our feelings, they unconsciously consume us and we become burdened by them. Accepting our truth is the only path to freedom.

Water stands on its own as the ubiquitous liquid of life. Roughly 60% of our body composition is made up of water, making this resource a rather vital substance for healthy development. We absorb water from many different factors, including our food and environment. The quality of water we ingest and absorb is pertinent because it has the capabilities of enhancing or harming our well-being. Our taps are contaminated with traces of heavy metals, synthetic minerals, and even pharmaceutical drugs. For that reason, I strongly advocate for water filtration systems. Some systems are equipped to increase the alkalinity of the water, which is a benefit that's been recently revered for reducing inflammation in the body. Bottled water is also equipped with detriments due to the plastic it's housed in. If the plastic is not BPA free, the chemicals will leach into the water at raised temperatures, affecting us internally. Externally, our planet is so overbearingly polluted with plastic, that it makes up 40% of our ocean's surfaces. Needless to say, bottled water is not a viable option for those reasons, alone.

Other liquids that would support the sacral chakra are beverages, broths and soups. Juices, teas and coffee each promote the flow of energy in their own unique way. Juice surges the body's cells with an energetic charge via enzymes and nutrients; whereas coffee offers an adrenaline high via caffeine boost. Tea may offer a dose of nutrients, caffeine or both!

Broths and soups are notably the most efficient vehicles of vitamins and minerals. Through the process of osmosis, all of the vitality of the plants and proteins will transmute into the liquid they're cooked in. Soup is also ideal, due to its warming and soothing nature on the digestive tract, which is necessary for efficient absorption and assimilation of nutrients.

Eat the rainbow (orange): oranges, acorn squash, butternut squash, nectarines, peaches, persimmons, guava, papaya, sweet potatoes, cantaloupe, mango, apricots, carrots, turmeric, pumpkin, and salmon.

SOLAR PLEXUS CHAKRA

The solar plexus resides at the center of the torso, just below the ribcage. This area is known as our "power house" and it is responsible for how we metabolically synthesize energy. This chakra governs the relationship we have with ourselves, through ego. It is here that we learn the aforementioned importance of a solid root foundation. If the individual is not grounded, their sense of self will be amplified here, creating a substantially overactive solar plexus. Emotional imbalances will cause the individual to exercise their use of power over others. They will view themselves in a higher regard, believing they are somehow superior. Alternatively, an underactive solar plexus will cause an individual to experience shame and self-hatred. Physical manifestations of an imbalanced plexus will generally result in digestive malfunction, ranging from acid reflux, to liver toxicity, to IBS. A distended belly is an unsuspecting indication that the individual has a need for control, while paradoxically lacking it themselves.

Much like the sun at the epicenter of our universe, the element associated with the solar plexus is fire. Conveniently, our very own "digestive fire" is located in our stomach, the preliminary site of the GI tract, where we process food. The gland that is associated with this chakra is the pancreas which plays a quintessential role in digestion. Digestive enzymes produced by the pancreas are secreted into the small intestine, promoting the further breakdown of food after it has left the stomach. The pancreas is also subject to producing and supplying the blood with insulin, which regulates blood sugar. When the production or response of insulin is impaired, the individual faces elevated glucose in the blood; this suggests that diabetes is also a physical manifestation of an imbalanced solar plexus.

Carbohydrates are the macronutrient that is responsible for providing energy to the body, thus making starches the designated food group of the solar plexus. Starch is a vast generalization for any food that is comprised of polysaccharides, also known as glycogen. Glycogen is multi-branched glucose that is only formed once it interacts with water (hence, the significant role of water in the diet, which supports the interdependence of the chakras). All carbs are not created equal, however.

There are two classifications of carbohydrates: simple and complex. Simple carbs are clinically defined as possessing only one or two sugar molecules. In dietary terminology, simple sugars are carbohydrates that lack dietary fiber. They are readily available and quickly metabolized by the body, providing little sustenance. Refined sugar is the apex of all simple carbs. It is generally extrapolated through the manufacturing processed, and is often disguised as one of its 60+ aliases, such as high fructose corn syrup, or any ingredient that has the suffix "-ose" (maltose, dextrose, sucrose, etc.). Even within the classification of simple sugars, sweeteners cause varying responses in the body. Some simple sugars such as local maple syrup or raw local honey possess natural occurring vitamins, minerals and enzymes that manufactured sugar and syrups do not.

Complex carbohydrates are made up of sugar molecules that are strung together in long, complex chains. They are found in plant matter, in their natural state, accompanied by the flesh or dietary fiber. Dietary fiber is comprised of soluble and insoluble components, both of which provide the sensation of satiety in the individual. Without fiber, our appetites become insatiable, which is evidently dangerous. Complex carbohydrates can be found in fruits, vegetables and grains, preferably in an unadulterated form.

Eat the rainbow (yellow): corn, lemon, bananas, pineapple, spaghetti squash, summer squash, delicata squash, mustard, nutritional yeast, yellow peppers, yellow tomatoes, yellow apples, yellow potatoes, chickpeas, lentil, eggs.

HEART CHAKRA

The heart is the one chakra that needs no introduction. Each of us has identified the vital life force centrally located in our chest, since that first time a love interest graced our presence. The heart is a magnificently strong, yet ever-so-fragile part of the body that carries indelible marks of those we have loved. The heart may arguably be the most relevant of all the chakras because of the boundless capacity of love it can contain. This philosophy is exemplified through the chakra system the same way a reservoir provides as irrigation. When we are depleted in most aspects of our lives, the heart sends an electric current of love to the areas of our body and soul that need healing. If the site of that resource is dry, then the being will suffer; either imminently, or even worse, in a prolonged state.

The heart is the fourth or middle chakra, signifying a point of convergence. Whether the individual is enduring a liberating current (root to crown) or a manifesting current (crown to root), the heart is what stabilizes our development. It is the control center that facilitates balance. One teaching we must ascertain, is well illustrated by the phrase "you can't pour from an empty cup." Choosing to love yourself before anyone else is not selfish, it is responsible and compassionate. If we do not have a healthy relationship with ourselves, we are incapable of giving anything more to others.

Do you ever wonder how love is conceived? How it mysteriously travels through the ether and nestles its way into your heart? For that reason alone, I feel it's no surprise that the element associated with this chakra is air. Just like love, we cannot taste, touch, see, smell or hear air- nor can we live without it. Love is what unifies us, and is aptly displayed through our social identity. Emotionally, a balanced heart will righteously practice self-acceptance, promoting peace as its mantra. An underactive chakra will allow the individual to be consumed by grief, from lack of healing and empathy. An overactive chakra will inhibit discernment, provoking codependency and loose boundaries. Physical imbalances will result as chest pains or weakened lung capacity, which can be precursors to asthma, coronary disease, hypertension and lung disease.

The gland that is associated with the heart is the thymus, which is extremely unique in relationship to the other endocrine glands. The thymus only secretes hormones until puberty is reached and then it is converted to adipose tissue. This gland is responsible for the maturation of T cells which helps the body fight off antigens that attack it. The most nutrient bearing food group that supports this process is vegetables. Vegetables provide as the most abundant sources of vitamins and minerals, due to the absorption of nutrients derived from the soil and sea. In the circle of life, organisms decompose, transferring minerals into the Earth. When a seedling grows into a plant, it's built-in uptake system absorbs those minerals, while also photosynthesizing the energy from the sun, creating vitamins. In this process, the plant takes in all four elements: earth, air, water and sun (fire), which is the summation of all the chakras corresponding elements that have been previously referenced. It is at the heart, where they all conspire to form one balanced entity.

As formerly stated, mostly organic vegetables should be consumed, only. Ideally, eating produce that is local, and in season should also be practiced. When we regularly eat foods that are not indigenous to the area we inhabit, our body becomes confused, consequently compromising our immunity. In the grand scheme of human evolution, we have only been able to eat whatever we want in the last few decades, which hasn't permanently affected our DNA, quite yet. In short, this means the body expects to only eat food from the land that it lives on, enabling it to be primed accordingly. There are several online guides that can track your location, and advise of the produce closely available to you. Farmer's markets and food co-operatives are ideal shopping alternatives that predominantly offer local, sustainable goods.

Lastly, it is preferred to diversify your intake of (all foods, but especially,) veggies as much as possible. There are hundreds of vegetables in the world, but in any given region, there are dozens in season to accommodate your palate and nutritional requirements. Habitually changing your diet introduces a range of nutrients and benefits, including an advanced microbiome. As briefly mentioned in the root chakra segment, the microbiome is an ecosystem of mutually beneficial bacteria, viruses, parasites and fungus that is housed in our small intestine. The more populated that ecosystem is, the healthier we become.

Eat the rainbow (green): spinach, broccoli, kale, arugula, peas, green beans, zucchini, green peppers, dandelion greens, swiss chard, collard greens, parsley, cilantro, sage, thyme, basil, rosemary, chives, green onions, asparagus, cabbage, celery, limes, green tea, brussel sprouts, seaweed, avocado, pear, kiwi, green apples, green grapes, starfruit, honeydew melon, tomatillo.

THROAT CHAKRA

The throat chakra is unmistakably located in the throat, specifically at the site of our larynx, or "voice box". Predictably, this chakra governs our communication, both inward and outward. It is the forum from which our expression is conveyed. The element that is designated to this chakra is sound, which suggests that the energy state is vibration. Through vibration, the transmission of ideas is exchanged, which is also known as language. There are several forms of language, some of which require no linguistics at all. This notion will be further explored in the succeeding chakras.

The throat is associated with our sense of creativity and self-expression. Through dictation, we actively manifest our world that both reside within and outside of us. Every idea that's conceived, every word that's spoken and every action performed defines our character. Through these processes, we are creating our reality. Conscious communication is a practice that is under-utilized in today's society. Many individuals are unaware of the consequence our words can have on others, and especially, ourselves. Overactive throat chakras are readily displayed through gossiping, posturing and dishonesty, while under activity is indicated through flaky, unreliable and inconsistent communication. Physical malfunctions will result in ear, nose and throat discomfort, or severe pain in the neck and shoulders.

Anatomically, the larynx is enclosed by the thyroid, indicating that the throat chakra is responsible for the healthy development and maintenance of this gland. The rate of thyroid disease has been on the rise exponentially, and I firmly believe the prevalence of it is both diet and environment related. While I have mostly touched on the impact of balanced nutrition on the chakra system, I feel that noting the environmental factors that affect the thyroid is critical. Radiation or EMF (electromagnetic field) is an invisible force field that emanates from any electrical or wireless device. Every day we hold our cell phones to our face to make a call. To further exacerbate this issue, handheld devices such as bluetooth earpieces are now being implanted into the sides of our brain (via ear canal), sending electromagnetic frequencies into the cranium. While this is likely to affect the subsequent 6th and 7th chakra more, this new development undeniably impacts how we communicate and metabolize our very own thoughts.

According to ancient literature, the food group that best supports the throat chakra is fruit. The theory behind this is that fruit is viewed as "highest on the food chain" because when it is ripe, it will naturally fall to the ground, thwarting the need to disrupt the plant's life cycle. Fruits also contain natural occurring sugars in conjunction with fiber, so they provide as a means of sustainable energy.

Through personal experience, I have found that the food that best supports the thyroid is seaweed. Before the environmental factors of Fukushima and radiation, the ocean was the best source of trace minerals that were available to us. Now that we have polluted our own waters with waste and toxic chemicals, we must be very conscientious of where our sea vegetables are sourced from. Seaweed is not only abundant in iodine, it also quantitatively contains vitamin K, iron and calcium, which many of us have deficiencies in as well. There are several varieties of seaweed that offer different flavors, textures and cooking uses. Kelp is generally the most nutrient dense, and I often put a sheet or two of it in almost every pot of soup I make. It marginally seasons (salts) the soup, but more importantly, all the nutrients transfer into the liquid.

Eat the rainbow (blue): blueberries, blue corn, indigo milkcap mushrooms, blue potatoes, blue majik spirulina, blue cheese, blue lobster.

THIRD EYE AND CROWN CHAKRA

These two chakras are deliberately grouped together because neither can be nourished by nutritional means. This is due to the fact that these two chakras are not associated with any bodily processes. In other words, the third eye and crown are perceived to be a separate entity from the chakras that precede them. In fact, it is believed that the only way to enhance the ability of the upper chakras is to avoid food altogether.

The third eye is located between the brows, at the center of the forehead. The element associated with this chakra is light, which transcends as luminescence in its energy state. The third eye houses our intuition and imagination- both being neglected concessions in our fast paced existence. Through this vantage point, we are granted the ability to inwardly reflect, while also identifying with others. The third eye captures what we cannot view through sight, however, should we choose to deny it, illusion may breed.

When the third eye is imbalanced, individuals suffer from vision impairment, headaches, sleep disorders and nightmares. The corresponding gland is the pineal gland, which is responsible for producing melatonin and stabilizing the circadian rhythm. When the circadian rhythm is off course, the entire body is negatively impacted. Disrupted sleep most prominently affects the hormones, causing a domino effect on stress and subsequently, body mass. Having a consistent sleep pattern is paramount in the development and maintenance of our health. Consider 8 hours of sleep to be the "food group" that is required for optimal well-being. The human adult needs 7-9 hours of sleep a night. When we sleep for any less than 6 hours, our body feels stressed and we start to store fat. Of course, this should only be a concern if compromised sleep is habitual; infrequent, curtailed sleep sessions will not render the same consequence.

The crown chakra is the seventh and final chakra, located at the top skull. The element that correlates with the crown is thought, which then conceives consciousness in its energy state. Consciousness is unequivocally the most pertinent practice to apprehend in our time here on this planet. While I have held love and grounding in the highest regard, nothing quite compares to the bliss that consciousness can grant us. Our present day culture has conspired to put all human beings on auto pilot. There is a theory that suggests that certain ideologies have been institutionalized to keep citizens of the community regulated for the betterment of society. Many of us are raised to be conformists, without even realizing it. We are instructed to go to school, get good grades, go to college, get a well-paying job, have a family, work until retirement, then live a few short years before we pass. What happens if we don't do those things? What if we feel called to independently think? We are outcast, judged, and ridiculed. This is where the liberation of consciousness can relieve you. Each of us are souls bound by the body we are born into, but it is our choice to remain captive or to be free through our thoughts.

When the crown chakra is imbalanced we are harnessed by attachments. Attachments can be anything from material items, to people, to substances. We hold onto things outside of ourselves because we lack connection and understanding within us. They are a means of sought out distraction, disabling inward reflection. There are no physical manifestations of a crown imbalance, but depression, alienation and confusion are all severe emotional discourses that inevitably will affect the entire individual.

The pituitary gland is the final gland at the top of the endocrine system, providing as the correspondent to the crown. As mentioned above, there is no sustenance that can sufficiently support the crown. It is recommended that the individual experiment with a regimented meditative practice to stimulate the pituitary gland. Meditation has been a traditional discipline observed for thousands of years. It is true that can be a very challenging method, but much like everything else that is worth experiencing in life, patience must be exerted. Meditation grants us the ability to hone many skills, particularly the psychological function that each chakra requires: grounding, desire, willpower, love, communication, intuition, and understanding. It also increases our attention span, focus, patience, stress management, impulse control, and self-acceptance. Countless studies have rendered that the brain can be rewired through meditation. If there is something we don't love about ourselves or others, we have the power to alter it, but only after surrendering to our consciousness.

In opposition to nourishment, fasting is also considered to be another instrument that may be utilized in supporting the crown chakra. Fasting is also a prehistoric technique that has been utilized for myriad health benefits. The belief supporting this practice starts with the digestive system. There are 365 days of the year, and we spend each of them consuming, day in and day out. Of course, we are relieved when we sleep at night, but while we are awake and active, we almost always have food metabolizing within us. The benefits of fasting result in reduced hunger levels, reduced cravings, cannibalized toxins, the promotion of detoxification, normalized insulin levels, cleared complexion, reduced blood pressure, and boosted immunity.

Again, these benefits must be implemented as a result of preceding chakra imbalances. Although the correction of these metabolic impediments would alleviate discomfort in the individual, nothing transforms a person more than the clarity they receive in their mind. When we deprive ourselves of the habit of eating, we learn to appreciate so much more out of life- not just the food we eat, but the relationships we uphold and the character we possess. Stripping ourselves of everyday luxuries, teaches us gratitude and awareness. So much of our lives revolve around the ritual of eating, that we become further distracted from everything else that holds importance in our lives. Analogous to meditation, fasting teaches us discipline and self-control. These ancient practices have diminished over time because our lifestyle has become so fast paced that we are perpetually overstimulated. Our attention spans are dwindling because we allow them to. Through these modalities, we have the power to expand and evolve.

Eat the rainbow (purple): eggplant, blackberries, plums, purple cabbage, red grapes, figs, purple cauliflower, purple carrots, purple asparagus, purple kohlrabi, elderberries, purple kale, murasaki (Japanese sweet potato)

Everything that is intended to nourish us is gifted from the Earth or provided within us. Our society has become so far removed from what is innately intrinsic to us that we have subscribed to the confines of its evolution. After all of the insight and advice I offer, please take away this one notion: be mindful. Mindful of the food you eat- the way you select it, chew it, absorb it, digest and become it. Mindful of the thoughts that dwell in your mental space that become your everyday actions. Mindful of your emotions, how you express them and how they impact others. Our time here is limited but not limiting. The choice is yours to make what you will of it!

© Ashley Sperber

ABOUT ASHLEY SPERBER, INHC

Website: www.ashleysperber.com
Contact: ashley@ashleysperber.com

Ashley Sperber is a holistic health coach and chef that inspires her clientele to achieve balance through mindful nourishment. In her NYC based practice, Ashley combines her skilled training along with her developed intuition to create personalized programs that facilitate her client's transformations. Outside of her practice, she curates and hosts integrative wellness workshops, plant based cooking classes and educational speaking engagements, utilizing her diverse breadth of healing modalities.

Ashley earned a Bachelor of Science in Sociology and Hospitality Management at the University of New Hampshire, followed by her continued education at the Institute of Integrative Nutrition. After acquiring her Holistic Health certification at IIN, she was then certified in Western Herbalism, Level II Reiki, and Emotional Freedom Technique at the NY Open Center. Ashley has also obtained a certification in Aromatherapy at the NY Institute of Aromatherapy, and is presently earning her 200 hour Registered Yoga Training certification.

Amidst all of her practices, Ashley has always been most passionate and experienced in preparing healthy, innovative culinary creations. She believes that the relationship we each have with food corresponds with the relationship we uphold with ourselves. Most recently, Ashley has refined her psychic and mediumship abilities, which enables her to target the root cause of emotional eating imbalances. She believes that once we break free of the holding patterns we confine ourselves to, we can live a freeing and fulfilling existence with ourselves and each other.

Roasted Root Vegetables Recipe

Yield 6-8 servings
Time 45 minutes

Ingredients
2 cups root vegetables (carrots, parsnips, beets, rutabaga, etc.)
chopped into 1 inch cubes
1 tablespoon + 1/2 teaspoon coconut oil
2 cloves garlic, chopped
1 tablespoon freshly chopped herbs (parsley, basil, dill, sage, rosemary, thyme, chives, etc.), plus more for garnish
Sea salt and fresh ground black pepper to taste
1/4 cup pumpkin seeds
1/4 teaspoon smoked paprika
2 tablespoons blackstrap molasses

Directions
(vegetables**)**
Set oven to 400 degrees
Line a baking sheet with parchment paper.
Toss root vegetables in 1 tablespoon coconut oil, garlic, herbs, and salt and pepper in a medium sized bowl.
Place vegetables in the oven for 15 minutes
Remove from oven and toss
Return to oven for another 15 minutes.

(pumpkin seeds)
Toss pumpkin seeds in 1/2 teaspoon coconut oil and smoked paprika, and place on a separate baking sheet
Place sheet in the oven for 3-5 minutes or until golden brown
Remove sheet from the oven
Remove seeds from sheet and allow to cool
Once root vegetables are done roasting, transfer to a serving dish and drizzle molasses on top, then add pumpkin seeds and fine herbs.

© Ashley Sperber

ELIZABETH TRIPP
Intuitive Healer and Certified Nutritionist/Dietitian

The chakra system has an integral role in my professional and personal life. As a spiritual being the chakra system is a tool to continue my soul's growth on this Earth journey. Personally and professionally, it is important I'm in tune with the energy flow of my body. I believe the body serves as a mirror to see myself and others clearer - mentally, physically and spiritually.

The chakras, especially the crown and third eye, are my gateways to the spiritual dimension. They are my access points to the infinite knowledge available to the soul on the Earth Journey from the Universe. I use the information that flows through my crown and third eye to assist my clients and myself to transcend on this soul's journey. As an energy worker I keep the energy flow of my body, mind and soul balanced by clearing my energy through earthing, nutrition, showers, oils, candles, long walks, nature, yoga, the beach, music, spending time with loved ones and writing.

With my clients I assist them to receive the true sustenance of life by using food as a tool to learn their soul's lessons. As each client uncovers the true vitality that already exists deep within, they learn to nourish his or her soul and lead a life of freedom and ease.

To Nourish the Soul is to truly feed the essence of your being with love and light. It is through the process of uncovering the root of your life's physical and emotional imbalances you gain the power to cultivate optimal health and well-being.

My heart chakra is beaming with love to be walking in my soul's purpose and I am filled with such joy to be able to help the souls who find their way to me each day. Life is truly a magnificent gift.

THE CHAKRAS
Elizabeth Tripp

We are souls living a human experience. I believe the human body is merely a collection of energy and the foods we eat are an extraordinary tool to learn the lessons of the soul. How does food relate to the chakras? Well, everything has its own vibration - a table - a car - a lamp - a rock - an orange - even our thoughts and feelings. The chakras are energy vortexes within the human body serving as points of attraction for energy. The seven main chakras are the foundation of a deep and strong energy flow that runs from above the crown of the head to the outside of the bottom of the feet. The chakras, like eddies in the ocean, draw energy in and out and support the body to have a distinct shape and form. The chakras store information for the soul and have different vibrations. This collective energy emits a frequency which attracts energy outside of the body to move towards us. As we attract energy we store it within us.

The human body is a highly intellectual machine designed by the soul to serve as an additional tool to transcend on this journey. The body is not intrinsically crafted to release all the energy it absorbs, thus much of our early life experiences are stored as energy in these vortexes. These stored memories create a disruption in the energy flow and trigger energy information present in the chakra from past lives to be activated. It's in these moments the human mind creates a dialogue between present and past pain. The mind constructs a way to describe its current circumstance – I feel bad, I feel unsafe, I feel sad, I feel upset. Here we are beginning to see the root cause to an imbalance in the chakra system. Much of the work I do in my private practice, Nourish the Soul, is about finding the root energy that has caused the body an imbalance in the energy flow of the chakra system. Once the energy flow has been disrupted the body compensates by responding with dis-ease. This is a signal to the body something is off and a message from the soul to look closer. This is where an individual's body may develop an infection, an illness, or even create padding to protect itself. As the energy imbalance becomes bigger so does the dis-ease and the mind's dialogue.

Everything emits energy and this includes the foods we eat. As humans, when we start to have uncomfortable feelings in tandem with an uncomfortable internal dialogue we find ways to escape. Since food is a source of fuel for the body it's naturally the number one way to cope with these feelings. Many people begin to use food as early as childhood to stuff down uncomfortable energy. In the act of stuffing this energy down it, creates an even bigger imbalance within the chakras. The more energy you put in your body, the more energy will be present. The body becomes overwhelmed and for some it responds by gaining weight, or rather a padding to hold it. I have found the energy that an individual is stuffing in to its body also attracts the energy of foods that are of its same vibration. Fear, sadness, pain and upset are of similar food vibrational frequencies found in chocolate, sweets, candies or processed foods.

For example, a client of mine grew up in a household with two alcoholic parents would often witness her parents arguing and yelling at each other when they got home from the bars. Unknowingly, this client felt the vibration of the anger and rage her parents were emitting. Being too little to understand what to do with this energy she started to feel a sense of unsafety. This energy was attracted to her root chakra -- the powerhouse of safety and security. The vibration from her parents triggered emotions from her past life in her root chakra that she was not complete with, and her body reacted by wanting to curl up in a little ball and hide. While holding onto to this energy her mind started to tell her "I am not safe." From that moment on my client started to feel anxious and unsafe. She described it as a sense of discomfort or confusion. She didn't like this feeling and wanted to make herself feel better. What did she do? Well, almost instinctually she noticed certain foods gave her a sense of comfort like bread and butter, or cookies and milk. While talking about this with her in session she started to see that as a little girl she used food to alleviate the uncomfortable feelings she had picked up from her parents. It is important to state that the client does not necessarily realize this energy had activated a past life experience and therefore she was reliving a situation that her soul wanted her to grow and learn from in this lifetime. Instead, the client started to see that she used food to push down these feelings to avoid feeling them and to avoid learning a sense of safety from within. Hence, this is how food is an amazing tool to learn the soul's lessons. We can start to see our behavior with food reflects how we are feeling and is also a reflection of the health and well-being of chakras.

Once this client became present to the event that caused her to disrupt her root chakra, she was ready to let go of this energy. This is the part of the work where I hold space for clients to release energy and clear it from their bodies. In her case, I guided my client into a meditation where she was able to create a sense of safety and peace within her body. She was given a personal declaration and new tools to practice building upon this new-found freedom. It was in that moment she released the energy that was stuck in her root chakra and allowed for the chakra to flow freely once again. This has incredible short-term and long-term effects. For this client she soon felt calmer. She stopped binge eating. She was less attracted to sweets and candy. Over a few weeks, she was able to begin to lose the extra weight she had been carrying without dieting. This was extraordinary for her and what I attribute to as a huge shift in her vibrational frequency.

© Elizabeth Tripp

ABOUT ELIZABETH TRIPP, RD, CDN

Website: www.elizabethmtripp.com

ELIZABETH TRIPP is the owner and founder of Nourish the Soul. She is an intuitive healer who has a tremendous amount of passion for working with people. At an early age, she discovered she had a unique capacity for sensing and understanding the feelings of others as well as the ability to feel and communicate with spiritual energy. Today, she embraces her gifts to work with clients deeply and profoundly. She is grateful to share her gifts with you, and is proud to say, "I'm living my soul's true purpose guiding individuals to live a happier and healthier life!"

She has studied the healing arts of the mind, body, and soul in the New York Metropolitan Area for ten years. By trade she is a Registered Dietitian (RD) and a Certified Nutritionist/Dietitian (CDN) since 2010. She is not your traditional nutritionist. She believes food and the body are incredible tools to uncover the root of our physical and emotional imbalances. Throughout her studies, she's expanded the breadth and depth of her understanding of mind, body & soul connection and along the way empowered herself to live a life of freedom with her whole self - her nutrition, her body, her mind and her spirit. It is her mission to provide her clients with permanent solutions to their life issues while changing the conversations people are having about food, the body, and how to cultivate true health and well-being.

Today in her practice, she enjoys witnessing my clients Nourish the Soul while walking into freedom with not just their body and food but relationships, career, and soul purpose too! As a spiritual teacher, speaker, healer, radio talk show host, and consultant her work brings her great joy. She is over the moon excited to share her revolutionary approach with the world. She looks forward to working with you!

CARMELA VILLAROMAN VELARDE
Holistic Intuitive and Integrative Therapist

Behind a veil of unabridged faith, I began my retreat to Peru on 8/8/8. The retreat, organized through my-then yoga studio and wellness center in New York City, originated after my spiritual guides advised me to put together a group to bear witness to a vision I had: of a shaman, who was to be attuned to a mountain god, leading the event.

I remember the retreat like a chapter, all-important in its passing, unfolding like a page meant to be voiced. I felt youthful, alert and responsive. The shaman to be attuned, Kay Dougherty, an esteemed colleague, and five other shamans led the retreat. We hiked at an altitude that I was not accustomed to, so we were instructed to chew the leaves of a sacred coco plant that acted as a pain reliever. Being an astrological earth, sun, and moon sign woman, I am heavy in my lower body. This has kept me resourceful when in trouble, as in this retreat which required surviving inclement changes of weather.

I felt honored to be walking with people so humble and supremely focused on the retreat's mission- to attune Kay. For two weeks, we performed ceremony upon ceremony along the sacred valley on route to Mount Ausingante. I felt the connection to this spiritual practice immediately. I was curious to see where this space would take me. I knew that there was a greater calling to my being present. One of our shamans, Adolpho, gave all the guests stones. I was given three. We were told to go back to our tents to connect with our stones. I was advised by my tent-mate, Jackie, a seasoned shaman from New Jersey to weave the stones into my chakras. I knew chakra is a Sanskrit name for "wheels" and that there were seven main chakras aligned along the spine from the coccyx to the top of the head. I knew each chakra spun at different speeds, but not until this moment did I witness such a blatant display of how these chakra wheels of life were connected energetically.

I placed the heaviest stone on the top of my head while I sat warmly in my sleeping bag. The cold air from the top of this mountain snuck through the tent and I breathed in its freshness. Suddenly, I felt the stone turn on my head in a clockwise direction to the point where my hair was getting tangled. I felt the turning of these wheels to the extent that they rotated. I can name two that were mildly stuck. They were the throat chakra (the fifth chakra) and the sacral chakra (the second chakra). As I felt the stones turning, I called in shock to my tent-mate to tell her what was happening. She sat up and said simply, "An apu has entered the tent." An apu is a mountain god. I felt the air circulate through the tent as the wheels turned. Some stones stuttered and that's when I went deeper into meditation and breath-work to balance into a smooth flow of rotation.

Upon returning home and much later on as I continued my studies in acupuncture and herbology, energy healing and nutrition counseling, I delved deeper into studying the chakras.

ENDOCRINE SYSTEM

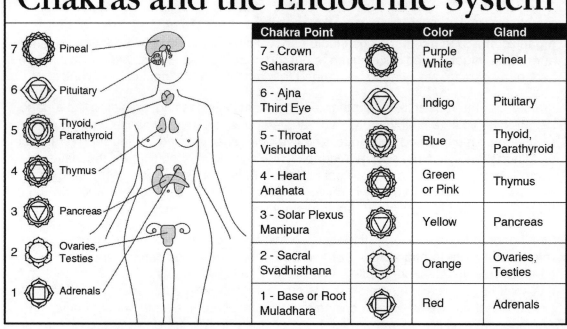

Chakras and the Endocrine System

Chakra Point		Color	Gland
7 - Crown Sahasrara		Purple White	Pineal
6 - Ajna Third Eye		Indigo	Pituitary
5 - Throat Vishuddha		Blue	Thyroid, Parathyroid
4 - Heart Anahata		Green or Pink	Thymus
3 - Solar Plexus Manipura		Yellow	Pancreas
2 - Sacral Svadhisthana		Orange	Ovaries, Testies
1 - Base or Root Muladhara		Red	Adrenals

Diagram labels:
7 Pineal
6 Pituitary
5 Thyroid, Parathyroid
4 Thymus
3 Pancreas
2 Ovaries, Testies
1 Adrenals

EATING WELL TO LET YOUR CHAKRAS THRIVE
Carmela Villaroman Velarde, BS, LMT

The best way to balance your chakras is to eat foods that will feed your cells the nutrients they need to thrive. The health and wellness industry is awakening to this way of thinking. Many people suffer from metabolic syndromes due to their hormones being imbalanced due to lifestyle stress, poor diet and lack of a regular fitness regimen or overexertion of the body. Throughout my studies and almost two decades in private practice in holistic self-care, I have viewed our movement in preventing bad health and illnesses as dharma work to educate others as to how survival should not mean only financial security. The demands of modern society led me to focus inward, to train and inspire individuals with global impact in mind and to raise healthy families. I honor people's desire to align with their higher purpose. Everyone dies but not everyone lives well. I educate with tools to help others better understand their imbalances with integrative therapies and modalities. As a holistic counselor, I am inspired to give seekers the picture as I see it so that they can become awakened to their whole self in the most natural way - mind, body and spirit.

I am grateful for the ancient wisdoms that have allowed me and others to heal our bodies naturally. In other words, to do what they do naturally, allowing the body to do what it needs to do. I have witnessed many miracles that I am grateful for. Education of food as medicine is my current focus for client work, through a certified organic superfood movement. Many health issues are due to the rise of the chemical warfare within our food system. Herbicide, insecticide and genetic modification have poisoned our food supply so much so that there are no natural nutrients left because our national soil and crops are adulterated. Our gut microbiome, located in the solar plexus, the 3rd chakra, is the seat of where the damage is being done. It affects not only our physiology through our gut,(also known as the second brain,) which governs our immune system, neurotransmissions and our serotonin production, but also our emotions. The gut, in the solar plexus, also governs our personal power source and emanation of self-love.

Prevention and intuition, along with our body's ability to defend foreign invaders, can be strengthened by us with daily detoxification* along with sourcing pure whole food and non-processed food choices. I will continue to find gateways to unlock, unleash and empower others through further studies of how our time on this planet can be optimized through lifestyle education.

* Please consult your health care provider before starting any detoxification program.

Your endocrine system (pineal gland, pituitary, thyroid, parathyroid, thymus, pancreas, reproductive organs and adrenals) is linked to all kinds of functions in your body. It regulates mood, growth development, metabolism, tissue development and reproduction.

To keep it at optimal function, avoid:

- Processed Foods
- Sugar
- Pesticides
- Unhealthy Fats
- Stress
- Diet Drinks

To keep it at optimal function, add more:

- Exercise
- Fruits
- Vegetables
- Good Fats
- Quality Protein (as amino acids are also the building blocks for hormones)
- Iodine (important in forming thyroid hormones)
- Adaptogenic Herbs (Asian ginseng, holy basil, milk thistle, rosemary, aloe vera)

1. The root chakra (Muladhara which in Sanskrit means "root support") is red in color. It is located at the pelvic floor of the body located at the base of the spine associated with your feelings of security. The glands represented in this first chakra are the adrenals, associated with survival ("fight or flight"). The earth element is associated with this first chakra. You should eat foods that are grounding, like root vegetables such as parsnips, turnips, and rutabagas, proteins like lentils, red beans and bone broths, fruits and vegetables such as beets, apples, watermelon, raspberries and pomegranates. Add in spices like paprika, ginger, cumin, garlic, and onions. All are very nourishing for your adrenals.

2. The sacral chakra (Svadhishthana, which in Sanskrit means "one's own residence") is located just below the navel and is associated with the reproductive organs. This water element chakra governs our emotional body and allows us to sense pleasure. Fluidity in this space through the lymph and bodily fluids like blood creates a life force center for balance. Creativity will flow with pure filtered water and juicy orange foods like mangoes, tangerines, papaya, clementines and melons.

3. The solar plexus chakra (Manipura, which in Sanskrit means "City of Jewels") is located in the soft space between the rib-cage, beneath the sternum and the belly. I immediately think of the color yellow with the sun beaming out of this chakra as a power source of confidence and balancing your self-esteem. It is associated with the pancreas and the outer adrenal glands. The fire element is known to be the engine of this third chakra as it regulates how our bodies secrete enzymes to properly digest and absorb our food and the energy from the world around us. Foods that help to activate this chakra and that are digestive aids include kombucha, kefir, yogurt and fermented foods like sauerkraut and kimchi. Also great for the solar plexus are lemons, yellow peppers, yellow squash, papaya, jackfruit, pineapple, raw seeds, chamomile tea and slow burning whole grains like brown, black or yellow rice.

4. The heart chakra (Anahata, which in Sanskrit means "unstuck") is located at the exact center of the chest and is associated with the thymus gland, so important for our immune system. It is the center chakra, the bridge between your upper and lower chakras and is the seat of your love and compassion. The color green offers a symbol of vitality and reproductive life and is also connected to the season of springtime. The air element is associated with this fourth chakra so get out and breathe balance into this chakra with green foods. Add spirulina, wheatgrass, chlorella, limes, green apples, thyme, basil, arugula, sprouts, kale and broccoli to your diet. In addition, choose foods like grapefruit, avocados and lemons as well as omega-rich foods like wild caught salmon, walnuts, chia seeds, flax seeds and hemp seeds all which aid a healthy heart.

5. The throat chakra (Vishuddha, which in Sanskrit means "especially pure") is blue in color. It is located at the center of the throat and at the base of the neck on the spine. What opens this chakra up is truthful essence of communication through purification. It is associated with the thyroid gland so please avoid acidic foods that trigger inflammation such as meat, dairy, caffeine, alcohol and all processed foods. When possible, select organic foods for their purity from pesticides and their ability to strengthen thyroid function. Ether is associated with this fifth chakra, so consider healing foods like raw juice from nutrient-dense fruits and vegetables. Blueberries, taro and plums add the color blue to the menu.

6. The third eye chakra (Ajna, which in Sanskrit means "to perceive") is indigo in color. It is located between the eyebrows and slightly above in the forehead. It is associated with the pituitary gland which is called the 'master gland' because it controls the other glands' functions. Intuition is the defining strength of the third eye chakra. Light is associated with this sixth chakra. Meditation and proper sleep can assist in balancing it. Bring in foods rich in anthocyanin like tart cherries, goji berries, blackberries, acai and blueberries.

7. The crown chakra (Sahasrara, which in Sanskrit means 'thousand-petaled') is purple or white in color. It is located on the top of the head and slightly back from the crown. The pineal gland is associated with this chakra and is connected to melatonin production, reproductive hormones, mood stabilization, cardiovascular health and possibly cancer prevention. The energy is about being able to experience universal oneness with its shining purple-colored light connected to the higher powers. Silence and focusing on spiritual practices like cleansing will assist in bringing the seventh chakra into balance. Like the third-eye chakra, sunlight is also associated with this seventh chakra so I recommend meditation in fresh air and high grade pure organic hemp CBD oil. Its main role is to increase the connection to your body's homeostasis that focuses on the endocannabinoid system. It is nature's stress reducing system that regulates our response to all forms of stress and pain, calms our nerves and grounds us. Every cell of our body has a CBD receptor site to feed, and it will shut off if not fed. When we are in our most enlightened state in the seventh chakra our body works optimally.

© Carmela Villaroman

ABOUT CARMELA VILLAROMAN VELARDE, BS, LMT

Social Media: Naturally Wholistic
Contact: carmelavelarde@gmail.com

CARMELA VILLAROMAN VELARDE is a holistic health practitioner, licensed massage therapist, certified pre-natal yoga teacher, Reiki master, acupuncture and herbology student, and health coach with the brand partnership of Purium, holding a BA in Psychology from the New School of Social Research in NYC.

She is currently the chapter president for the Health and Wellness Network of Commerce in King of Prussia, PA.

Upon meeting an individual for a consultation in person or by phone, she assesses their health goals, health history and commitment level and guides individuals through the path to self-discovery and healing.

She often utilizes a variety of tools such as astrological natal charts, the Five Element Theory of Chinese medicine and the chakra system.

She resides in her hometown in Pennsylvania along with husband Antonio and their children Kitana and Neo.

You can reach her directly through www.iamnaturallywholistic.com and on social media under the moniker, Naturally Wholistic.

The
Sound Healer,
The Cantor &
The Painter

CARLOS CUELLAR BROWN
Music Therapist

I have both professional and personal experience balancing and retuning the vital body energy centers. In my practice I have used the solar harmonic spectrum frosted crystal bowls and tuning forks to recalibrate the chakras as well as self-generated tones such as humming and toning. I also incorporate mindfulness to my sound healing practice. The experiential quality of these methods allows you to notice and permit relevant emotional issues to emerge and consequentially dissipate.

I work with the general population but also have clinical experience with: Adult Day Care, Long Term Care, AIDS-Dementia and Alzheimer's. My clients regularly report positive outcomes which include improved moods, stress reduction, release of muscle tension, pain management, increased focus and productivity, transcendental experiences and emotional resolution. When you practice sound therapy you can expect an increase in your overall wellbeing as you activate your healing response.

My chapter entitled "Emotionally Tuning Your Inner Instrument" explores the origins of healing frequencies present in nature and in our bodies. It also describes the outer skin surrounding our body which acts more like a bio-field that interacts with our energy meridians. Our bodies are like a musical instrument with nodal points that resonate with each other. These natural frequencies can recalibrate and rebalance our body back to harmony.

EMOTIONALLY TUNING YOUR INNER INSTRUMENT
Carlos Cuellar Brown MT-BC

The first step in addressing emotional issues many times is compassionate love and forgiveness. This emotional state is what the body needs to retune with its vital self.

A complementary approach to the healing process is centered on the properties of sound as medicine. Although this has yet to be accepted and verified, there is a growing body of evidence that suggests that sound can in fact affect the body in multiple ways.

We can begin to experience the healing properties of tones by using tuning forks, crystal bowls, humming, toning vowel chanting techniques, and other tools.

On the journey back to wellness, our bodies will vibrate in a bath of energy transformation. When done appropriately, these modalities will revitalize and retune the vital body back to universal wholeness.

Vibrations of color and sound are associated with specific chakras. The chart below shows each chakra, the sound frequency in which it best vibrates at, the color associated with it, the basic emotions, natural properties, Bija Mantra (a one-syllable sound used in meditation or yoga practice), and the vowel sound.

As a music therapist who has worked with a variety of people in various settings, I believe in these sound healings and welcome you to explore how they can benefit you in a session.

Root Chakra
A=432 Hz
Color=Red
Basic Emotions=Anger
Natural Properties=Physical identity
Bija Mantra=LAM
Vowel=UH

Navel Chakra
B=456 Hz
Color=Orange
Basic Emotions=Vigilance
Natural Properties=Desire
Bija Mantra=VAM
Vowel=OO

Solar Plexus Chakra
C#=540 Hz
Color=Yellow
Basic Emotions=Loathing,
Remorse, Disgust
Natural Properties=Self-Esteem
Bija Mantra=RAM
Vowel=OH

Heart Chakra
D=576 Hz
Color=Green
Basic Emotions=Love, Compassion
Natural Properties=Empathy
Bija Mantra=YAM
Vowel=AH

Throat Chakra
E=648
Color=Blue
Basic Emotions=Fear
Natural Properties=Self-Expression
Bija Mantra=HAM
Vowel=AY

Third Eye Chakra
F#= 720 Hz
Color=Indigo
Basic Emotions=Grief, Sadness, Awe
Natural Properties=Insight
Bija Mantra=OM
Vowel=OM

Crown Chakra
G#=792 Hz
Color=Purple
Basic Emotions=Ecstasy, Joy, Serenity
Natural Properties=Bliss
Bija Mantra=MMM
Vowel=EE

ABOUT CARLOS CUELLAR BROWN

Website: https://carloscuellarbrown.wixsite.com/music-and-wellness

CARLOS CUELLAR BROWN is a board certified music therapist with over nine years of experience implementing Music Therapy modalities in a variety of clinical populations that include: adult day care, nursing homes, long term care, children hospitals, AIDS Dementia, hospice and NICU.

His interventions are designed to promote wellness, manage stress, alleviate pain, improve and maintain motor strength, promote socialization and mediate emotional trauma. His relaxation groups, Guided Imagery and Music, and Mindful Meditation sessions offer a unique experiential approach that integrates voice, breath, imagery and ancient solfeggio frequencies. These methods will affect your human physiology and endocrine systems and they can create a powerful agent in the healing process.

To book a session with Carlos and learn more about him, visit his website.

DAVID PRESLER

Cantor, Voice Coach, Classical Performer, Composer, Conductor and Talent Manager

I believe that we are all on a path of growth. As we learn in life to master our health, careers, and our emotional and spiritual well-being we find ourselves at different levels climbing the mountain of spiritual evolution.

Balancing my chakras as part of my health clears the way for me to achieve what needs to be achieved. Eliminating stress and surrounding myself with positive people is just as important. Negative people can shift greatness into a downward direction. This mind-set of wellness is vital to my life and to aligning my chakras.

In addition, Ziji Kaufman, one of the most important guides in my life, is a master at balancing chakras and helping one's aura to shine. My commitment to frequent aura-healing sessions with Ziji allows me to be ready for all that I do.

My path has been a unique and interesting one. I have been a cantor in Jewish synagogues for 40 years, many of them part time, which allowed me to pursue studies in jazz, show tunes, piano, opera, composition, conducting and producing.

As a performer and a vocal coach, my approach is definitely in conjunction with the idea of being fully alive.

When I am singing I am conscious of the fact that my heart is ever evolving and expanding. My intention is to bring the divine into my singing. It enables me to achieve miracles in my live.

SEEKING THE DIVINE EXTERNALLY AND WITHIN US
David Presler

I was born in East Stroudsburg, PA to Rabbi Bernhard Presler and Lily Spanlang. Dad was born in Stetin, Germany in 1936 and Mom in Belgium in 1939. Dad fled to England, and Mom was hidden in Switzerland. I grew up as a Rabbi's son in conservative congregations, learning to read Torah and leading services while Mom cooked chicken soup and lit the Shabbos candles. I felt the aura of the candles when they flickered every Sabbath on Friday night.

My mom was the true seeker, the more Spiritual one. She guided me to follow my passion, which was music. Since I was her first born, and because of the entire trauma she went through, we were very close, and still are. We are very much the same spiritually, yet different.

My mom has been working on a channeled spiritual book of guidance, which is going to be published this year. She lives in Delray Beach, FL and I am close by in South FL. Dad now lives in Israel.

I am someone whose life unfolded while working to discover what is possible. I put myself through school and all of my achievements have been accomplished by sheer effort. I tried many different avenues and paths, only to discover a passion for music. My loves in music are cantorial, opera, and Broadway and I also put on recitals each year singing German lieder and other art songs. Performing, composing, conducting and producing is when I vibrate at my highest. I am certainly on a Spiritual path. I am committed to growth, to excellence and to success.

I am always working on several projects at a time. I'm an entertainer of jazz, show tunes, piano and opera. I manage and teach music and I have been a part-time cantor in Jewish synagogues for 40 years. Being a cantor comes easily to me.

Great achievements take focus. I grapple with mastering my craft, staying healthy, making a living and moving the game forward. I may have performed seven characters in a Nutcracker musical to great acclaim. Yet, I then need to turn my attention back to the basics of cleaning my apartment, keeping up an active Facebook page, staying healthy and keeping my body in shape.

 I have found that many people are hooked into social media, the news and politics. These can lower our vibrational frequencies to the outside world. However, to reach success we must be tuned to an inner truth that pulls us heavenward and towards our destiny and inheritance. I am committed to growth, to excellence and to success. When performing, there often exist issues involving nerves and confidence. A lack of confidence is usually related to stories we make up in our heads that often aren't true. I have taken numerous courses in leadership and communication at Landmark, and they have opened my mind to realizing when I am truthful and when I am not.

For me, success has been a long time coming, and every day I experience miracles and new doors opening. This is a result of consistent crafting of who I am and what I am present to in my life.

In the end, we must follow our passion, and if we can survive as artists, fabulous. I am grateful for the opportunity to perform each week, to learn new repertoire and to stretch my talents far beyond my own expectations. We must reach for the stars and keep our bodies and minds healthy. We must be open to the resources available and take advantage of the tools at our fingertips—and at the same time strive to be unique, to be different and to be our authentic selves!

© David Presler

ABOUT DAVID PRESLER

Website: preslerproductions.wixiste.com/mysite
Contact: preslerproductions @gmail.com or 347-571-1740 (What's App)

DAVID PRESLER earned his B.A. and M.S. Degrees at Queens College in Music Education and his S.C. in Jewish Education and Administration at Yeshiva University

David is a voice instructor and works with aspiring singers who are committed to their career and to their practice. He sticks with the more traditional Bel Canto exercises for working with the voice.

As a concert artist, he has appeared in numerous venues performing art songs, opera arias, Broadway favorites, jazz standards, sounds of Sinatra and classic repertoire in various languages -- French, Italian, Spanish, German, Hebrew, Yiddish, Ladino and Russian.

He has served numerous congregations for the past four decades in the New York and Florida regions. His creativity, passion and experience make him one of the most unique and versatile cantors in the field. He also books local cantors year-round.

He is a student of Spirituality, having studied with several spiritual teachers and greatly influenced by his mother, Lily, a Holocaust survivor.

Cantor Presler is a prolific composer of liturgical music with *Sim Shalom* as his first published work in the Shabbat Anthology 2005, published by Transcontinental Music Publication. He continues to compose new liturgical works for Shabbat and holy days, and often records and posts new material on YouTube.

YouTube: https://www.youtube.com/watch?v=2fVt7w2Re48
Listen to *60 Years Ago*, Presler's original song on the Holocaust, including mention of the camps including Auschwitz.

Featured Album: *Time for Moshiach* - A Jewish Jazz CD.

JO JAYSON
Painter, Author, Teacher of Physical and Emotional Wellness and Empowerment.

I am able to scan an individual remotely or in person, and have an accurate knowing which chakra may be off-balance or sluggish. I don't really know how I do this except that I can, and I'm pretty much always accurate. Most people, including myself, will have shifts and changes to their energy centers throughout their days and weeks. It's not normal to have seven fully-functioning healthy, open chakra energy centers 24/7, although it would be lovely. Our energy centers are completely managed by our inner thoughts, beliefs and overall vibrations that we are broadcasting. One of the most important centers to always give your attention to is your solar plexus, for this is where we shine with inner power or don't. I try to personally be always aware and tuned in to my solar plexus through the day and make sure that I am fully charged, much like my cell phone. I find that if I am powered up, then I move through my day much easier than if I was running on empty and with the lights switched off.

FINDING BALANCE, HARMONY AND WELLNESS THROUGH YOUR CHAKRAS
Jo Jayson

Finding balance in our busy lives and attaining and maintaining harmony in our mind and body seems to be a never-ending challenge for most of us. The craziness of our own schedules and our personal experiences can leave us feeling frazzled, depleted and victims to the circumstances around us.

The truth is that we are consciously and subconsciously creating our realties all the time; the good, the bad and the ugly. Our thoughts and our beliefs dictate the vibration and frequency we emit, and this creates our physical and emotional experiences.

Our physical bodies have energy around them called the subtle body. This is our energy field and it's where the vibrations of what we feel and think emanate from. They are in fact actually what make our aura the color that it is, which is constantly changing depending on our mood and thoughts. The chakra energy points in our body however are not the same as the overall aura. Our chakra energy points are centers of prana (life giving force) within wheels of energy that allow this life force to flow and circulate within and around us.

We have around 80,000 chakras in our bodies but we work primarily with the main seven chakras from the root to the crown of the body. The root chakra spirals downwards and connects with the feminine mother earth energy and the top crown chakra spins and spirals upward toward the heavens, connecting to the masculine divine consciousness. All the other chakra points spiral outwards from our spines out of the front of our bodies. Each one of these chakra points corresponds to particular emotional and physical realms. When these chakras are flowing and spinning clear, we feel balanced and aligned. When these chakras are not flowing but are sluggish and blocked, we feel misaligned and disconnected from our own natural state of peace and harmony.

Each chakra energy field has a color and sound vibration and frequency. The color frequencies often used in western society to illustrate the chakra system are the seven colors of the rainbow. Each center corresponds to emotional and physical aspects. If you are working on confidence and self-worth for example, you would focus on your solar plexus, your third chakra. If you were dealing with breast cancer or lung and heart issues you would put your focus on your heart and fourth chakra. Any issues with speaking your truth or expressing your feelings, you would be giving energy to your throat and fifth chakra. There are many ways to help shift and clear the chakra energy points in the body. Yoga, color therapy, essential oils, gemstones and crystals and working with nature's elements are all valid and wonderful ways to help energize the centers, but the most direct and permanent effect on your frequencies is focusing directly on your thought processes and belief systems. Energy healing from a practitioner can help somewhat. But without personal focused work on your own vibration on a daily basis through self-development and meditation, the chakra energy system can easily fall back into disharmony and misalignment.

Working on healing the chakra system within you is a primary way to achieve autonomy over your own energetic frequency. Understanding that one's physical and emotional condition is directly associated with the health and state of your chakra centers is important, but ultimately your thought and belief patterns are imperative to finding wellness and health from within.

To achieve ultimate wellness and balance I recommend that, in addition to working with the chakra system, you work on self-development and health through classes or with coaches. Doing both will benefit you enormously.

© Jo Jayson

Artwork: © Jo Jayson – to view this image in color visit: jojayson.com

ABOUT JO JAYSON

Website: www.jojayson.com
Contact: info@jojayson.com or 917-748-1903

JO JAYSON was born in the United Kingdom and is a self-taught painter. She began her career as a muralist and decorative painter in London, Sydney, and New York. In 2008, she started working with the Divine Feminine energies. Since then, she has worked as a professional intuitive painter, channel, and teacher. Upon completion of her much-loved *Goddess Chakra Series of* paintings, Jo went on to complete the internationally acclaimed *Sacred Feminine Series* of paintings depicting thirteen "Divine Feminine" channeled archetypes. The images and wisdom that Jo receives and shares has helped women all over the world find empowerment, healing and inspiration. She is the author of the award winning book *Self-Love Through the Sacred Feminine*, the companion to her *Sacred Feminine Guidance Cards and Guidebook*. Jo has spent six years teaching workshops and online courses for healing and self-development in the United States, and offers paintings, prints, meditation kits and CD's for physical and emotional wellness and empowerment.

The
Coaches

TRENT RHODES
Mindfulness Coach, Career Developer and Literary Artist

Learning about the chakras became a natural progression from my experience working with energy, in meditation, martial arts, Qigong and yogic breathing. The term, chakras, came up quite often and so I gravitated towards learning about it.

Chakras are energy centers and we use them (or neglect them) in our daily lives at every moment. And because they correspond to particular thought patterns and actions, it makes sense to me that gaining knowledge of chakras and practicing how to strengthen them would influence my daily manifestations. For example, the solar plexus chakra is of importance in career development. Its energy reflects personality, magnetism, ego strength, self-perception and charisma. The throat chakra corresponds to communication, self-expression and speaking (or acting) one's truth. These are qualities that support the "people skills," so often said to be lacking in potential candidates for jobs; they had the skill and the expertise but struggled to build good work relationships. These "people skills" are of the utmost necessity for leadership roles, where the tasks are about strategy and human relations. So instead of just focusing on the raw skills that people possess, we can augment those abilities on a holistic level by tapping into the metaphysical energy that surrounds them.

I tend to discuss these metaphysical topics in open-minded spaces. Meaning, I don't force anyone to absorb my thoughts, nor would I voluntarily describe chakras unless I recognized the person's consciousness was open to it. The person asking related questions, bringing up the topic on their own or showing a general openness to spirituality can signal this.

I think it's easier than ever to learn about how we are made of energy, that all material life has an energetic origin, and that quantum physics shows us very clearly how all matter is energy at the base. So from that initial understanding, one hopefully would be open enough to recognize that saying we have ENERGY centers when we are MADE OF energy isn't woo-woo.

Chakras are part of my conscious career development practice. What distinguishes my approach is this element of metaphysical knowledge and how applying it transforms what can seem like a mundane experience, such as job searching and professional development, into one of self-discovery. By arming oneself with metaphysics and the chakras, all that one does in career development enhances in quality. Life and the vocation evolve together.

THE CHAKRAS AND THE PSYCHE
Trent Rhodes

INTRODUCTION: HOW I ARRIVED AT THIS STUDY

I'm a solitary scholar-practitioner in the spiritual sciences. To me, the world is a fine blend of matter and energy and I've been drawn to the metaphysical since I was young. The fascination began with television shows like the X-Men and martial arts-oriented games like Street Fighter. These media have distant origins but the themes were common: overcome challenges, win the battle within, self-evolve, tap into your potential, fortify your energy, and become magical.

While attending formal school, I took advantage of the first Internet access at home to research to my mind's content. That began around age thirteen. Three years prior, I urged my mother to enroll me in a martial arts school and Taekwondo was the most accessible in the phone book. I had a sample class shortly after and fell in love with the experience, environment and energy. Moving the body in such a focused-yet-instinctual way felt natural to me despite taking just one class. My passion was ignited nonetheless, and that first day sprouted into a 23-year long-term love with martial cultivation.

As my metaphysical interests grew, so did my martial competency and I began intuitively sensing the relationship between the body and mind, and the spiritual influences upon daily living. I recognized the stronger I became internally, the more efficient my desires manifested, and the ease with which I handled situations that before would be deemed struggles.

My learning became more precise with time, acquiring definitions and terms, becoming comfortable with words like qi, prana, life force, kundalini, tantra, Qigong, Wu Wei, Jin… the list continues.

A consistency I recognized was no matter where my private learning took me, there was a reference to energy centers housed within the physical and spiritual bodies. Often they were grouped in sevens with some traditions alluding to more. These were the chakras, the energy vortexes that formed houses for specific energy frequencies the human being stores and radiates. Each chakra was associated with a particular realm in the body, with both health and disease indicators.

I also recognized there were psychological health and disease indicators as well; certain mental states would correlate to a high-functioning chakra while the more chaos-inducing states reflected energetic blockages in the corresponding chakra.

In my professional life, I recognize the value of incorporating chakra knowledge into my element. Working as a career advisor for a college, and a career developer in my own business practice, there are ample opportunities for understanding how chakras work to benefit clients, college graduates and anyone seeking to elevate their professional platform.

The core focus of my work in this area is: marry energy and matter, alchemy with analysis, magic to the mundane and the chakras with professional performance.

Everyone's professional challenges differ, but the common theme I recognize is the barrier manifested from within. Because of either a lack of knowledge in this space or disinterest, professionals do not merge concepts of energy with daily living. Often, I've coached people on mindset and transmuting emotions before covering resumes or interview practice, without using the specific language. These inner blocks form an initial locked door that, without attention and resolution, prevent the client from excelling in a career development sphere: as above, so below, as within, so without.

In this chapter, I briefly explain how the chakras influence conscious career development.

NOTE: As a solitary scholar-practitioner, I propose no certainties in this chapter, but outlooks, insights and challenges for the reader to recognize the chakras' psychological patterns and how they relate to professional development. This chapter is a challenge to the western learner, whose paradigm sways in favor of the logical approach to conclusions. It is designed to ellicit the possibility of synthesizing and further observing the states of consciousness we are inclined to call healthy and those harmful, or ill-sufficient for well-being.

Lastly, this chapter aims to bring a stronger focus on mindfulness and the importance of observing our inner states so that we remain balanced, with chakras energetically moving and flowing, and applying that understanding to our professional lives.

ROOT CHAKRA

SANSKRIT: MULADHARA CHAKRA
Color: Red
Number: 1

"Root" is an adequate name for this energy center, as its position is located at our tailbone. This rooting connects to our instinctual motives including survival, food, shelter, safety and an overall grounding feeling.

Balanced Root Chakra

When this chakra is balanced, we feel safe enough to live within the world without a constant fear of loss or danger. Our emotions are secure in that we have enough to sustain our lives nutritionally. We feel capable of earning the income necessary to produce what we require for living expenses. An older caricature of this root chakra balance is the American Dream: married couple, pets, children and a gated home. The children go off to school happily and ace their classes. The pets have just enough to eat and are openly happy about their lives. The couple hugs and kisses and dances, not to mention take vacations alone and with the rest of the family. In this scenario, there are none or very few material trifles.

A more modern version may be the financially independent Millennial, who lives in an open loft. She sips her Starbucks coffee and ventures off to work, headphones in ears, casually strolling to the destination. At home, she relaxes and surfs the Internet. At work, she's a tech wiz. Challenges that come her way can be given optimum attention because her basic needs are met.

This mental state reinforces the inner locus of control, or experience of self-empowerment to influence life in one's favor. There's a sense of inner agency, solidified enough so the person of balanced root chakra can face a situation that might otherwise cause an imbalanced root chakra to emotionally crumble.

Grounding is a keyword of focus for the balanced root chakra. Stability is actualized, and this provides the possessor with the reserve energy to handle higher-level considerations.

Unbalanced Root Chakra

Imagine the same couple from the American Dream stuck with major debt. They owe on the mortgage, the car, the school tuition and their personal credit cards. The children are not producing high grades. During the parent-teacher meetings, the couple verbally spars with the instructors. They host a blame game for the kids' poor performance. Now, the couple begins blaming each other for their lack of attention to guide their children. Each feels they're doing all they can. And seeing the results of "all they can," they feel even less successful as parents, spouses and in life.

One of the pets falls ill; it seemed sporadic to the husband, and the wife believes it was from the new food they bought. In her opinion, they never should have changed their diet. This adds another stress layer for the couple. The entire household is on unstable grounds.

This is a rather extreme-but-realistic example of what an unbalanced root chakra can produce. An ungrounded muladhara shakes up the locus of control, causing the person to give her power to outside forces. Psychologically, she is at the mercy of everything external. There is no change, unless something outside of her changes for her. Needless to say, this mental state is incapacitating and potentially a factor in the feelings of hopelessness we can experience when we believe nothing in our lives go our way. An unbalanced root chakra is the epitome of the victim mentality.

Root Chakra – Conscious Career Development

Professionals have a visceral feeling when personal survival is at stake. Before considering any vocation, we aim to ensure our basic needs are met: shelter, food, an overall feeling of safety. More adventurous souls might be willing to go without these needs guaranteed, but generally we feel comfortable and more capable of seeking higher-level pursuits when we can reasonably say our security is handled. In the work sphere, this comes in the form of a consistent paycheck, medical benefits, insurance, a place to call work, a place to live, feeling our skills are valued and utilized.

The struggle to progress from a job to a vocation often involves securing this foundation, ensuring we will have food the next day and enough money to get by. It is when we face scenarios that threaten our financial / resource stability that we tend to experience the stress involved with a ruptured root chakra.

Acquiring a consistent cash flow, whether through a formal occupation or self-employed business can assist with amplifying this root center.

While we may feel passionate about a cause, practicality may require that we attain a job so that we can financially sustain ourselves while building our private enterprise. Based on weighing the options, ensure that your choice considers strengthening the root.

SACRAL CHAKRA

SANSKRIT: SVADHISTHANA CHAKRA
Color: Orange
Number: 2

Balanced Sacral Chakra

The sacral chakra houses what is commonly known as the sexual energy. The sex force is our creative energy, the power that gifts us with the ability to bring our imagination into physical existence. Often "fertility" is perceived as solely a result of sexual union, but all

of our ideas that manifest in the material world are "conceived" through energetic fertilization. So we then can say, a fertile mind is a creative mind. Consequently, this force is essential for all of our activities in the world. It provides the raw fuel to operate with abundance and zest. Traditions throughout the world offer practices, arts and sciences to cultivate this potent energy because of its vital necessity for living.

When the svadhisthana chakra is balanced, there is a deepened quality of life. Psychologically, there is reserve energy to handle mundane tasks with enough left over without a drain.

The healthy sacral chakra also manifests healthy beliefs and actions around sexuality and sensual expression. The individual is comfortable within and this reflects externally. There is an understanding of the sexual functions and the relationship between the sexual energy and life force, or creative energy. There also is an empowered sense of creation; the person can conceive and manifest ideas without the common mental blocks often associated with an inhibited imagination.

Unbalanced Sacral Chakra

This chakra unbalance can be summed up with the word addiction. Tibetan tantric practitioners, because of how rapidly one can elevate, and how fast one can fall if abused, consider cultivating the sacral energy, the "lightning path" or "left-hand path."

Addiction, the inability to control impulses, is common to the abused sacral creative force. These addictions range from drugs to sex to gambling to death-defying experiences. They all come from the need to express the sensual energy, to gain a high and altered state of consciousness.

Addictions can damage the sacral chakra due to its overstimulation and weakening willpower. The ability to say no decreases, so each temptation results in an indulgence. Results of an unbalanced svadhisthana include ruined careers, relationships, businesses and personal lives.

The Sacral - Conscious Career Development

Any level of career growth will require significant amounts of creative energy. This energy is the same as the sex force and can be harnessed by a process called transmutation. Transmutation involves developing energy in one area and refocusing it on another endeavor. That same energy fuels our drive to pursue a new project, position or growth.

One method to igniting this energy in a non-sexual way is to discover a passion. This activity or experience moves us to exuberance; we can do the work for free and rarely if ever feel drained. We love it. This passion sparks the sacral chakra in a way that allows us to use its force to produce creations other than children. Professionally, the passion we have is ideally associated with our work. We convert that sacral energy into career-oriented pursuits, so that we emanate that same exuberance in our craft.

SOLAR PLEXUS CHAKRA

SANSKRIT NAME: MANIPURA
Color: Yellow
Number: 3

Balanced Solar Plexus Chakra

The "solar" aspect of this energy center refers to its ability to project strong light; that light manifests in the form of many intangible qualities connected to the masculine principle, including confidence, self-control, a sense of agency, willpower, focus, charisma and forward movement. This chakra houses the energies often required for successful ventures involving people.

In a balanced manipura, a person has a well-integrated personality. Beliefs are formed in such a way as to enable an individual to function within an environment, and to do so with a considerable level of influence. There is recognition that environments require certain quality emergence and the person is capable of adjusting when necessary. Both this chakra and the anahata chakra play a vital role in establishing empathic connection with people. The heart-to-heart and solar radiance form a general charisma that creates likability based on rapport.

Unbalanced Solar Plexus Chakra

When this chakra is out of control, we witness the creation of excessive ego. Overt strength of personality, charisma and will without the empathy or moral grounding can lead to a domineering persona capable of capturing the hearts and minds of people, swayed by the alluring energy, yet unaware of potential malicious intent. By masking the malevolent intentions, this persona embodies a public character that makes people says, "She understands me. I understand her and will follow her."

If allowed to continue, such a force can rise to high positions of influence and ensnare ever-larger audiences. The more people believe in him or her, the more power they attain and the more ego-gratification the experience brings.

Solar Plexus Chakra – Conscious Career Development

Of the many chakras available for our use, the manipura is one of the most professionally vital, as it pertains directly to our charisma and personality. Self-belief requires that we understand our talents and purpose, and how we desire to project them into the professional environment.

What does your successful-self appear like?

What do you envision as your ideal occupation?

What are your beliefs?

What kind of company matches the beliefs that you hold?

What type of company do you see yourself designing?

What are your values?

These are questions the yellow power helps you to propose and clarify. Once you decide upon these ideas and commit to embodying, your personality will amplify, radiating into how you handle your business and professional relationships. Quickly people will realize you're in alignment: body, mind, spirit and values, the definition of integrity.

The solar plexus chakra is also involved in how you apply your willpower. This means setting professional boundaries for what you stand for and what you choose to not tolerate. This challenge often manifests in choosing service / product pricing. Sometimes we can feel uncomfortable about telling someone there is a cost to have our product or service. In these moments we face an emotional dilemma, and this becomes more of a challenge when we're dealing with those closest to us. If we've been accustomed to assisting friends and family using our talent, it may feel uncomfortable for us to suggest they now have to invest in it monetarily. If we don't activate this chakra power, we face being overused and miss out on opportunities for energy exchange: talent for money or some other form of return.

HEART CHAKRA

SANSKRIT NAME: ANAHATA
Color: Green
Number: 4

Balanced Heart Chakra

Quotes throughout the centuries speak of the power of love, and love is universally associated with the heart. This energy center forms the seat of our relationship possibilities. From this vortex, we radiate magnetic energies that pull or attract relationships at all levels to us: people, animals, opportunities, materials and experiences. The famed law of attraction has its source in the anahata. It is from here that a healthy anahata can manifest desires that bring personal evolution, an ascension process, while it transmutes negative experiences into energy most useful for the person. A person with a balanced heart chakra is capable of meeting new people, creating connections and maintaining long-term relationships. Increased connection makes each moment fuller, providing the person with an enriched existence.

Unbalanced Heart Chakra

Coldness, unwarranted personal reserve and an inability to maintain relationships are signs of an unbalanced or weakened heart chakra. The wall created prevents other warming energies from spiritually "touching" the person; harmony becomes difficult to establish. Consequently, this spiritual isolation can produce physical effects we commonly recognize as depression, social anxiety, jealousy and a victim mentality. These states manifest as a result of a lack of love and the healing energies it provides.

Heart Chakra: Conscious Career Development

"Heart" in this view refers to the ability to develop professional rapport. Imagine attending a professional event and each contact you make there is a visible connection. Eyes reciprocate, energies match, the topics you cover are seen with like-mind. There is a clear resonance and you exchange business cards, eager to assist each other with talent or information. This is an example of what an awakened heart chakra can do for a professional.

The anahata enables you to shift from a self-focused (yellow chakra) vibration to another vibration where you reach out to someone else. Your interest in another's occupation, their abilities and what they desire to accomplish becomes a focus, and this energy projection dissolves the mental distance between you. What we call "networking" involves potent heart chakra resonance.

THROAT CHAKRA

SANSKRIT NAME: VISHUDDHA
Color: Blue
Number: 5

Balanced Throat Chakra

The vishuddha vortex manifests through our communication skills and overall self-expression. To sing, to dance, laugh, argue, persuade, and speak our truth are all forms emerging from this chakra. When healthy, we express our inner world externally with clarity; what we think, we say with precision. The audience who understands this can digest this precision, and this strengthens our rapport connected to the anahata chakra. We can flow with the impulse to voice our opinions when angry, sad or feel moved to be present for another in counsel.

Unbalanced Throat Chakra

If you've felt shy, timid or need to hold back your knowledge, these are symptoms reflecting a weakened throat chakra. To dodge the experience of revealing a truth, we tend to opt for lies. The lies build upon each other, and because they are fabricated information, we feel our truth is more protected behind this armor. What lying accomplishes, however, is deeper suppression of the throat chakra. It becomes more difficult to speak truth as lying becomes more habitual.

Throat Chakra: Conscious Career Development

Technical skills and knowledge aside, one of your most effective tools in professional life will be communication. This is not just your ability to read and write; it also involves your body language, tonality, diction and timing the environment to know what to communicate and when to do so. A strong throat chakra will empower you to project your messages with clarity. Imagine yourself performing at your best in a presentation. You've practiced several times. Your mind is calm. Your technology works just right. You hit all of the accurate points in the slideshow, answer the audience's questions and deliver this engaging presentation in a way that everyone leaves with new insight. This is an example of the throat chakra at work.

An inhibited vishuddha can show up as shying away from speaking opportunities in meetings, being bashful about your skill sets when asked the famous question, "What do you do?" or uncertainty when discussing matters of personal value and how you assist people. When empowered, this communication arrives to the conscious mind directly from the intuitive nature, our inner truth. As the channel to the truth emerges, we begin communicating with greater passion and purpose and this can be reflected throughout our work.

THIRD EYE CHAKRA

SANSKRIT NAME: AJNA
Color: Purple
Number: 6

Balanced Third Eye Chakra

The third eye is given a location between the two eyes spiritually and deemed as the pineal gland biologically. Described as being a seat for multidimensional thinking and wisdom, this chakra houses our intuition. When activated, we tap into nonlinear thinking, capable of extracting solutions in holistic downloads rather than analytical steps. Understanding can pour into our minds in chunks or we can receive the famous "A-ha" moments of insight.

Unbalanced Third Eye Chakra

A weakened ajna can give us situational blindness; we become unable to read experiences in layers or creatively. Restricted to logic, we function with a narrow-minded agenda that cannot see the dimensions necessary for a total solution.

This can influence our personal lives and relations with family, friends, lovers and the environment.

Third Eye Chakra – Conscious Career Development

We can study knowledge for a considerable amount of time and eventually realize that the gut feeling can surpass this type of information. Especially in leadership positions, we may receive advisement from staff. As we sit upon this information, we come to a conclusion about a course of action based on a combination of this knowledge and our own intuition. This is an example of the ajna at work.

When we give an interview or receive one, we're meeting someone for the first time. We assess the physical, the energy, the environment and intentions and form a synthesized vibe. This is the ajna at work.

When we have a sample coaching session with a potential client, we assess based on the experience's feedback. We then sense that this person is a fit or not. We also may sense exactly how our gifts may be of service to them. This is ajna at work.

Our third eye is a powerful perception expander. Applying this chakra in one's career elevates the level of insight we gain in a given experience. We can penetrate a process, application or system with both a creative and analytical mindset. It gives rise to original thinking often contrary to structural maintenance organizational life.

CROWN CHAKRA

SANSKRIT NAME: SAHASRARA
Color: Pink
Number: 7

Balanced Crown Chakra

The upper three chakras take a person to the more energetic, spiritual realms of perception. The crown manifests body-mind connection and a holistic perception that encompasses inner sight as well as an experience of fullness with all creation. This may manifest as joy, inner contentment or the energy of cosmic love for all beings. At this level, one sees the self in others and a unity in all things.

Unbalanced Crown Chakra

When this vortex is dormant, dualistic thinking rules. Competition overtakes cooperative mental states, and the individual sees separation of self from everything else. With this distance, it becomes easier to harm another or pillage an environment without concern for the consequences. Only the rational calculations, equating the means justifying the ends finds value in an unbalanced crown chakra.

Crown Chakra – Conscious Career Development

The crown chakra endows us with the power to see connection in all things. As a consequence, we may feel less motivated to continue working in a company that does not support our inner truth, and we may experience a new level of soul-searching to discover the right vocation that does match. After 10 years in a job, crown chakra emergence can crash down on all of those years of beliefs and attachments. Suddenly, we're off on a new path, ready to leave the old and begin a new vocation.

Professionally, the sahasrara will keep you focused on the root mission of your career. Your purpose will remain present in consciousness as you develop it into a business or practice. With your spiritual purpose as the guiding light, rather than solely material gain, the quality of your service will expand along with how you elect to assist others.

© Trent Rhodes

ABOUT TRENT RHODES

Website: www.iamtrentrhodes.com
Contact: tr@iamtrentrhodes.com or 973.818.7279

TRENT RHODES is a Mindfulness Coach and Literary Artist with a focus on empowering clients to achieve their highest self-image in their careers. As a coach offering a bespoke service, he challenges the powerful, conscious and driven to take the next step and transform to their highest level.

Experienced in the Gestalt-style coaching methodology, he combines his passion for tapping into the powers of the subconscious mind with modalities including a level 2 Reiki certification, meditation, martial arts and the power of words through writing and speech.

Trent also connects with men driven to become their highest masculine self, serving as a private mentor in the art of becoming a gentleman. His Instagram page, @The.Divine.Masculine presents the layout for his philosophy on how men can manifest their native energy based on knowledge and wisdom of the ancients in the contemporary world.

As an educator, Trent's written extensively on perceiving life experience as the true classroom. His blog CrownOfMind.com and his books provide learners with a source of insight on how to guide one's own education.

Trent was initiated into his spiritual path at the age of 16 and claimed the mantle of an autodidact. Through connection with the God-source, self-study, experience and consistency in workshops, he's synthesized the principles of metaphysics, alchemy and ancestral wisdom with practicality for 18 years.

He received his coaching education in a nine-month program with Coaching for Transformation, a Law of Attraction Certification from the Global Sciences Foundation, and Etiquette Certification from IAP Career College.

OLIVIA WHITEMAN
Meditation Guide and Project Fulfillment Coach

As a meditation guide and project fulfillment coach, it is important that I am 100% present, patient and purposeful. Meditation has been the go-to method I use for myself and my clients to regain composure and clarity. Having this practice offers so many benefits to handle life in a way that leaves us with peace and joy.

The chakra meditation I do is very simple. I sit in a chair with my feet firmly planted on the ground, hands on my lap, palms facing up, and I close my eyes. I then imagine a red silk scarf at the base of my legs, swirling around me until it reaches the base of my spine. The color of the scarf then turns orange and wraps around my body until it reaches my navel. At this point, I take slow deep breaths, inhaling all that is good. I then see the color of the silk scarf change to bright golden yellow as it encircles my stomach area from two inches above my navel to right below the tip of my sternum. I allow the yellow silk scarf to penetrate all my cells with warmth. When I am ready, I continue watching the silk scarf turn green as it gently embraces my back and heart, then move into a turquoise blue covering my throat, neck, and face. The vision continues with the scarf now indigo in color covering the area above my eyes and forehead, and finally it moves up above my head and turns purple. Once again, I hold my breath releasing a big sigh. I then envision a white light surrounding me in protection, connecting me to heaven and earth. I relax into the white light and when I am ready, I open my eyes, wiggle my fingers and toes and begin or end my day with peace and tranquility.

When I meditate, I only need to see the colors, because I know what they represent. When I work with people new to chakra meditation, I give more details. For example, I start by saying, "focus your energy on the first chakra also known as the root chakra. It is red and is located at the base of the spine. You feel stable and secure. You have an innate sense of belonging and are part of a tribe. Now, say out loud or inside your head, "I am grounded and secure." I continuing sharing other attributes of the root chakra and move up giving similar details for each chakra until we travel from the base of the spine and reach the top of the head.

My chapter focuses on the solar plexus chakra, as this chakra when aligned offers us the drive and confidence to get things done. It will benefit you in setting goals in any area of your life.

I would love to get emails at lifecoacholivia@hotmail.com with your thoughts.

GOAL SETTING, MEDITATION AND CHAKRAS
Olivia Whiteman

Once most people move forward in pursuit of a goal they have been thinking about for a while, they always say the same thing. "I should have done this a long time ago." If you have a project that you want done and aren't making the amount of progress you need or want, ask a professional for help. When we recognize we need assistance and do something about it, it is the best thing we can do for our overall well-being.

We often hire people to teach us to drive, make gourmet meals, handle our taxes and so much more. We know that singers, actors, sports figures, and other professionals hire coaches to make them better. Yet when it comes to completing a goal, people seem to think they need to do it themselves or they can ask a friend for help. Often, this method results in things left undone. A common reason people give for not completing what they started is that they have too many other priorities. If this reason resonates with you, I suggest taking advantage of the benefits that goal setting, time management and meditation offer. You will definitely see an improvement in getting things done.

Another reason why people don't complete something they start that is not often mentioned, however, has to do with chakra imbalances.

The word chakra comes from an ancient Sanskrit Indo-European language, and means spinning wheel of light. Chakras are like wheels. They spin--some slowly and others more quickly. Chakras are thought of as symbolic funnels in which energy flows into and out of a person. There are many chakras but our focus will be on the seven main chakras. These chakras or spiritual centers are associated with many attributes. A few chakra attributes are color, location on the body, one of the six senses, a sound, and the number of lotus (chakra) petals.

Order	Color	Location	Sense	Element	Sound	Lotus Flower
1st	Red	Root/Base	Smell	Earth	LAM	Four-petals
2nd	Orange	Sacral/Navel	Taste	Water	VAM	Six-petals
3rd	Yellow	Solar Plexus	Sight	Fire	RAM	Ten-petals
4th	Green	Heart	Touch	Air	YAM	Twelve-petals
5th	Blue	Throat	Hearing	Sound	HAM	Sixteen-petals
6th	Indigo	Third Eye/Brow	Insight	Light	OM	Two-petals
7th	Purple	Crown of Head	All	Thought	OM	Thousand-petals

When our chakras are blocked, it can result in problems if not brought back into alignment. The longer the obstruction remains, the worse the issue can become. Problems or issues can manifest physically, mentally or spiritually. As it relates to goal setting, when one or more of our chakras are blocked, it is reasonable to assume that it can result in being unable to finish what we start. However, we don't often attribute our lack of progress as stemming from a blocked chakra. If we did, then we would do something about it and the result would be that we would accomplish more and have more positive outcomes with our projects.

The chakra often out of alignment when we are unable to take action is the solar plexus. It is located in the area two inches above the navel to right below the tip of the sternum.

Do you know if your solar plexus is out of alignment? One hint, as I already mentioned, is that you can't finish what you started. There are others. The chart below shares some of the other signs to clue you in.

IS YOUR SOLAR PLEXUS BALANCED?

Excessive Solar Plexus Charka	Deficient Solar Plexus Chakra
1) Do you anger easily? 2) Are you critical of others? 3) Are you judgmental? 3) Are you controlling? 4) Are you aggressive? 5) Are you focused on how things benefit you? 6) Are you focused on how people benefit you?	1) Do you please others, before yourself? 2) Are you afraid to speak up? 3) Do you lack confidence? 4) Is your self-esteem low? 5) Do you seek approval from others? 6) Do you follow the crowd? 7) Do you feel you've been victimized? 8) Do you feel lethargic?
Do you suffer from any of the following? - Pain in the neck, head or lower back - Anorexia or bulimia - Hypoglycemia or hyperglycemia - Fibromyalgia	

After people view this list, I often get asked, "What if I possess some of the above signs, but not others? How many traits must I possess for my solar plexus chakra to be out of balance? How will I know if I need to balance my solar plexus?" What I reply is, "How do you feel about yourself and your life? What is in harmony and what is missing?" As a person who often has blocks in her solar plexus, I know when my blocks are cleared. This is because when I am in balance, I behave differently.

- I know and ask for what I want
- I demonstrate self-confidence
- I am not afraid to assert my own identity
- I do not judge myself or others, critically
- I am not easily irritated, angry or frustrated
- I am energetic
- I have no issue with sleeping, digestion or fatigue
- I am overall healthy
- I feel happy with my life

The one thing to note is that our energy will shift depending on the people or environment we are in. At work we may feel guarded but at home we may feel relaxed or vice-versa. If something feels like it's an issue or a problem or has you constantly thinking about it, this is the biggest sign that your chakras need balancing.

So, how do we balance our chakras? There are many ways, and I will share with you some of them. To help illustrate my points, I am including a case study.

CASE STUDY: MONICA

When I first met one of my clients (let's call her Monica) she complained of earaches, sore throat, headaches, and digestive issues. She had difficulty completing chores and trouble sleeping. Her mind would race all night and she often woke up fatigued. Although she had a strong spiritual practice, she often felt sad. It was clear by her symptoms alone, that she had issues with several chakras, including her solar plexus. It was imperative that no matter what else, our time together should focus on bringing her chakras back into balance.

Monica's dream was to become a successful makeup artist, whose clientele included celebrities. She started working on creating a portfolio with an aspiring model who was also a friend. For a variety of reasons, the project was put on hold. A year after they stopped, Monica wanted to resurrect the project. However, she was too nervous to ask her friend who was now making money modeling to resume what they began. She came to me for assistance in moving forward with her dream. What follows are what we focused on in our sessions. They provide tools and suggestions that can help almost anyone move forward.

1) FINDING SOLUTIONS

When we have issues that block us, it is important we address ways to resolve them and ways to shift any thinking we may have from the negative to the positive. Luckily there are many options; a few of these include:

- starting a daily meditation practice
- writing in a gratitude journal
- developing a sleep routine
- re-evaluating eating habits
- creating a vision board
- checking in with a physical or mental healthcare provider.

For more options see the chart: Ways to Strengthen & Balance the Solar Plexus Chakra

2) SCHEDULING & ACCOUNTABILITY

We often know what we need to do. However, do we? Using a scheduling and accountability system to get you going can help.

Monica was familiar with all the wellness options I presented to her, yet she wasn't doing any of them. We started by scheduling her calendar to take advantage of what we both knew would give her benefits. We arranged to talk twice a week to assess her progress. When she didn't do what we talked about, we explored what was going on for her and what she could do that might help move her forward.

For Monica, using the calendar and having the accountability portion worked well. She liked having tasks assigned to her and follow-up phone sessions.

3) UNDERSTANDING BEHAVIORAL PATTERNS

Once we know our patterns, when we decide we are tired of repeating behaviors that don't bring us results, we can then commit to a transformation. When we know how we like to work, we can then tap into the best results for our unique way of accomplishing things.

Monica needed to take lots of breaks as fatigue was an issue for her. Therefore, she had to be mindful of times in her day when she was most energized and schedule her calendar to work on high priority tasks during these moments.

4) ACKNOWLEDGING PAST SUCCESSES

It is really important to remind ourselves that we can and do accomplish things. *I, therefore, encouraged Monica to think about her past successes, and even write out a list of all that she had accomplished.*

5) CREATING A VISION

It is great to be driven by vision; knowing and imagining how accomplishing a goal will change your life can push us through times when we want to give up.

I recommended Monica write something that she could look at often that would inspire and drive her to complete her vision. To get her started we used a worksheet I created called, "Manifesting a Vision." It is a set of questions that help with goal setting.

A copy of the worksheet is available in the Handout Section at the end of this chapter.

6) FOCUSING ON DETAILS

Success increases when we put our thoughts in writing and include the details. The goal setting plan should include answers to how, what resources, with whom, and by when.

Monica's project was to highlight her editorial makeup skills. Editorial makeup is makeup that is used for runway and magazine spreads. It is not worn every day. It was very important that as a makeup artist, Monica communicate her viewpoint with the photographer, hair-stylist, model and her assistant, to bring her vision to life. Monica had many components to consider and to take care of to complete her project successfully, including:

- Analyzing her budget and time-constraints for the shoot
- Deciding the looks she would be executing and how long each look would take
- Preparing a mood board to give to everyone involved in the concept of the shoot

- Hiring a photographer and letting the photographer know what she had in mind so the right lighting would be available (intensity, natural, filtered, up, direct, reflected, silhouette, etc.) and confirming his work days availability
- Booking a photo studio for a realistic number of hours to do all that was needed
- Booking a hair-stylist, sharing how many styles she wanted and how much time she had for each style
- Making sure who was providing hairspray, brushes, blow dryers, an extension cord, hair accessories, etc.
- Contacting her friend to model for her and checking her work days availability
- Confirming her model's skin is clear, and if not, what is going on with it
- Making sure of her model's dress size
- Selecting what clothes, jewelry and accessories she wanted at the shoot
- Checking her make-up kit had clean brushes, make-up remover, and enough pencils, brushes, pigments, lip color, loose powders with cream/liquid foundations
- Thinking when breaks would be, for how long, planning and providing refreshments
- Arranging for an experienced assistant to help her at the shoot, sharing her schedule and vision for the shoot ahead of time, enhancing her assistant's success in making sure everyone stayed on schedule
- Arranging for transportation to the shoot

7) KNOWING & UNDERSTANDING THE STORIES WE CREATE & WHY

Fears are so varied. Some people are afraid of success, others of failure. Also, there are two types of fears; those that we know of and those that are hidden in our subconscious. Fears are stories we tell ourselves. Stories create our past. They impact our present and possibly our future. As it relates to obtaining a favorable outcome for your goals, it's imperative you know the stories you create around accomplishing what you say you desire.

Monica's fear was that her friend would reject her request to model for her. Eventually, the call she dreaded was made. Guess what? There was no resistance. Her friend was looking forward to reconnecting. It was only after the call that Monica realized all that she feared was just a story she created in her head. Knowing this allowed us to focus on other stories she may be creating that prevent her from accomplishing what she said she wants for her life.

8) ALLOWING THINGS TO BE WHAT THEY ARE

It is necessary to follow our own path. Yet, it sometimes leads us astray. When that happens, accept it. Suffering ends when we give up wanting to change what cannot be undone.

After Monica's session, we looked at contact sheets and I was speechless. I was going to give her feedback when her friend popped by. Monica was buzzing with excitement and wanted to share the photos with her friend. After her friend looked at all the images, there was silence. Her friend expressed exactly what I was thinking. "Did you ask the photographer to let you see the frames so you could make adjustments as you were working?" Monica responded that she did. Her friend continued by asking, "What happened to the mood board you originally showed me?"

Monica's response to her friend's question was that at the photo studio she decided to try a different look then what was planned. Wow! It was as though she wanted to sabotage herself was all I thought. We looked at the photos several more times before the excitement of being in the studio with her now famous friend wore off, and it hit her that she should have stayed focused on executing her original plan. She had spent all her budget on a professional photographer and studio, hair-stylist, makeup, cabs, refreshments, and now had very few photos she could use.

9) CROSSING THE FINISH LINE

It is amazing how often we overlook options that are available to us from day one. Sometimes urgency opens us to creative opportunities. When failure presents itself, we need to be gentle with ourselves. If we use disappointments to learn from and have the courage to continue, then we are winners.

When Monica and I reconnected to discuss how to move forward, we worked on formulating a new plan. It didn't take long before she came up with a solution. Monica's friend was willing to work with her again and she ended up finding a photographer and a hairstylist willing to work with her. It was a wonderful collaboration and so was the result.

Result: One completed project and one happier and healthier Monica.

© Olivia Whiteman

the Magic Is In You

WAYS TO STRENGTHEN & BALANCE THE SOLAR PLEXUS CHAKRA

Sunshine Sit Out in the Morning Sun	**Clothing & Accessories** Wear a Yellow Top or Scarf Place a Yellow Ribbon in Your Hair
Crystals Place Crystals around your Home, Office or in your Bag Amber Golden Topaz Citrine Yellow Calcite Tiger Eye	**Essential Oils** Work with Nature's Plant Essences Cinnamon Clove Geranium Ginger Grapefruit Lemongrass Peppermint Rosemary
Exercise Do Yoga, i.e. Sun Salutations Belly Dance Take a Groove Dance Class	**Flowers** Plant Sunflowers Buy Daisies Get Flower Essence Therapy
Jewelry Put on Yellow or Gold Earrings, Pendant, Necklace or Cufflinks Wrap a Golden Belt around Your Waist	**Treatments** Visit a Reflexologist Book a Crystal Healing Session Take a Reiki Class
Affirmations Say Affirmations Daily & Often I Am Enough I Accept Myself I Am an Individual I Achieve Great Things I Speak Up for Myself	**Foods & Drinks** Nourish Your Body with Yellow Food and Liquids Yellow Fruits Yellow Vegetables Pasta Corn Lemon Bananas Turmeric Milk Ginger Tea

CHAKRAS SUMMARY

7th   **Crown Chakra** / Thousand Petal or Spoked Wheel/*Sahasrara Chakra*
Location: just above the crown of the head
Color: encompasses all colors
Mantra Seed Syllable: encompasses all sounds

Element: the ultimate reality of all truth
Number of Petals: 1000 (symbolic for unlimited)
Focus: detachment from ego and illusory nature of the material world, attaining the goal of yoga (self-realization).

6th   **Third Eye Chakra** / Rule or Command Wheel /*JAjna Chakra*
Location: in the middle of the forehead, between the eyebrows
Color: indigo
Mantra Seed Syllable: *om*

Element: the universal mind
Number of Petals: 12
Focus: intuition, decision-making, and the surrendering of egocentric intellect in favor of attaining nondualistic wisdom

---

5th   **Throat Chakra** / Especially Pure Wheel/*Vishuddha Chakra*
Location: throat
Color: turquoise or blue
Mantra Seed Syllable: *ham*

Element: ether/space
Number of Petals: 16
Focus: self-expression and communication

4th   **Heart Chakra** / Wheel of the Unstruck or Singular Sound / *Anahata Chakra*
Location: within the center of the chest
Color: green
Mantra Seed Syllable: *yam*

Element: air
Number of Petals: 12
Focus: peace, love, and empathy

3rd   **Solar Plexus or Navel Chakra** / Wheel of the Jewel City / *Manipura Chakra*
Location: solar plexus
Color: yellow
Mantra Seed Syllable: *ram*

Element: fire
Number of Petals: 10
Focus: power, will, and self-esteem

2nd   **Sacral Chakra** / One's Own Self-Based Wheel / *Svadhisthana Chakra*
Location: sacrum
Color: orange
Mantra Seed Syllable: *vam*

Element: water
Number of Petals: 6
Focus: emotions, desires, and creativity

1st   **Root Chakra or Root Wheel** / *Muladhara Chakra*
Location: base of the spine
Color: crimson
Mantra Seed Syllable: *lam*

Element: earth
Number of Petals: 4
Focus: physical survival, self-preservation, and security

HANDOUT: MANIFESTING A VISION WORKSHEET

1) Do you have a goal that you are blocked in manifesting? If yes, take the time to answer the following questions.
   - What is the one thing you want to accomplish?
   - How long have you had this goal?
   - Is this your vision or someone else's?
   - Who would be most disappointed if you did not accomplish this?
2) What is your process when setting goals?
   - Do you need motivation to get started?
   - Do you do it right away? (If it depends on the goal, explain.)
   - Do you keep starting and stopping?
   - Do you prefer to work in small units and in spurts or do you prefer to dedicate hours or weeks to a project?
   - Do you estimate how long it will take to complete?
   - Do you wait until the last minute? (If yes, are there any exceptions?)
   - Do you ask for help or company?
   - Do you schedule it into your calendar?
   - Is there flexibility in the way you like to work? In other words, if you are best in the morning but only have free time in the evening, can you work or are you too exhausted and just need to decompress and go straight to sleep?
   - Do you make sacrifices so you can work on your goals? What are they?
   - How do you feel about your process with things you are excited or passionate about?
3) What is your process when setting goals that you are excited or passionate about?
   - Do you need motivation to get started?
   - Do you do it right away? (If it depends on the goal, explain.)
   - Do you keep starting and stopping?
   - How do you prefer to work: in small units, spurts or until the project is donet?
   - Do you estimate how long it will take to complete?
   - Do you wait until the last minute? (If yes, are there any exceptions?)
   - Do you ask for help or company?
   - Do you schedule it into your calendar?
   - Is there flexibility in the way you like to work? In other words, if you are best in the morning but only have free time in the evening, can you work or are you too exhausted and just need to decompress and go straight to sleep?
   - Do you make sacrifices so you can work on your goals? What are they?
   - How do you feel about your process with things you are excited or passionate about?

ABOUT OLIVIA WHITEMAN

Website: HealingSpace.info
Email: healingspaceinfo@hotmail.com
To Order More Books: harmonyinchakras@gmail.com

OLIVIA WHITEMAN is focused on using practical and realistic steps to guide you to getting your projects done. She is available to meet face-to-face with clients located in New York, New Jersey, Connecticut and Pennsylvania. She also provides corporate motivational sessions, and does this throughout the United States.

At the Healing Space in Montclair, N.J., she offers meditation classes. Check her website for more information.

Olivia Whiteman feels giving a person what he or she needs is key—one person may need confidence, while another may need to stop imagining negative conversations, and still another may want an accountability partner. She is proud of her clients' achievements and has many testimonials like the one given by artist Alise Loebelsohn.

> *"Olivia can help you manifest the life you want to live. She has given me the confidence to push forward." ~ Alise Loebelsohn, aliseloebelsohn.com*

To learn about upcoming events and get tips on meditation and goal setting, subscribe to Olivia's free newsletter by sending her an email.

Anyone who subscribes will receive *21 Tips to Win at Goal Setting*.